The Psych[illegible] in Life

This book offers an inspiring exploration of current findings from the psychology of meaning in life, analysing cutting-edge research to propose practical, evidence-based applications. Schnell draws on psychological, philosophical and cognitive perspectives to explore basic concepts of meaning and to introduce a multidimensional model of meaning in life.

Written in an accessible style, this book covers a range of topics including the distinction between meaning and happiness, the impact of meaning on health and longevity, meaning in the workplace, and meaning-centred interventions. Each chapter ends with exercises to encourage self-reflection and measurement tools are presented throughout, including the author's original Sources of Meaning and Meaning in Life Questionnaire (SoMe), to inspire the reader to consider the role of meaning in their own life.

The Psychology of Meaning in Life is essential reading for students and practitioners of psychology, sociology, counselling, coaching and related disciplines, and for general readers interested in exploring the role of meaning in life.

Tatjana Schnell is an associate professor at Innsbruck University, Austria, and adjunct professor at MF Specialized University, Oslo, Norway. As head of the Existential Psychology Lab, she focuses on fundamental questions of how to conceptualise and measure meaning in life, and on the nexus of meaning in life and health, suffering and dying, religion, secularity, work, and civic engagement.

The Psychology of Meaning in Life

Tatjana Schnell

Routledge
Taylor & Francis Group
LONDON AND NEW YORK

First published 2021
by Routledge
2 Park Square, Milton Park, Abingdon, Oxon OX14 4RN

and by Routledge
52 Vanderbilt Avenue, New York, NY 10017

Routledge is an imprint of the Taylor & Francis Group, an informa business

British Library Cataloguing-in-Publication Data
A catalogue record for this book is available from the British Library

Library of Congress Cataloging-in-Publication Data
A catalog record for this book has been requested

ISBN: 978-0-367-42281-3 (hbk)
ISBN: 978-0-367-41585-3 (pbk)
ISBN: 978-0-367-82316-0 (ebk)

Typeset in TimesNewRoman
by Apex CoVantage, LLC

Visit the eResources: www.routledge.com/9780367415853

To Ivo and Jona

Contents

List of figures xi
List of tables xii
Acknowledgements xiii

1 Searching for meaning? 1

1.1 Why a feel-good society is not a meaningful society 1
1.2 (Facing up to) questions of meaning 3
1.3 Know thyself! 3
1.4 Literature 4

2 Defining meaning 5

2.1 Etymology 5
2.2 Philosophical definition 5
2.3 Meaning in life: a multidimensional construct 6
2.4 A brief discourse: why achieving meaningfulness is a demanding task in our time 8
2.5 Know thyself! 9
2.6 Literature 11

3 Measuring meaning in life 13

3.1 In-depth research: qualitative studies 14
3.2 Broad-based research: quantitative measurement 18
3.3 At the interface: the SoMe-Card Method 25
3.4 Literature 26

4 Meaning as attribution 28

4.1 The hierarchic model of meaning 29
4.2 Vertical and horizontal coherence 32
4.3 "No man is an island": the environment's role 33
4.4 And how does it feel? 34
4.5 Know thyself! 35
4.6 Literature 37

5 Varieties of meaning 38

5.1 Interindividual differences in meaningfulness and sources of meaning 38
5.2 Meaning is dynamic: changes over the lifespan 40
5.3 Meaning in life and sources of meaning for men and women 42
5.4 Meaning in life, education and intelligence 47
5.5 Meaning is dynamic: changes across activities and days 51
5.6 A brief discourse: studying – often pointless, usually no fun? 55
5.7 Know thyself! 56
5.8 Literature 56

6 Sources of meaning 60

6.1 The strongest predictors of meaning 60
6.2 Breadth, balance and depth of sources of meaning 62
6.3 Many roads to meaning 66
6.4 Brief discourse: on worldview and meaning 77
6.5 Know thyself! 83
6.6 Literature 84

7 The social dimension of meaning in life 88

7.1 Asked directly: social relationships as primary sources of meaning 88
7.2 Family and friendship as sources of meaning? 91
7.3 Meaning and marital status 92
7.4 Children as a source of meaning 93
7.5 Social inclusion 95

7.6 From social inclusion to meaning – or vice versa? 97
7.7 Social inclusion at work 98
7.8 Know thyself! 100
7.9 Literature 100

8 Crises of meaning – when foundations shake 105
8.1 A lack of meaning 105
8.2 Are Western societies in a crisis of meaning? 106
8.3 Overcoming crises of meaning 109
8.4 A brief discourse: pilgrimage – on the way to meaning 111
8.5 Know thyself! 113
8.6 Literature 114

9 Existential indifference 117
9.1 Whatever! 117
9.2 How to assess existential indifference 118
9.3 Relationships and explanatory approaches 118
9.4 Ways out of indifference? 126
9.5 Know thyself! 129
9.6 Literature 131

10 Meaning and happiness 134
10.1 Hedonic and eudaimonic well-being 134
10.2 Meaning without happiness 141
10.3 Know thyself! 143
10.4 Literature 144

11 Meaning, health and illness 147
11.1 Can meaning in life improve your health? 147
11.2 From mind to body 156
11.3 "I can't go on!" Crises of meaning prevent recovery 163
11.4 Posttraumatic growth 168
11.5 Know thyself! 171
11.6 Literature 172

12 Meaning-centred interventions 178

12.1 Gaining meaning from a meta-perspective – life reviews 179

12.2 Meaning-oriented psychotherapy 187

12.3 Know thyself! 199

12.4 Literature 199

13 Meaning in work 207

13.1 The search for meaning in work 207

13.2 What is meaningful work? 211

13.3 Correlates of meaningful work 220

13.4 You can't save the world every day! Risks of meaningful work 222

13.5 The job as a source of meaning? 226

13.6 Brief discourse: voluntary work – meaningful commitment 228

13.7 Know thyself! 230

13.8 Literature 231

14 Outlook 237

14.1 Caught in the system? 238

14.2 Meaning is subjective – eudaimonia calls for justice 243

14.3 Literature 244

Index 247

Figures

2.1	Varieties of positions within different social subsystems	10
3.1	Scales and dimensions of the Sources of Meaning and Meaning in Life Questionnaire (SoMe)	20
4.1	What do you see?	29
4.2	The hierarchic model of meaning (Schnell, 2009, 2014)	30
4.3	Personalised model of meaning	36
5.1	Characteristics of the five dimensions of meaning over the lifespan	41
5.2	Degrees of meaningfulness over the lifespan (N = 1,291)	42
5.3	Different importance of sources of meaning for men and women (N = 1,123)	44
5.4	Different importance of sources of meaning for female and male convinced atheists (N = 102)	46
5.5	Degrees of meaningfulness in relation to education (N = 1,291)	48
5.6	Frequencies (in %) of activities perceived as meaningful and pleasant	54
8.1	Crises of meaning (%) in six age groups (N = 1,291)	107
9.1	Existential indifference (in %) in six age groups (N = 1,291)	119
11.1	Meaningfulness motivates health-related behaviour in the hierarchic model of meaning	151
11.2	Meaning in life as a moderator of the relationship between stressor and experienced distress	153
11.3	Crisis of meaning as a mediator between stressor and alcohol and drug use	163
12.1	Life-review exercise: my life as a book	199
13.1	Vertical coherence and horizontal coherence at work	212
13.2	Predictors of meaningful work (beta weights)	214

Tables

3.1 Measuring meaningfulness and crisis of meaning 21
3.2 Interpretation of your meaningfulness score 22
3.3 Interpretation of your crisis of meaning score 22
3.4 Authenticity profile of sources of meaning 23
5.1 Prediction of sources of meaning through personality traits (multiple regression, N = 310) 39
6.1 Sources and dimensions of meaning, with annotations 61
9.1 Identification of four types of meaning (mean scores) 118
9.2 Existential Indifference (%) – Legatum Prosperity Index (ages 16–25; data collection 2010–2014) 123

Acknowledgements

With special thanks to Henning Krampe, Peter la Cour, Martin Gaedt, Tini Seykora, Lars J. Danbolt, Monika Radecki, Lucy Kennedy, Charlotte Mapp and the Existential Psychology Lab team, University of Innsbruck.

Chapter 1

Searching for meaning?

You won't find the meaning of life in this book. Whether it exists and what it could be is not scientifically ascertainable – at least not from a psychological perspective. What you will find, however, are insights into how people give meaning to their lives. Thus, this book is about personal meaning, or "meaning in life." Many people experience their life as meaningful without resorting to a universal meaning of life. Others believe they know the meaning of life and thereby gain fulfilment. Some "simply live" and find the question of meaning rather superfluous. In critical moments, however, the question of meaning arises for almost everyone. It goes hand in hand with doubts about fundamental beliefs. Our foundation is questioned: "Am I on the right path?" "Can my worldview stand up to hard times?" "Why am I doing all this?"

Such questions can be exhausting and are often painful to deal with. In general, we try to avoid them. Who is prepared to rebuild a ship on the open sea? To dispose of rotten planks, find suitable new ones and attach them to the others, all while living life and fulfilling its daily requirements: working, educating one's children, taking care of relatives, cultivating relationships, staying healthy yourself and so on.

In many cases, the impulse to deal with the meaningfulness of one's own life comes from an upsetting event: an illness, a separation, an accident, a death, an experience of personal failure. All of these events interrupt the continuity of our experience. They change our perspective and sharpen our vision. They evoke the question why.

1.1 Why a feel-good society is not a meaningful society

In a world marked by great inequality and driven by opaque dynamics, it may be better not to ask why. Better here means lighter, more pleasant or smoother. The question why holds the danger of previous illusions being dismantled. If "because that's how you do it" or "that's the way things are" is no longer sufficient as an answer, you are faced with your own responsibility. This realisation implies either a call for change or a conscious decision for what *is*. Both require reflection. And sometimes, this confronts us with the challenge of drawing consequences. Such questions and the changes that may accompany them are not easy, pleasant and smooth. Nevertheless, they are important and valuable.

But why? Wouldn't it be much better to just live and enjoy life? When I talk to others about my field of research, I often hear, "The purpose of life is simply to live!" Apart from the fact that some of us like to question and reflect in principle, a desire to "just live" is certainly understandable. And a meaningful life depends neither on cognitive ability nor on a personal affinity for headaches. However, if we take a closer look at our society, it becomes clear why it is difficult today to equate a life of "just do it" with a good life.

We live in a multi-optional society. At every fork in the road, a wide variety of possibilities open up. We are inevitably spoiled for choice; no way of life is self-evident. Questions arise: Which type of school? What kind of education, and where? Which form of life, which form of love? Man or woman, long term or spontaneous, marriage or not? No child, a child or children? What occupation? The list is almost endless. Under these conditions, what does "just do it" mean? Those who avoid reflection will often take the path of least resistance, will choose options that offer themselves. It is unlikely that the path taken will actually correspond to the person's abilities, interests and values.

Furthermore, our present culture is based on an image of the human being that conveys to us that happiness is feasible – through consumption, diet, wellness or trendy lifestyles. The promises of happiness are manifold. And anyone who is still not happy despite all these possibilities has only themselves to blame. The supposed availability of happiness causes happiness stress. Those who do not question the more or less subtle influence of advertising and mass media will fall into the well-being trap: Short-term satisfaction leads to long-term dependency and frustration.

Last but not least, people who live unquestioningly give away their creative potential. The fewer objections we make, the more one-sided developments become. The fewer citizens who ask "why?", the more remote the logics of political and economic decisions become. Questions of meaning are the basis of indignation and commitment (Hessel, 2008; Hessel & Vanderpooten, 2011). They demand a change of perspective and challenge supposed impossibilities, necessities and constraints. Asking questions about meaning means questioning ourselves – with all the potentially disturbing (and thus productive) consequences.

1.2 (Facing up to) questions of meaning

"Just do it" doesn't guarantee well-being. It may prevent conflicts, but will rarely lead to a life that is experienced as good or fulfilling. What philosophers have been demanding for a long time has been confirmed by empirical research on meaning in recent years: The confrontation with ourselves and the meaningfulness of our actions is beneficial and sometimes necessary for a good life.

Many people are pushed to authenticity by crises. Viktor Frankl even described suffering as an opportunity: It can trigger growth and maturation processes that would otherwise not have taken place. But there is nothing to be said against posing questions of meaning on one's own initiative. Or – in a better formulation by Viktor Frankl – to see ourselves as being questioned by life (Frankl, 1986). The book in hand offers an introduction to the reflective examination of life's meaning on the basis of scientific findings. On the one hand, it promotes personal reflection, and on the other hand, it should help to constructively take up and deal with questions of meaning in patients and clients. At the end of each chapter, you will have the opportunity to question yourself. Greek antiquity assumed that those who asked big questions would do well to understand and recognise themselves: *Gnothi seauton*! (Know thyself!) was an inscription at the entrance of the oracle of Delphi.

1.3 Know thyself!

ESSENTIAL QUESTIONS

Have you ever dealt with the question of meaning in your life?

- If so, when and why?
- If not, why not?

WHAT IS YOUR OPINION ON THE FOLLOWING STATEMENTS?

Life's but a walking shadow, a poor player,
That struts and frets his hour upon the stage,

And then is heard no more. It is a tale
Told by an idiot, full of sound and fury,
Signifying nothing.

(Shakespeare, 2015, p. 77f)

We "must find out the meaning that is objectively there."

(Frankl, 2000, p. 113)

Life that had meaning would not ask about it.

(Adorno, 2003, p. 516)

FOR CONTEMPLATION

With Heidegger, Rüdiger Safranski criticises an understanding of meaning as

> something that exists in the world, or in some imaginary Beyond, as something present-at-hand, something that one can hold on to and orient oneself by – God, a universal law, the stone tables of morality. . . . That kind of nonsense was then rampant – "meaning" was being practiced; there were meaning research programs; there was talk of the shortage of sense-and-meaning resources, which therefore should be used economically. It was a particularly foolish metaphysics of existence.
>
> (Safranski, 1998, p. 151)

1.4 Literature

Adorno, T. W. (2003). *Can one live after Auschwitz? A philosophical reader*. Stanford, CA: Stanford University Press.

Frankl, V. E. (1986). *The doctor and the soul: From psychotherapy to logotherapy*. New York: Vintage.

Frankl, V. E. (2000). *Man's search for ultimate meaning*. Cambridge, MA: Perseus Publishing.

Hessel, S. (2008). *Time for outrage: Indignez-vous!* London: Twelve Hachette Book Group.

Hessel, S., & Vanderpooten, G. (2011). *Engagez-vous!* La Tour d'Aigues: Editions de l'Aube.

Safranski, R. (1998). *Martin Heidegger–between good and evil*. Cambridge, MA: Harvard University Press.

Shakespeare, W. (2015). *Macbeth*. London: Penguin Books.

Chapter 2

Defining meaning

Empirical research on meaning deals with meaning *in* life. It is therefore a question of whether, how and when people find meaning in their lives, what sources they draw on and which purpose they pursue. The fact that many people believe that there is a meaning *of* life is not questioned by this approach. However, such concepts are empirically examined exclusively from the perspective of the individual. How can personal concepts of meaning be grasped? And what does "meaning" mean at all?

2.1 Etymology

Let us begin with the etymology of the German term for meaning (*Sinn*), since it is particularly revealing. Originally it meant "walk, journey, way." The Germanic word group is based on the Indo-European root, whose original meaning was again "to take a direction, to seek a trail" (Duden Etymologie, 1989). Etymologically it is thus the taking of a path, the decision for a direction that determines meaning or meaninglessness. A dynamic quality of meaning is implied. Meaning cannot be fixed. Meaning is the journey, not the reward.

The English term "meaning" was inherited from the Germanic: terms like *mena*, *menen*, or *menian* meant to "signify, intend, think, or have in mind" (Oxford English Dictionary, 2001). The ampler background of the German term *Sinn* is thus not covered by the English term "meaning" (see also Leontiev, 2013).

2.2 Philosophical definition

In a philosophical dictionary, Schischkoff (1991) emphasises the subjectivity involved in the perception of meaning. Meaning, he contends, is not an essential property. It is attributed to a thing, action or event by a person in a specific situation. Therefore, "a thing can be meaningful to one person, but meaningless to another, or meaningful to me today and meaningless a year later" (Schischkoff, 1991, p. 667, transl. TS). This definition confirms the dynamic character of meaning mentioned earlier and further defines it as subjective and relational.

2.3 Meaning in life: a multidimensional construct

With reference to the etymological and philosophical aspects, meaning in life can be determined as the direction – or purpose – that someone pursues, and the ensuing subjective and dynamic evaluation of their life as more or less meaningful (Schnell, 2009, 2014). This concept entails several dimensions: On the one hand, it is about the perceived quality of meaning as meaningful, meaningless or lacking meaning; on the other hand, it is about the origins of this experience, the purpose which is attached to life. These dimensions will be examined in more detail in the following.

2.3.1 *Meaningfulness and crisis of meaning: two relatively independent dimensions*

The first empirical studies on meaning in life used scales based on the assumption that meaningfulness and crisis of meaning were two sides of the same continuum (e.g. Purpose in Life Test, PIL; Crumbaugh & Maholick, 1964). This implied that an absence of meaningfulness would inevitably be accompanied by a crisis of meaning. This assumption fitted Viktor Frankl's theory, which proposed a universal will to meaning (Frankl, 2014). Accordingly, Frankl concluded that not fulfilling the need for meaning would be accompanied by frustration, in the worst case by a noogenic neurosis triggered by the lack of meaning.

For a long time, the one-dimensionality of meaningfulness/crisis of meaning was not tested. Only a separate measurement of both constructs, as made available by the Sources of Meaning and Meaning in Life Questionnaire (SoMe; Schnell & Becker, 2007; Schnell, 2014; Section 3.2.1), allowed for an empirical examination. The result clearly spoke in favour of a two-dimensional solution. The presence of a crisis of meaning could predict quite well the absence of meaningfulness, but this did not work vice versa: When meaningfulness was low, no conclusions could be drawn as to whether a crisis of meaning was present. In many cases, low meaningfulness and low crisis of meaning occurred together (more on this in Chapter 9; Schnell, 2010). Statistically, this fact is expressed in an (only) moderate negative correlation. The two constructs of meaningfulness and crisis of meaning are examined and defined in more detail next.

2.3.2 Meaningfulness: a definition

Meaningfulness is the basic trust that life is worth living. It is based on a (mostly unconscious) evaluation of one's life as coherent, significant, oriented and belonging (Schnell, 2009, 2014).

Coherence means a sense of consistency and comprehensibility. It is based on the experience that our perceptions, acts and goals make sense to us, that they are not inconsistent with one another but instead (ideally) complement and build on each other (horizontal and vertical coherence; Schnell, 2009; Sheldon & Kasser, 1995; see also Section 4.2). A coherent view of self and world have been identified as relevant to the experience of meaning in life (Emmons, 1996; Heintzelman, Trent, & King, 2013; Reker & Wong, 1988).

Significance refers to the perception of resonance to our action (or non-action). If our decisions or acts remain without consequences, we feel irrelevant, insignificant and thus meaningless (Bandura, 1997; Grant, 2008).

Orientation represents the availability of a direction or purpose. Having a purpose, knowing the way one's life should take, serves as a compass when decisions have to be made, when goals are chosen and pursued. Likewise, access to such a compass facilitates the rejection of possibilities which do not correspond to personal values or goals. In our multi-optional society, a form of rejection competence has become a vital skill to prevent a loss of self and perspective. A sense of direction is considered indispensable in the active pursuit of meaning in life (Emmons, 2005; Wong, 1998).

Belonging means perceiving oneself as part of a larger whole, as having a place in this world. It refers to an existential experience rather than a social kind of belonging. It can be viewed as a response to existential isolation, which Yalom (1980) calls one of the four existential givens. Existential isolation means fundamental isolation, brought about by the idea that I alone am responsible for my life and that I am the sole author of my life. A sense of belonging counters this imposition by engaging nevertheless. It can be expressed in many different ways, such as by taking responsibility for family, friends, colleagues, religion, nation, nature or humanity (Schnell, 2009, 2012).

These four criteria – *coherence*, *significance*, *orientation* and *belonging* – can be understood as central elements of meaningfulness. They are closely related to and highly correlate with a subjective understanding of meaning (see Schnell & Becker, 2007; Schnell, 2009). They specify the experience of meaning without referring to its sources, which vary between individuals. The presence of meaningfulness is usually not conscious, but it can be made conscious.

2.3.3 *Crisis of meaning: a definition*

A crisis of meaning is defined as a judgement on one's life as frustratingly empty, pointless and lacking meaning (Schnell, 2009; Schnell & Becker, 2007). It is accompanied by disorientation and disintegration of self-view and worldview. In contrast to meaningfulness, crises of meaning are consciously experienced as a painful state.

2.3.4 *Sources of meaning: a definition*

Meaningfulness depends on active involvement in life. Coherence, significance, orientation and belonging cannot arise from reflection alone; rather, they are qualities of engagement and action. This can take many forms, and people differ in which purpose they perceive as significant. Sources of meaning represent a variety of orientations that give meaning to life when being actively pursued. They thus give form to meaning; they are "meaning in action" (Leontiev, 1982; Schnell, 2004/2009).

2.4 A brief discourse: why achieving meaningfulness is a demanding task in our time

If I had asked a Tyrolean farmer 50 years ago about the meaning in his life, he would have looked at me in astonishment. Until quite recently, meaning was not questionable. Tyrolean farmers lived as part of a Christian-Catholic community. Belonging to this community and the resulting orientation were not a question of choice or conviction; they were self-evident. Equally self-evident was daily action. The cycle of the seasons dictated what was to be done and when. The importance of these activities became manifest in the successful harvest. Family life, profession, politics and church followed a unified view of the world. Those who were integrated into this system lived coherently and consistently.

Today, Western societies are largely characterised by super-diversity (Vertovec, 2007) and functional differentiation (Luhmann, 1977). Social processes do not follow a superordinate concept; instead, a large number of autonomous subsystems have developed that interact with the overall system according to their own codes and rules. Individuals must locate themselves anew in each of these subsystems, deal with the options available there and make a choice. *Coherence* is therefore not present from the outset but instead represents an achievement of the individual. Figure 2.1 illustrates this by means of a selection of societal subsystems and corresponding options.

Orientation and *belonging* also depend on personal choice. It is up to the individual to find their purpose, to prioritise certain values over others. The choice is large; because almost everything is possible, sanctions are unlikely. Also belonging does not just happen; it follows a decision, and in most cases, it requires personal initiative. At the same time, the *significance* of one's own actions is becoming less and less noticeable. The effects of decisions disappear in the opacity of complex global processes. At the national level, a feeling of powerlessness is spreading among citizens. Political decisions remain opaque. Increasingly more processes are centralised, which seems to reduce the opportunities for citizens to have a say. Under these conditions, it should become clear that meaningfulness cannot be taken for granted but instead can effectively be viewed as an achievement.

2.5 Know thyself!

ESSENTIAL QUESTIONS

- Do you differentiate between the meaning of life and a personal meaning in life?
- Does your life seem coherent to you, or does it exhibit contradictions? If so, which ones and why?
- Can you say in which direction your life should go? Do you pursue a life goal or purpose?
- Do you feel that your actions (or non-actions) are noticed and have consequences?
- Do you experience yourself as part of something greater than yourself? If so, what is this "greater whole"?
- Can you identify conditions in your environment that you experience as conducive to living a meaningful life? And can you identify obstructive circumstances?

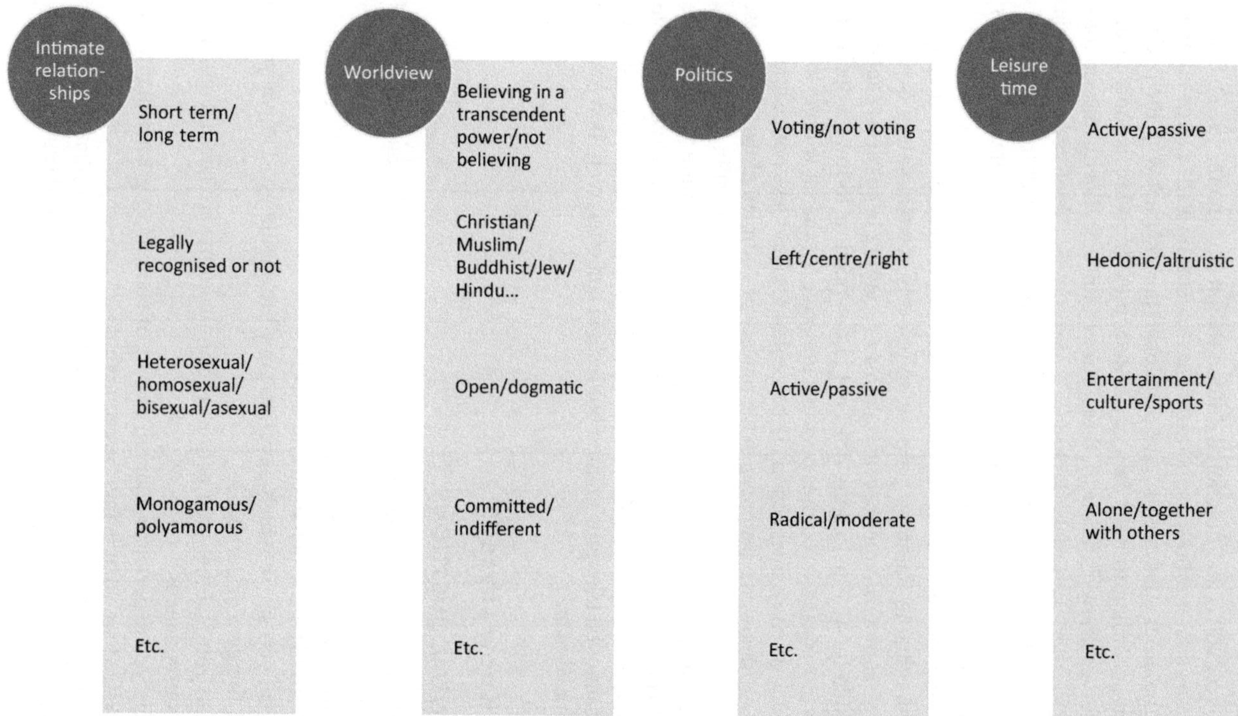

Figure 2.1 Varieties of positions within different social subsystems

2.6 Literature

Bandura, A. (1997). *Self-efficacy: The exercise of control*. New York: Macmillan.

Baumeister, R. F., & Leary, M. R. (1995). The need to belong: Desire for interpersonal attachments as a fundamental human motivation. *Psychological Bulletin, 117*(3), 497.

Crumbaugh, J. C., & Maholick, L. T. (1964). An experimental study in existentialism: The psychometric approach to Frankl's concept of noogenic neurosis. *Journal of Clinical Psychology, 20*(2), 200–207.

Duden Etymologie. (1989). *Herkunftswörterbuch der deutschen Sprache 2* (völlig neu bearb. und erw. Aufl. von G. Dosdrowski, Der Duden, Bd. 7). Mannheim, Wien and Zürich: Duden.

Emmons, R. A. (1996). Striving and feeling: Personal goals and subjective well-being. In J. Bargh & P. Gollwitzer (Eds.), *The psychology of action: Linking motivation and cognition to behavior* (pp. 314–337). New York: Guilford.

Emmons, R. A. (2005). Striving for the sacred: Personal goals, life meaning, and religion. *Journal of Social Issues, 61*, 731–745.

Frankl, V. E. (2014). *The will to meaning: Foundations and applications of logotherapy*. New York: Plume Books.

Grant, A. M. (2008). The significance of task significance: Job performance effects, relational mechanisms, and boundary conditions. *Journal of Applied Psychology, 93*(1), 108.

Heintzelman, S. J., Trent, J., & King, L. A. (2013). Encounters with objective coherence and the experience of meaning in life. *Psychological Science, 24*(6), 991–998.

Leontiev, A. N. (1982). *Tätigkeit, Bewusstsein, Persönlichkeit*. Köln: Pahl-Rugenstein.

Leontiev, D. A. (2013). Personal meaning: A challenge for psychology. *The Journal of Positive Psychology, 8*(6), 459–470.

Luhmann, N. (1977). Differentiation of society. *Canadian Journal of Sociology, 2*(1), 29–53.

Meaning. (2001, January 9). *Oxford English dictionary* (3rd ed.). Retrieved from www.oed.com/view/Entry/115440?rskey=2itcSs&result=1&isAdvanced=false#eid

Reker, G. T., & Wong, P. P. (1988). Aging as an individual process: Toward a theory of personal meaning. In J. E. Birren & V. L. Bengston (Eds.), *Emergent theories of aging* (pp. 214–246). New York: Springer.

Schischkoff, G. (1991). *Philosophisches Wörterbuch*. Stuttgart: Kröner.

Schnell, T. (2004/2009). *Implizite Religiosität–Zur Psychologie des Lebenssinns* (2nd ed.). Lengerich: Pabst.

Schnell, T. (2009). The sources of meaning and meaning in life questionnaire (SoMe): Relations to demographics and well-being. *Journal of Positive Psychology, 4*(6), 483–499.

Schnell, T. (2010). Existential indifference: Another quality of meaning in life. *Journal of Humanistic Psychology, 50*(3), 351–373.

Schnell, T. (2012). "Für meine Freunde könnte ich sterben" – Implizite Religiosität und die Sehnsucht nach Transzendenz. In U. Kropac, U. Meier, & K. König (Eds.), *Jugend–Religion–Religiosität. Resultate, Probleme und Perspektiven der aktuellen Religiositätsforschung* (pp. 87–108). Regensburg: Pustet.

Schnell, T. (2013). Mehr als angenehm – über Partizipation und Sinnerleben. In T. Köhler & C. Mertens (Eds.), *Jahrbuch für Politische Beratung 2012/2013* (pp. 39–49). Wien: Böhlau.

Schnell, T. (2014). An empirical approach to existential psychology: Meaning in life operationalized. In S. Kreitler & T. Urbanek (Eds.), *Conceptions of meaning* (pp. 173–194). New York: Nova Science.

Schnell, T., & Becker, P. (2007). *Der Fragebogen zu Lebensbedeutungen und Lebenssinn (LeBe)*. Göttingen: Hogrefe.

Sheldon, K. M., & Kasser, T. (1994). Coherence and congruence: Two aspects of personality integration. *Journal of Personality & Social Psychology*, *68*, 531–543.

Vertovec, S. (2007). Super-diversity and its implications. *Ethnic and Racial Studies*, *30*(6), 1024–1054.

Wong, P. T. P. (1998). Implicit theories of meaningful life and the development of the personal meaning profile. In P. T. P. Wong & P. S. Fry (Eds.), *The human quest for meaning: A handbook of psychological research and clinical applications* (pp. 111–140). Mahwah, NJ: Erlbaum.

Yalom, I. D. (1980). *Existential psychotherapy*. New York: Basic Books.

Chapter 3

Measuring meaning in life

Because of its abstract and complex character, measuring meaning in life is not an easy undertaking. But the same is true for many psychological characteristics. Psychology's psychometric inventory comprises a multitude of methods that give us access to subjective lifeworlds. They include explorative methods related to individual cases and the quantitative operationalisation of latent constructs. Qualitative methods and quantitative methods are both helpful in assessing meaning in life.

And yet it remains a challenge to select and develop adequate instruments. Several scales used over the past half-century (Antonovsky, SOC, 1993; Battista & Almond, LRI, 1973; Crumbaugh & Maholick, PIL, 1964) were limited in their validity by the assumption of the one-dimensionality of meaningfulness and crisis of meaning. An additional problem was the choice of items. Meaningfulness was measured by items that related to positive affect and life satisfaction, and meaninglessness was operationalised by items that measured depression and boredom. A clear understanding of what distinguishes meaningfulness from neighbouring constructs and possible correlates was apparently lacking.

As a consequence, the research findings suffered, such as with regard to the connection between meaning in life, mental health and well-being. If the scale that measures meaning in life does so through items that capture depression, there is inevitably a high correlation with depression scales. We also get confounded results when a meaning scale that contains items tapping life satisfaction or positive affect is correlated with measures of subjective well-being. It can therefore be assumed that the majority of the research results of the last centuries which deal with the topics of meaning in life, mental health and well-being report artificially elevated correlations (Schnell, 2009, 2014).

It is equally difficult to identify the sources on which people draw for their meaning. A procedure frequently applied in international research was simple but possibly misleading: People were asked questions like "What makes your life meaningful?" or they were asked to write down the three most important things that gave meaning to their lives. This approach is problematic because of the implicit nature of sources of meaning. What gives meaning or purpose to our lives is rarely conscious. It is embedded in our actions and tacitly guides decisions (Schnell, 2011, 2014). When asking directly for sources of meaning, we get the same limited responses all over the world. They typically include family, friends and happiness/well-being (e.g. Debats, 1999; Delle Fave, Brdar, Wissing, & Vella-Brodrick, 2013; Lambert et al., 2010). It is not possible, with this kind of survey, to determine what these terms actually signify; whether they refer to actual or desired sources of meaning; or to what extent these responses might be stereotypes, mentioned due to a lack of deeper knowledge.

3.1 In-depth research: qualitative studies

To avoid the pitfalls just described, my team and I at the University of Trier chose to follow a grounded theory approach (Glaser & Strauss, 1998) to reliably and validly identify the various dimensions of meaning in life. This method represents a systematic approach to develop theoretical concepts on a broad empirical basis by using content analytical techniques. In other words, extensive, unbiased exploration precedes test development. This prevents a questionnaire from measuring exclusively what the researcher thinks is possible and useful.

3.1.1 Structured exploratory interview

What gives meaning to our lives is expressed in many ways. It shapes our *beliefs*, influences our *actions* and comes to light in special *experiences*. Therefore, these three perspectives were analysed in a foundational qualitative study. The means of choice was a structured exploratory interview. Our aim was to record the diversity of possible sources of meaning, identified through the "detour" of personally relevant convictions, meaningful actions and extraordinary experiences. In addition, we wanted to know what was really significant about the content mentioned, because one content – such as family – can have different meanings. We arrived at these meanings by using a laddering technique, a variation of the ultimate meanings technique developed by Dmitry Leontiev (2007). "Laddering" here means that all the answers given by our interviewees were questioned again: "And why? What does that mean for you? What exactly does that signify? What does it stand for?" These questions were repeated until a fundamental meaning was reached that could no longer be questioned – until we arrived at an "ultimate meaning" (ultimate concern). Within the framework of this study, the process of laddering fulfilled two functions: First, it increased the objectivity and reliability of the summary and interpretation of the interview data, since the respondents themselves provided a large part of the interpretation of their answers. Second, the sources of meaning thus identified formed the basis for our psychometric questionnaire, the SoMe (to be discussed later).

3.1.2 Findings from the interview study

We conducted interviews with 74 people. A high heterogeneity of the sample with regard to age, gender, education, occupation and religious background was aimed at and achieved through the use of various sampling techniques. All interviewers had completed a three-day interview training and were well acquainted with content and technique. Our experiences were consistently positive, and the same was also reported by the respondents: It is apparently possible to capture such an abstract topic as meaning in life on the basis of simply formulated, concrete questions (a detailed description of the interview process, the analysis and the evaluation can be found in Schnell, 2004/2009).

We experienced the laddering technique as particularly helpful, since it enforces a process of consistent probing and clarification. One of the participants described it poignantly as a way of "tidying up in your head." (In Section 3.1.3, you can practise laddering.) Here are some examples of answers to two of our interview questions and the meanings that the interviewees arrived at after laddering:

A 61-year-old woman answered the question about what she thought her child (or grandchild or other close child) should ideally do in the future:

> "Ideally that what they do best, and that they are happy with it. What they like most about their job."

- What does this mean? "This is the only way to feel comfortable when you do what you do best. I always tell them that money doesn't matter; money is transient. Feeling good and comfortable is important to me, because what good is a job for me where I earn a lot of money and then have to go with displeasure?"
- What does this mean? "Comfort."

Asked if there was something that was important to her and that she regularly advocated, she said,

> "I have children's meetings in the parish, and they also come to my home, the children from the surrounding area."
>
> - What does this mean? "That they have someone to talk to, there are so many children these days, they really don't have anyone to listen to them and sometimes, when I say to them, 'Take it home and do it at home,' they say, 'Nobody will help me.' If they have anything, they come, if they hurt their knee, they come and get a Band-Aid, they come."
> - What does this mean? "Care, social commitment."

A 46-year-old man answered a question about his child's (or grandchild's or other close child's) future as follows:

> "Stay a learning person."
>
> - What does this mean? "Because that guarantees flexibility. This is a very important characteristic – that you are and remain flexible. Because simply the world changes quickly, not only the big world, but also the small world around you."
> - What does this mean? "Development."

When asked about a regular engagement, he said,

> "I'm constantly advocating for the insights that come from art, for other people who otherwise have nothing to do with art, that they can also be used by others."
>
> - What does this mean? "For example, in conversations with other people or in lessons with pupils, I try to explain to people how important it is to perceive the designed and natural environment and draw conclusions for their own lives: How do I design my environment? From architecture to objects, etc. Where I know a little, where you can learn lessons for life, I try to pass that on a little. As often as possible, at every opportunity."
> - What does this mean? "Creativity, development, passing something on (generativity)."

A 49-year-old woman answered our question about her child's future:

> "He should become a lawyer."
>
> - What does this mean? "This may also come from my childhood. My mother was always quite clumsy about her rights, and I always felt like a champion for her."
> - What does this mean? "Then I have a very strong sense of justice, and I have also put it on my son, and today I fight for my acquaintances. I always orient myself immediately: what rights do they have? This is such a 'hobby' of mine."
> - What does this mean? "Morality, social commitment."

Asked if there was anything that was so important to her that she regularly advocated it, she said:

> "Yes, I'm in the [X] organisation, I've been doing this child and youth telephone helpline for the last few years, and I'm now doing public relations work there. And I'm volunteering in [Y]. I'm committed to it and I'm happy to do it."
>
> - What does this mean? "That I can give something back to society. I often have the feeling that especially at a young age I got a lot from friends, from people around me who helped me and I just want to give something back. In the past, it wasn't so important to me to give back, I did it more in a close environment, but today it's very important to me that I give something back to people who aren't connected to me or my family at all."
> - What does this mean? "Social commitment, passing something on (generativity)."

3.1.3 Know thyself!

SELF-EXPLORATION: TREES OF MEANING

According to Dmitry Leontiev, the choice of starting questions for laddering is not crucial, because the process will always open up access to our existential foundation. Next are some sample questions. These are already tapping existential issues, so you probably won't have to descend too many rungs to get down to your foundation.

Ask yourself one question at a time and make a note of the answer(s). A graphical representation in the form of a tree of meaning is helpful for this. Take some large sheets of paper (DIN A4 or larger), put them upright in front of you and note your first answer to each question on top of each sheet (if you have several answers to a question, use several sheets).

From this answer, uncover the roots. Each of your answers should be questioned, asking "Why?" and "What does that mean for me?" Repeat these questions until you cannot find further meanings. The first why question will usually lead to several meanings. Each of these will have further meanings. So there will be multiple branches of the roots. This demonstrates that our beliefs, actions and experiences are multiple, have different meanings for us and are based on different motives. When you approach the ground, you might find a slight reduction in meanings again, due to overlaps. Try it out:

A What is a good person, according to you? (Why?)
B What is your motto in life? (Why?)
C What does an ideal day look like for you? (Why? What do the individual things mean to you?)
D When and where can you be completely at ease, feel at one with yourself? (Why? What does the activity/situation mean to you?)

By the way, this exercise works best with two people: If another person asks the questions, they may do so even more consistently than you do.

The process of laddering helps to clear the mind, as some of our interviewees mentioned. The examination of the lowest level can lead to further insights. Here you will find concepts that drive and steer you in your life, that are particularly important to you. Subsequent considerations could include the following: Do I give these meanings enough space in my life? Do I put them into practice the way I think is right? If not, what is stopping me?

3.2 Broad-based research: quantitative measurement

Whereas qualitative methods give us rich insights into personal life worlds, quantitative measurements have many other advantages. As soon as a subjective construct can be expressed in numbers, it is possible to compare different people or groups of people or to associate the collected values with other interesting characteristics. We can check whether the results we obtain in a conversation or in individual case analyses apply only to the interviewees or whether we can transfer them to certain groups.

I have experienced that some qualitatively oriented researchers radically reject the questionnaire methodology and some quantitatively working colleagues do not believe in qualitative research at all. Both approaches answer different questions, and both are necessary to get a complete picture. The development of the Sources of Meaning and Meaning in Life Questionnaire (SoMe) was based on extensive individual case analyses, such as the interviews described earlier (including consensus-based, cyclical content analysis), triangulation through photo studies and communicative validation based on discussions of the study results with the respondents (for details, see Schnell, 2004/2009). This qualitative basis resulted in a questionnaire, which has since proved its worth in numerous national and international studies.

3.2.1 The Sources of Meaning and Meaning in Life Questionnaire (SoMe)

The Sources of Meaning and Meaning in Life Questionnaire (SoMe) is an objectively evaluable procedure for the comprehensive and differentiated measurement of meaning and purpose in life. It assesses degrees of personal meaningfulness and crisis of meaning and the extent to which 26 sources of meaning are being realised. The 26 sources of meaning can be assigned to five superordinate dimensions: vertical selftranscendence, horizontal selftranscendence, selfactualisation, order and well-being and relatedness (see Figure 3.1). On each scale or dimension, an average, below-average or above-average value can be achieved in relation to the reference group. The respective profile indicates whether there is a crisis of meaning, whether a person perceives their life as meaningful, which sources of meaning contribute to it and to what extent.

The SoMe is designed for use in research and practice. It consists of 151 items, which take about 20 minutes to respond to. If only the two meaningfulness and crisis of meaning scales (five items each) are employed, completion is possible in two to three minutes.

Since we are usually not aware of the sources of our meaning in life, a questionnaire must take this into account. The SoMe therefore does not explicitly ask for sources of meaning. Instead, it measures the degree

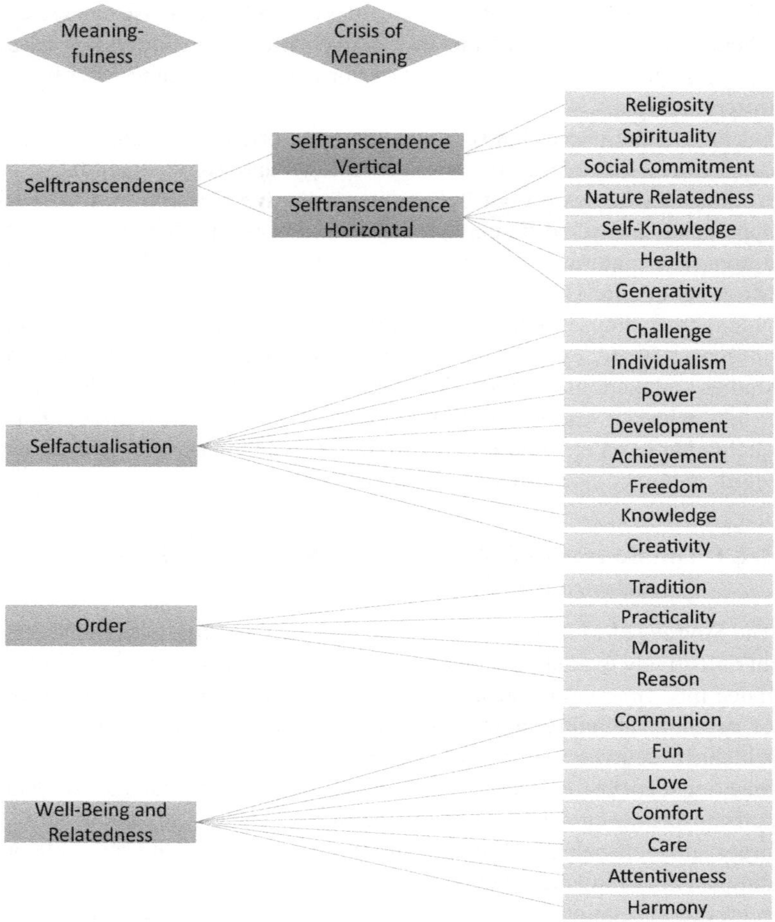

Figure 3.1 Scales and dimensions of the Sources of Meaning and Meaning in Life Questionnaire (SoMe)

Source: Courtesy of Tatjana Schnell 2020.

of self-attribution of activities and beliefs that represent the different sources.

The SoMe is currently used in at least 19 languages. Its use has led to many insights, which are presented in the following chapters.

In Section 3.2.2, you can use two parallel scales of the SoMe to record your degrees of meaningfulness and crisis of meaning and compare them with a (German-speaking) reference sample. (For the original Sources of Meaning and Meaning in Life Questionnaire, go to www.routledge.com/Psychology-of-Meaning-in-Life/Schnell/p/book/9780367415853)

3.2.2 *Know thyself!*

SELF-EXPLORATION: MY MEANING IN LIFE

Rate the statements shown in Table 3.1, according to how much you agree with them. Then calculate the sums. Reference values are available to help you determine whether your values are below, in or above the average.

Table 3.1 Measuring meaningfulness and crisis of meaning

		Do not agree at all					*Agree completely*
		0	*1*	*2*	*3*	*4*	*5*
1	I have a fulfilled life.	☐	☐	☐	☐	☐	☐
2	I feel pain from finding no purpose in my life.	☐	☐	☐	☐	☐	☐
3	Through my actions, I can make a difference in this world.	☐	☐	☐	☐	☐	☐
4	I am missing meaning in my life.	☐	☐	☐	☐	☐	☐
5	I experience myself as part of a larger whole.	☐	☐	☐	☐	☐	☐
6	My life seems empty.	☐	☐	☐	☐	☐	☐
7	I have a sense of direction in my life.	☐	☐	☐	☐	☐	☐
8	The different things I do in my life complement each other in a meaningful way.	☐	☐	☐	☐	☐	☐

Source: Courtesy of Tatjana Schnell 2020. All rights reserved

For calculation and interpretation (compared to a sample of N = 7,920 respondents who completed the German version of these scales), see the following:

Meaningfulness: Sum (1, 3, 5, 7, 8) = _____

Table 3.2 Interpretation of your meaningfulness score

		Below Average	*Average*	*Above Average*
Men	16–25 years	0–9	10–20	21–25
	26–50 years	0–9	10–20	21–25
	51–90 years	0–11	12–22	23–25
Women	16–25 years	0–11	12–20	21–25
	26–50 years	0–11	12–22	23–25
	51–90 years	0–13	14–22	23–25

Crisis of meaning: Sum (2, 4, 6) = ______

Table 3.3 Interpretation of your crisis of meaning score

		Average	*Increased*	*Critical*
Men	16–25 years	0–3	4–8	9–15
	26–50 years	0–2	3–8	9–15
	51–90 years	0–1	2–8	9–15
Women	16–25 years	0–3	4–8	9–15
	26–50 years	0–2	3–8	9–15
	51–90 years	0–1	2–8	9–15

SELF-EXPLORATION: THE AUTHENTICITY PROFILE OF SOURCES OF MEANING

In Table 3.4, you can see the 26 sources of meaning in the form of short statements. For each source, mark how important it is to you. Then mark in a different colour how much you actually put this source of meaning into action. Connect the crosses of one colour with each other. In this way, you get a profile that shows matches and discrepancies between your ideal and your actual orientation, and this can serve as an indicator of authenticity.

Table 3.4 Authenticity profile of sources of meaning

		0	1	2	3	4	5
Selftrans-cendence vertical	1. Religion and faith are an important part of my life.	•	•	•	•	•	•
	2. The belief in some other reality (fate, reincarnation) shapes my life.	•	•	•	•	•	•
Selftranscendence horizontal	3. I actively strive for justice and fair conditions for all.	•	•	•	•	•	•
	4. I have a close relationship with nature and am committed to protecting it.	•	•	•	•	•	•
	5. It is important to me that my body is fit and healthy, and I do a lot for it (e.g. healthy nutrition, sports).	•	•	•	•	•	•
	6. I regularly confront myself with my strengths and weaknesses because it is important for me to know myself.	•	•	•	•	•	•
	7. I orient my life towards passing on my experiences and knowledge to others.	•	•	•	•	•	•
Selfactualisation	8. I am looking for new things, variety and risk. Spontaneity and curiosity are the focus for me.	•	•	•	•	•	•
	9. I follow my own ideas and distance myself from the ideas of others.	•	•	•	•	•	•
	10. In my life, I want to use my strengths and thereby assert myself. I like to exert influence on others.	•	•	•	•	•	•
	11. It is important for me to focus on my own goals. For this, I am ready to learn and change.	•	•	•	•	•	•
	12. I strive for success and outstanding results; I set myself strict standards.	•	•	•	•	•	•
	13. I find it important to be free and unconstrained and take my life into my own hands.	•	•	•	•	•	•
	14. I scrutinise much, gather information and make a point of understanding everything I encounter.	•	•	•	•	•	•
	15. Creativity is my priority, and I arrange my life and environment as imaginatively and originally as possible.	•	•	•	•	•	•

(*Continued*)

Table 3.4 (Continued)

		0	1	2	3	4	5
Order	16. Traditions are of great importance to me, and I orientate myself on what has proved its worth.	•	•	•	•	•	•
	17. Standing with both feet on the ground is vital to me. I generally concentrate on what is useful and necessary.	•	•	•	•	•	•
	18. I consider clear norms and values to be important and orient myself accordingly.	•	•	•	•	•	•
	19. I find it necessary to make decisions out of consideration, leaving my feelings out of the equation.	•	•	•	•	•	•
Well-being and relatedness	20. Friendships and relationships are central to me. I enjoy being together with others.	•	•	•	•	•	•
	21. In my life, pleasure and cheerfulness play a big role. They make my life worth living.	•	•	•	•	•	•
	22. Romanticism, intimacy and passion are very important to me and shape my thoughts and actions.	•	•	•	•	•	•
	23. I usually pursue activities that make me feel comfortable, allow for relaxation and idleness.	•	•	•	•	•	•
	24. It means a lot to me to be there for others and to take care of them. I help when I am needed.	•	•	•	•	•	•
	25. I take care to be attentive to my surroundings and consciously and regularly carry out valuable activities.	•	•	•	•	•	•
	26. I strive for harmony in my life; it is essential for me to be in balance with myself and others.	•	•	•	•	•	•

Source: Courtesy of Tatjana Schnell 2020.

3.3 At the interface: the SoMe-Card Method

It is a challenge to deal with the subject of meaning in the context of therapy and counselling. It might be difficult to find words for this abstract topic. Moreover, awareness of one's own sources of meaning is often missing. Questionnaires are helpful in gaining a differentiated overview of personal sources of meaning. They are usually employed at the beginning of a consultation or treatment and possibly again at a later point in time to measure change. However, the questionnaire is completed by the client on their own, and the analysis then follows specific algorithms. Those who prefer a dialogical exploration of sources of meaning and who have enough time for it are well advised to use structured exploratory interviews, such as the one described earlier. In many settings, however, it may be necessary to use a procedure that is less time-consuming. The Sources of Meaning Card Method (la Cour & Schnell, 2019) is a good choice here. This instrument, developed by the Danish health psychologist Peter la Cour and me, represents an innovative way of integrating the exploration of personal sources of meaning into a therapeutic or advisory conversation in a structured way (la Cour & Schnell, 2020; Schnell & la Cour, 2018).

La Cour was involved in the development of the Danish version of the SoMe. Quite naturally, terms and constructs of the SoMe entered into his therapeutic work with pain patients – who reacted positively to this, as la Cour reported. He decided to systematise the exploration of personal sources of meaning in a dialogical context. Inspired by so-called Q-methods, we jointly developed the SoMe-Card Method. The Q-method, originally developed by William Stephenson (1953), presents a range of personal statements on cards. These must then be sorted by the client according to their relevance. The Q-method represents an interface between qualitative and quantitative methodology. It is particularly suitable for assessing complex attitudes from a subjective perspective (Müller & Kals, 2004).

For the SoMe-Card Method, the most informative items of all 26 sources of meaning were selected (i.e. the highest loading item on the factor representing the scale). The resulting 26 statements are presented on DIN A6 format cards. Clients or patients are asked to go through all 26 cards and select a maximum of five that come closest to their own orientations. Each of these cards is followed by a semi-structured conversation, which refers to the interpretation, significance, importance, threat and potential changes of the respective source of meaning. Finally, the therapist notes the chosen sources of meaning and summarises the main thoughts of the conversation in writing, focusing on possibilities for action and change. The client then receives the document to take along. In principle, the procedure can be completed within one hour.

The method has been carried out in various settings in Denmark, Norway, Germany and Austria. It was used with psychotherapists, nurses, clerics, students, volunteers, patients with various illnesses, people at the end of their lives and primary school children. In Denmark, the SoMe-Card Method has become an established element in training existential communication and care at hospitals and healthcare institutions. When asked, both applicants and conversational partners stated that the method provided insight into attitudes and beliefs that were otherwise difficult to access. The availability of printed statements to talk about personal meaning makes abstract apprehensions "tangible," as formulated by one client: "The cards make it easier. They open things, we can then talk about it. If they were not there, I would be embarrassed" (la Cour & Schnell, 2020, p. 13).

3.4 Literature

Antonovsky, A. (1993). The structure and properties of the sense of coherence scale. *Social Science & Medicine*, *36*(6), 725–733.

Battista, J., & Almond, R. (1973). The development of meaning in life. *Psychiatry*, *36*(4), 409–427.

Crumbaugh, J. C., & Maholick, L. T. (1964). An experimental study in existentialism: The psychometric approach to Frankl's concept of noogenic neurosis. *Journal of Clinical Psychology*, *20*(2), 200–207.

Debats, D. L. (1999). Sources of meaning: An investigation of significant commitments in life. *Journal of Humanistic Psychology*, *39*(4), 30–57.

Delle Fave, A., Brdar, I., Wissing, M. P., & Vella-Brodrick, D. A. (2013). Sources and motives for personal meaning in adulthood. *The Journal of Positive Psychology*, *8*(6), 517–529.

Glaser, B. G., & Strauss, A. L. (1998). *Grounded theory. Strategien qualitativer Forschung*. Bern: Huber.

la Cour, P., & Schnell, T. (2019). *The sources of meaning card method*. Innsbruck: Studia.

la Cour, P., & Schnell, T. (2020). Presentation of the sources of meaning card method: The SoMeCaM. *Journal of Humanistic Psychology*, *60*(1), 20–42.

Lambert, N. M., Stillman, T. F., Baumeister, R. F., Fincham, F. D., Hicks, J. A., & Graham, S. M. (2010). Family as a salient source of meaning in young adulthood. *The Journal of Positive Psychology*, *5*(5), 367–376.

Leontiev, D. A. (2007). Approaching worldview structure with ultimate meanings technique. *Journal of Humanistic Psychology*, *47*(2), 243–266.

Müller, F. H., & Kals, E. (2004). Die Q-Methode. Ein innovatives Verfahren zur Erhebung subjektiver Einstellungen und Meinungen [69 Absätze]. *Forum Qualitative Sozialforschung/Forum: Qualitative Social Research, 5*(2), Article 34.

Schnell, T. (2004/2009). *Implizite Religiosität–Zur Psychologie des Lebenssinns* (2nd ed.). Lengerich: Pabst.

Schnell, T. (2009). The sources of meaning and meaning in life questionnaire (SoMe): Relations to demographics and well-being. *Journal of Positive Psychology, 4*(6), 483–499.

Schnell, T. (2011). Individual differences in meaning-making: Considering the variety of sources of meaning, their density and diversity. *Personality and Individual Differences, 51*(5), 667–673.

Schnell, T. (2014). An empirical approach to existential psychology: Meaning in life operationalized. In S. Kreitler & T. Urbanek (Eds.), *Conceptions of meaning* (pp. 173–194). New York: Nova Science.

Schnell, T., & Becker, P. (2007). *Der Fragebogen zu Lebensbedeutungen und Lebenssinn (LeBe)*. Göttingen: Hogrefe.

Schnell, T., & la Cour, P. (2018). Von der Tiefe im Leben sprechen. Erkenntnisse der empirischen Sinnforschung und Exploration von Lebensbedeutungen mit der LeBe-Kartenmethode. *Wege zum Menschen, 70*(1), 33–47.

Stephenson, W. (1953). *The study of behavior: Q-technique and its methodology*. Chicago, IL: University of Chicago Press.

Chapter 4

Meaning as attribution

Let us return to the philosophical definition of meaning: Meaning is attributed to a thing, action or event by a person in a specific situation (Schischkoff, 1991). When we ask about the origin of meaning, we are thus talking about appraisal and attribution processes. Early on, gestalt psychology convincingly showed that people organise their world into meaningful patterns – also termed "gestalt" (Koffka, 2013). Consider Figure 4.1: What do you see? Almost everyone will see a cube. However, no cube is shown. In fact, there is just an assemblage of black and white areas. It is part of our perceptual repertoire that we interpret stimuli in such a way that they appear to us to be meaningful. And something appears meaningful if it is more than what is directly given: if we can see a significant *surplus*.

What does that tell us? The black and white areas shown in Figure 4.1 seem meaningless per se. A meaningful gestalt emerges when the perceived areas turn into a larger whole – in this case, a cube. In contrast to separate black and white areas, the perception of a cube is meaningful because we can allocate it to our repertoire of action, see its purpose.

Let's try to play through the definition on a different level. You are currently reading this text. Does it make sense to you? Whether it makes sense depends on the who and the when – the person and the situation. Imagine that you are a 12-year-old child who came across this book by chance. You probably wouldn't experience reading it as meaningful, because you couldn't understand many things. If you were a history student under time pressure, just before an important exam, then you could understand the text – but in your current situation, it would probably make less sense to read it. Let's say you are a therapist or a doctor who has been able to take some time off for reading. Some of what you read here will remind you of conversations with patients; other points will tie in with your experience. Through reading, your thoughts might be

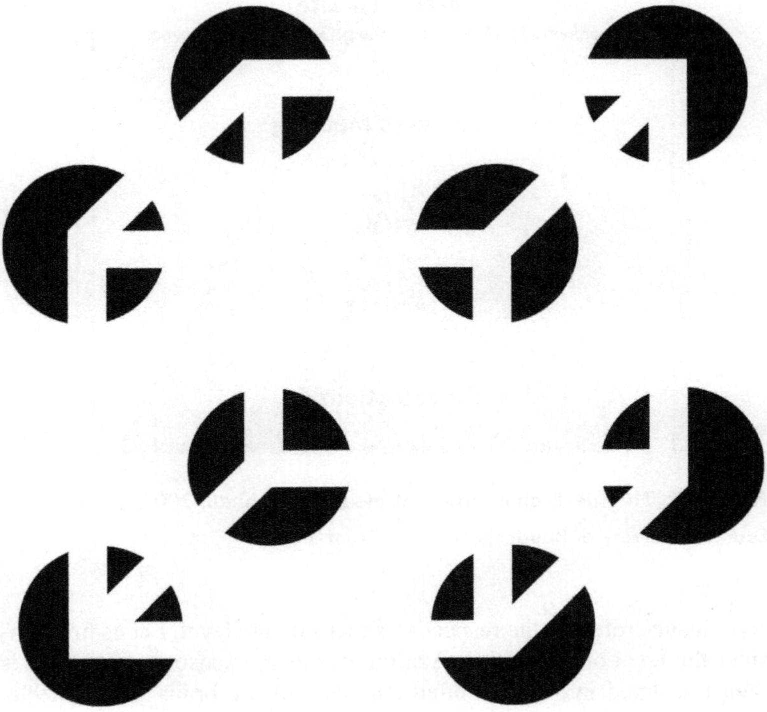

Figure 4.1 What do you see?

directed to new paths. Your insights will contribute to your superordinate goal – to accompany patients and support them in the healing process. In this case, reading would make sense.

Therefore, meaning originates in the perception of a surplus. A thing may be beautiful, an action boring or interesting; it becomes meaningful only once it has a further significance. The hierarchic model of meaning (Schnell, 2009, 2014) illustrates this.

4.1 The hierarchic model of meaning

Construction of meaning takes place incessantly, from the level of stimulus perception to the complex level of meaning in life. Reading the hierarchic model (Figure 4.2) bottom up suggests that a surplus of

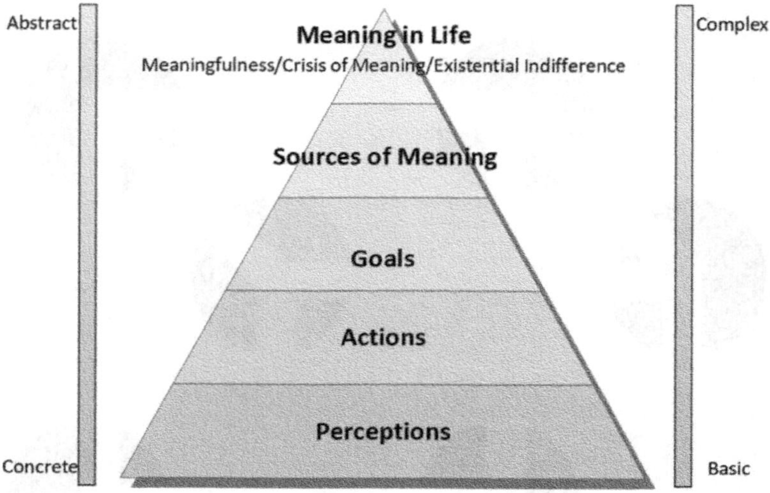

Figure 4.2 The hierarchic model of meaning (Schnell, 2009, 2014)

Source: Courtesy of Routledge/Taylor & Francis

significance refers to the respective superordinate level. Let us first consider the level of perception. A stimulus hits the sensory organs and is then translated into the "unified language of the brain" (Roth, 1998, p. 93, transl. TS) – that is, neurochemical signals which are then transmitted into certain brain areas. No meaning is inherent in these signals. It is constructed by filtering information, combining it and comparing it with existing schemata. All these processes serve to arrive at an understanding of the signals – a meaningful perception. A perception is typically perceived as meaningful when it suggests a reaction to the environment – a surplus referring to the level of action (Prinz, 2000).

Actions are experienced as meaningful when they serve superordinate goals. Aimless action is "mere" activity – which of course also has its place. Not everything we do has to be goal oriented and meaningful. If we move to the beat of music, sing to ourselves or aimlessly walk about, then this may be meaningless, but not in the sense of a negative evaluation. In meaningful action, however, meaning is generated from a surplus of significance that the action might have in relation to overarching goals. Thus, meaningless movement becomes meaningful movement if it serves goals such as health, achievement or enjoyment. Singing in the shower makes sense when, for example, the singer is practising for a singing competition or when their intention is to feel good – which can actually be achieved through singing, which stimulates the release of endorphins and the production of immunoglobulin A and oxytocin (cf. Janning, 2012).

Goals are often regarded as meaningful per se, because they activate a future orientation, motivate people and help to structure everyday life (cf. Emmons, 2003). But this view must be put into perspective: Goal pursuit can also be destructive or meaningless. It has negative consequences if we hold on for too long to goals that cannot be achieved (Brandtstädter & Rothermund, 2002). And goal pursuit can turn into a meaningless endeavour if the goals are extrinsic rather than intrinsic (Sheldon, Ryan, Deci, & Kasser, 2004). Extrinsic goals are those that are pursued in the hope of gaining advantages or avoiding punishment – not because they are considered right and good. So if I pursue a goal simply because my parents wanted it, because it is highly regarded in society or because otherwise I will no longer receive financial support, then sooner or later, it will lead to a sense of meaninglessness and thus to a decrease in motivation. Goals are perceived as meaningful when they are consistent with more-general sources of meaning in our life – that is, when they reflect a person's values and beliefs and enable a movement in a direction that is in line with personal sources of meaning.

Being oriented by sources of meaning stands for an active, involved life, for commitment to a purpose (or several purposes). The perception of sources of meaning as meaningful depends on an overall appraisal of (one's) life as meaningful and worth living. Without being connected to this highest level of meaningfulness, sources of meaning can lose their meaning and become empty commitment. This is particularly evident in situations of crisis, when traumatic events call into question the validity of previously viable orientations (Chapter 1, Chapter 8).

Meaning in life is arranged at the top of the pyramid. No personal level is superior to it. The surplus of significance in this case refers to the sociohistorical context. My life is perceived as meaningful when it takes shape as a story – integrated into the course of history/histories. Can I link my life story with those of the people around me, locate myself in the present social and historical situation? Or do I experience myself as isolated, alienated?

Another reading of the hierarchic model of meaning proceeds top down. In this case, it implies that, starting from the presence of a meaning in life, an active orientation towards sources of meaning is motivated. From these, the pursuit of specific goals suggests itself, which in turn fuels meaningful action and shapes perception accordingly. If, on the other hand, life is seen as meaningless, then nothing is worthwhile. Why get involved, pursue goals or try to do the right thing?

4.2 Vertical and horizontal coherence

The hierarchic model of meaning also illustrates the need for internal coherence: It suggests that lower levels must be integrable into higher levels to be perceived as meaningful. Kennon Sheldon and Tim Kasser coined the terms "vertical coherence" and "horizontal coherence" to describe a coherent system of meaning (Sheldon & Kasser, 1995). They refer primarily to goals, but the specifications can be applied to all levels. Vertical coherence refers to the aforementioned consistency with higher levels: Lower levels should be consistent with or regulated by higher levels. Horizontal coherence means that processes at the same level should complement and not contradict each other.

Here is a fictional case to illustrate vertical coherence and horizontal coherence: Paul says that he finds his *life meaningful*. He identifies communion, achievement and personal development as core *sources of meaning*. At the level of *goals*, he mentions maintaining relationships, work–life balance and speaking different languages. His *actions* include regularly spending time with friends, keeping weekends free from work, being concentrated and efficient at work, devoting one evening a week to learning a foreign language, being open to people from other countries and integrating them into his circle of friends. Paul's *perception* is characterised by the fact that he does not view things new or foreign as unpleasant or frightening but rather as an interesting challenge; that he regards conflicts as solvable through communication; and that he considers people to be primarily trustworthy.

Vertical coherence, here, is expressed in the way that Paul's meaningfulness is reflected in his orientation by sources of meaning. These are not only abstract values; they are also put into action through his pursuit of goals: The striving for relationship cultivation and work–life balance supports his interest in communion. The goal of speaking different languages represents the significance that achievement and personal development have for him. Also, Paul's actions are vertically coherent, since they serve to achieve his goals. His perceptions also correspond well with the higher levels. His openness to new experiences facilitates actions like learning foreign languages or inviting foreigners into his circle of friends. Paul's trusting view of people also agrees with this, and his understanding of conflicts as solvable interpersonal problems is coherent with his community spirit.

Is Paul's system of meaning also *horizontally coherent*? Paul's perceptions are based on compatible basic assumptions and expectations. His actions do not contradict but instead complement each other in achieving his goals. The goals are also chosen in such a way that they can be pursued in parallel without conflicts arising. At the level of sources of meaning, horizontal coherence is not immediately evident. Achievement and communion have the potential to conflict with each other, but they do not have to. The goals that Paul has chosen make it possible to reconcile his sources of meaning and thus to create horizontal coherence at this level as well. (In Section 4.5, you have the possibility to check your own system of meaning for vertical coherence and horizontal coherence.)

4.3 "No man is an island": the environment's role

Questions of meaning cannot be negotiated separately and solely on an individual level. At all levels, they need to be integrated into higher-level contexts – up to being integrated into social and historical processes. Philosophy understands an "individual" as an "independent and rational being who can command him- or herself but at the same time is a carrier of general human values in overarching contexts" (Schischkoff, 1991, p. 332 f., transl. TS). Processes of meaning take place in the confrontation with these overarching contexts. The environment influences every level of the hierarchic model of meaning described earlier, whether in a supportive, restrictive or moderating way.

To support meaningful living, environments should be sufficiently transparent and comprehensible on the one hand and provide sufficient resources – that is, contribute to manageability – on the other (Antonovsky, 1987). *Kafkaesk* environments and ambiguous stimuli complicate meaningful perception. Social and financial restrictions limit possibilities for action. Through expectations and learning experiences associated with them, these limitations also narrow the choice of goals and orientation towards sources of meaning. Meaningfulness is difficult to achieve if the environment impedes significant, coherent and value-oriented action and the experience of belonging.

Just as no meaning is inherent in a thing (but is attributed by a person in a certain situation), no environment can be understood as supportive or obstructive of meaning, per se. Here too, it is all about the relation between a certain individual and their environment. We could assume that today's liberal, pluralistic multi-optional society is an ideal basis for individual meaning-making, since every person has the chance to choose their own way. But are coherence, orientation and belonging not much more easily achievable in a society that offers fewer options, is oriented towards a common canon of values and demands and expects belonging – such as in authoritarian regimes? A cognitively complex person with a high tolerance for ambiguity (i.e. the ability to deal with uncertainty and contradictions) will probably experience the multi-optional society as conducive to meaning, especially if they perceive themselves as part of that society. Others, who feel marginalised in the multi-optional society, might yearn for an environment characterised by more-coherent structures and clearer orientations and belonging. European citizens who joined the terrorist militia Islamic State can be seen as an extreme example of this. Various analyses come to the conclusion that these decisions are based less on religious convictions than on a need for identity, belonging and meaning. Emigrants feel alienated from Western societies; they experience them as cold, inhuman, selfish and immoral. The Umma on the other hand – the world community of Muslims, represented here by the Islamic State – is regarded as synonym for order and belonging and satisfies the need for a shared orientation (Cesari, 2011).

These considerations again reflect the relativity of the concept of meaning. Instead of determining meaningful and meaningless environmental conditions, we find that people experience different conditions as meaningful. These may be conditions that violate human rights and ignore democratic principles and the rule of law. From a humanist perspective, it can be difficult to speak of meaningfulness here. Nevertheless, it might be necessary if we want to understand the existential dimension of individual worldviews and the actions that emanate from them. Focusing on shared existential needs can open up a basis for comprehension and communication. Even largely contradictory (political, religious, etc.) attitudes can gain in comprehensibility when we realise that the various parties are trying to satisfy a similar need for coherence, orientation, significance and belonging.

4.4 And how does it feel?

We now know a number of things about how meaning is constructed – but how does it actually feel? We generally don't feel it at all, because it is not an emotion. Let's look at the defining features of an emotion (Scherer, 2005):

- Cognitive appraisal: a cognitive evaluation of events and objects and the context they occur in.
- Physiological arousal: the biological component of emotional experience.

- Motor Expression: facial or vocal expression and gestures that arise with an emotion.
- Action tendencies: the motivation to strive for (pleasant) or avoid (unpleasant) feelings.
- Feelings: the subjective experience of an emotional state.

Meaningfulness is a great motivator, as explained in more detail in Section 11.1.1. Cognitions also play an important role, especially in the form of unconscious evaluation processes that check the coherence or incoherence with the respective superordinate context (see Figure 4.2). But a sense of meaning is not biologically activated. It is accompanied neither by physiological arousal processes nor by mimic or gestural expressions. The aspect of subjective experience is also largely absent, since meaningfulness is normally not perceived at all. A meaningful (life) situation is characterised by coherence and fit – that is, characteristics that usually remain below the threshold of perception. Our extremely economic perceptual apparatus draws our attention above all to things that require intervention. As long as everything runs such that it is adequate and consistent for us, there is no reason to point this out.

We can thus say that the presence of meaning is not a feeling. Rather, it is the result of subjective evaluation processes that remain below the perception threshold as long as the result is positive. When it comes to meaning, feelings have above all a confirmative function, such as the experience of joy when reaching an important goal (Klinger, 1998) or an affirmative feeling of closeness and belonging. By the way, this is similar in health: We are not normally aware of it either. It is also not a feeling. But there are critical characteristics that allow us to assess our health – just like our sense of meaning.

The situation is quite different, however, if the subliminal subjective evaluation processes turn out to be negative. In such a case, our attention is inevitably drawn to it: Meaning becomes conscious and can be experienced – but only in the form of its absence.

4.5 Know thyself!

SELF-EXPLORATION: MY PERSONAL MODEL OF MEANING

Fill in your personal model of meaning *from bottom to top* (Figure 4.3): Note the actions you perform daily, the goals you pursue, your sources of meaning (e.g. those with the highest "is" values from Table 3.4) and your

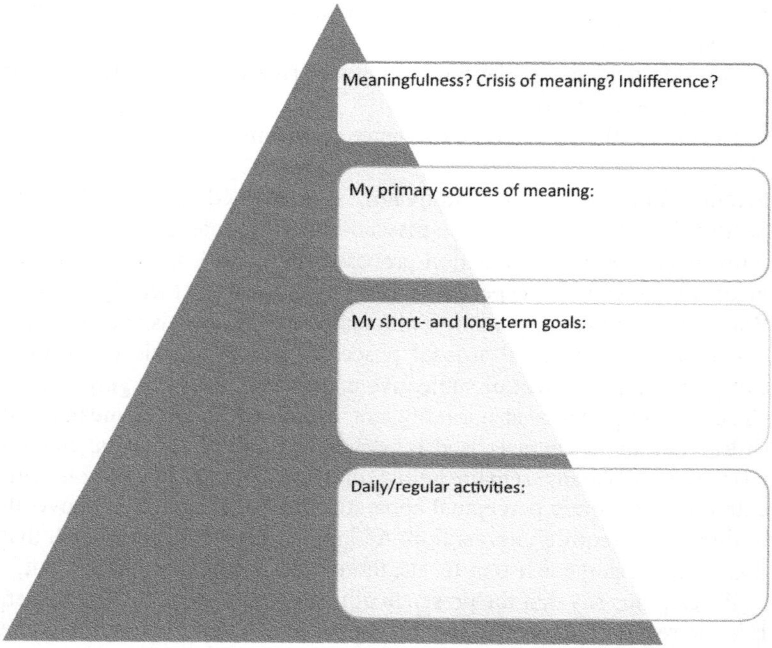

Figure 4.3 Personalised model of meaning

Source: Courtesy of Tatjana Schnell 2020.

meaning in life. Then analyse the pyramid in terms of vertical coherence and horizontal coherence.

VERTICAL COHERENCE

Do your actions serve to achieve your goals? Do your goals coincide with your sources of meaning? Are your sources of meaning motivated by the assumption that your life is meaningful?

HORIZONTAL COHERENCE

Do your actions match? Do they complement each other? Or do they contradict each other? Do your goals match? Do they complement each other? Or do they contradict each other? Do your sources of meaning match? Do they complement each other? Or do they contradict each other?

4.6 Literature

Antonovsky, A. (1987). *Unraveling the mystery of health: How people manage stress and stay well.* San Francisco: Jossey-Bass.

Brandtstädter, J., & Rothermund, K. (2002). The life-course dynamics of goal pursuit and goal adjustment: A two-process framework. *Developmental Review, 22*(1), 117–150.

Cesari, J. (2011). Muslims in Europe and the US: A shared but overrated risk of radicalism. In R. Coolsaet (Ed.), *Jihadi terrorism and the radicalisation challenge* (pp. 101–116). Farnham: Ashgate.

Emmons, R. A. (2003). Personal goals, life meaning, and virtue: Wellsprings of a positive life. In C. L. M. Keyes & J. Haidt (Eds.), *Flourishing* (pp. 105–128). Washington, DC: APA.

Janning, M. (2012). Vom Segen des Singens. *Heilberufe, 64*(4), 24–25.

Klinger, E. (1998). The search for meaning in evolutionary perspective and its clinical implications. In P. T. P. Wong & P. S. Fry (Eds.), *The human quest for meaning* (pp. 27–50). Mahwah, NJ: Erlbaum.

Koffka, K. (2013). *Principles of gestalt psychology.* Abingdon: Routledge.

Prinz, W. (2000). Kognitionspsychologische Handlungsforschung. *Zeitschrift für Psychologie, 208*, 32–54.

Roth, G. (1998). *Fühlen, Denken, Handeln. Wie das Gefühl unser Verhalten steuert.* Frankfurt am Main: Suhrkamp.

Scherer, K. R. (2005). What are emotions? And how can they be measured? *Social Science Information, 44*(4), 695–729.

Schischkoff, G. (1991). *Philosophisches Wörterbuch.* Stuttgart: Kröner.

Schnell, T. (2009). The sources of meaning and meaning in life questionnaire (SoMe): Relations to demographics and well-being. *Journal of Positive Psychology, 4*(6), 483–499.

Schnell, T. (2014). An empirical approach to existential psychology: Meaning in life operationalized. In S. Kreitler & T. Urbanek (Eds.), *Conceptions of meaning* (pp. 173–194). New York: Nova Science.

Sheldon, K. M., & Kasser, T. (1995). Coherence and congruence: Two aspects of personality integration. *Journal of Personality & Social Psychology, 68*(3), 531–543.

Sheldon, K. M., Ryan, R. M., Deci, E. L., & Kasser, T. (2004). The independent effects of goal contents and motives on well-being: It's both what you pursue and why you pursue it. *Personality and Social Psychology Bulletin, 30*(4), 475–486.

Chapter 5

Varieties of meaning

5.1 Interindividual differences in meaningfulness and sources of meaning

For Paul, socialising with lots of people is a pleasure; Paula tries to avoid group activities or parties. Bert is often worried, anxious and nervous, whereas Berta remains calm and serene. People differ in their personality traits. Do these interindividual differences influence whether someone sees meaning in their lives? Our investigations have shown that this is the case to a relatively small extent: In our study with 202 German participants of different age groups, approximately 16 percent of meaningfulness could be explained by personality traits (Schnell & Becker, 2006). Conscientiousness, extraversion, agreeableness and openness contributed to it. A study in the US with 275 undergraduate student participants found no relationship between a presence of meaning and openness; instead, they additionally established a negative correlation with neuroticism (Steger, Kashdan, Sullivan, & Lorentz, 2008). Another study (Halama & Dedova, 2007) interrogated 148 adolescents in Slovakia and found positive relationships between meaningfulness and extraversion, openness and conscientiousness, a negative link between meaningfulness and neuroticism and no correlation with agreeableness.

Summarising the results that were found in all three studies, it seems to be somewhat easier for self-controlled, optimistic and sociable people to lead a meaningful life. The nonexistent link between meaningfulness and neuroticism in the German sample might be attributable to age – since it is the only sample that included older adults. It suggests that even when people experience anxiety, vulnerability or self-consciousness, they can still see their lives as meaningful.

The connection between personality traits and sources of meaning is much greater. We are born with a predisposition towards certain personality traits; these strengthen or change through our experiences over the course of our lives. At all times, however, a certain pattern of personality traits forms the background for our confrontation with the world. This is expressed in an unconscious tendency to show or choose a certain behaviour and to reject others. Thus, people who are open to experience are more likely to find meaning in selfactualisation than in tradition, morality or reason. In contrast to an extraverted person, an introverted person will probably not invest their time and energy in power, communion or fun. Table 5.1 gives an overview of associations between the big

Table 5.1 Prediction of sources of meaning through personality traits (multiple regression, N = 310)

	% Explained by Big Five	*Neuroticism*	*Extraversion*	*Openness*	*Agreeableness*	*Conscientiousness*
Religiosity	5				+	
Spirituality	9	++	+		+	
Social Commitment	19			+++	++	
Nature Relatedness	15		− −	++	++	+
Self-knowledge	33	+	−	+++		+
Health	19		−	+	+	+++
Generativity	7			+		++
Challenge	28		+++	+	−	− −
Individualism	23		+	+++	− −	
Power	40		+++		− − −	+
Development	33	-		+++		++
Achievement	25	++	+		− − −	+++
Freedom	11			++	− −	
Knowledge	34		-	+++	−	++
Creativity	33			+++		
Tradition	35	++		− − −	+	++
Practicality	28		++	− − −		+
Morality	16	++		− −		+++
Reason	30			−		+++
Communion	35	++	+++		+++	
Fun	25		+++	−		−
Love	17	+++	++	+	+	
Comfort	15		++	+		− −
Care	31	+	++	+	+++	+
Attentiveness	12	+	++	+	+	+
Harmony	24	+		++	+++	++

Note: +) *beta* < 0.2; ++) *beta* 0.2–0.3; +++) *beta* > 0.3; −) *beta* < −0.2; − −) *beta* −0.2–0.3; − − −) *beta* < −0.3

five personality traits (neuroticism, extraversion, openness, agreeableness and conscientiousness; Matthews, Deary, & Whiteman, 2003) and sources of meaning.

The correlations show that some sources of meaning are shaped more strongly (e.g. for power, 40 percent) and others less strongly (e.g. for religiousness, 5 percent) by personality traits. The table can be of help when you are interested in identifying sources of meaning that are likely to correspond to a person on the basis of their personality dispositions. (It is helpful to have a big five personality profile of that person at hand for this.) Alternatively, it might also be appropriate to tackle such orientations that a person has avoided so far, since this might initiate positive changes.

5.2 Meaning is dynamic: changes over the lifespan

Personality traits are considered stable if they do not change over several months. In this sense, also meaningfulness and sources of meaning are stable. Nevertheless, it is reasonable to assume that at different stages of life, other themes become relevant. The developmental psychologist Erik H. Erikson sketched it out in his psychosocial development model: While childhood is about developing trust, autonomy, initiative and industry, puberty is focused on developing an identity. Young adulthood centres on learning intimacy, middle adulthood on developing generativity and late adulthood on accepting and integrating one's life course (Erikson, 1988). Accordingly, sources of meaning should also change with the phases of life.

Our data from a sample of 793 people aged 16 to 85 (M = 40, SD = 17) confirm this assumption (Figure 5.1). Figure 5.1 shows an increase in both vertical selftranscendence and horizontal selftranscendence from middle adulthood onwards – that is, the phase in which, according to Erikson, self-centring is reversed. In the same period, there is a decline in the importance of selfactualisation. Well-being and relatedness are important during adolescence and in young adulthood, but they remain relevant even into old age, despite a slight decline.

A particularly strong change can be seen in the dimension of order: Tradition, reason, practicality and morality clearly increase from age 30 and again from age 50. The first of these two trends might be related to the onset of parenthood. The average age of mothers at the birth of their first child in German-speaking countries is around 30. There are surprisingly few statistics on the age of fathers at the birth of their first child.

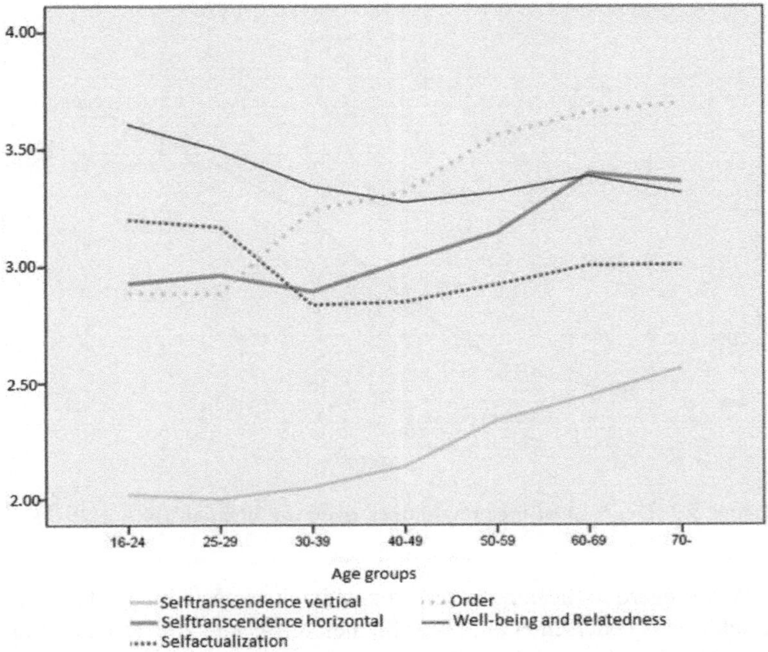

Figure 5.1 Characteristics of the five dimensions of meaning over the lifespan

According to Swiss statistics, fathers are between 30 and 39 years old in the majority of live births (Schweizer Bundesamt für Statistik, 2019). The birth of a child goes hand in hand with responsibility. With the arrival of the helpless baby, security, protection and rootedness take on a new meaning. Traditions offer important starting points for structuring everyday life with small children in a meaningful way, such as through rituals. In addition, the phase of young parenthood is a time when we often start reflecting on the conventions, customs and values that guide our parental actions and will thus be passed on to the child.

The second increase in the relevance of order, which can be observed from an age of about 50 years, may be related to the professional situation. At this stage, the majority of professionals are no longer concerned with career, development and advancement. Experience-based, prudent reason is more common than "youthful" risk taking. What has been achieved is consolidated; what has proved its worth is less questioned.

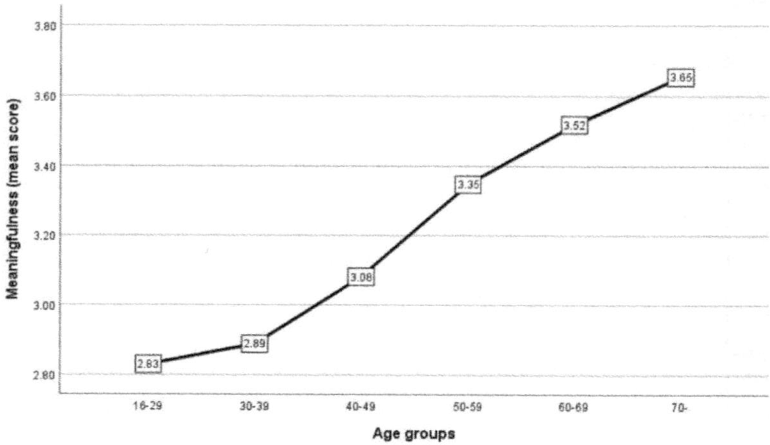

Figure 5.2 Degrees of meaningfulness over the lifespan (N = 1,291)

With regard to meaningfulness, a positive increase with age has been established (Pedersen et al., 2018; Schnell & Becker, 2007; Steger, Frazier, Oishi, & Kaler, 2006). Figure 5.2 shows merged data from recent surveys (N = 1,291), which, with regard to gender, age and education, approximates the German general population. Meaningfulness is lowest at ages 16 to 39; it then rises continuously into old age (r = 0.28). A rise of meaning with age was already observed in the 1980s (Reker, Peacock, & Wong, 1987) and in the beginning of this millennium (Schnell & Becker, 2007). It might therefore be an age effect, not a cohort effect. In other words, as we approach old age, we all could expect more fulfilment and existential stability; it is not just a characteristic of this age group at the present moment. But even if this should be the case, external events can always disrupt such developments. Thus, a "natural" increase in meaningfulness with age will probably not manifest itself in a world marked by climatic disasters, dramatic social injustice or a pandemic wich tragically affects the old ones, in particular.

5.3 Meaning in life and sources of meaning for men and women

In terms of reported meaningfulness, men and women differ either a little (Pedersen et al., 2018; Schnell & Becker, 2007; Pollet & Schnell, 2017) or not at all (Damásio, Koller, & Schnell, 2013; Steger et al., 2006). The differences found point in the direction of a slightly higher meaningfulness in women.

However, quite extreme gender differences can be seen when it comes to sources of meaning (Figure 5.3). On average, men and women seem to invest in quite different types of purpose. The pattern that emerges reflects the age-old "duality of human existence" (Bakan, 1966): agency vs communion. Agency manifests itself in the form of self-assertion and self-development, whereas communion manifests itself through cooperation and attachment. In the sources of meaning, agency is represented by selfactualisation. Empirical gender differences have been established with regard to challenge, power, freedom, achievement and knowledge. Also, reason (from the dimension of order) is preferred by men. Communion manifests itself above all in the form of care and communion. Empirically, these two sources of meaning clearly appeared as women's domains, just like most other sources of meaning pertaining to the dimension of well-being and relatedness: fun, love, harmony, comfort and attentiveness.

The gender profile also replicates the established finding that women are more religious than men and tend more towards different forms of spirituality. In Christian traditions, women are more likely to believe in a god or higher power, and they are more actively involved in religious events (Sullins, 2006). Accordingly, men more often identify as atheists (Keysar & Navarro-Rivera, 2013; Schnell, 2015a).

The causes of this gender difference have still not been clarified (Klein, 2012). Socialisation processes seem to play an important role here, and they seem to be connected to the aforementioned distinction between agency and communion. To a greater extent than men, women are responsible for raising children. They are therefore more often at home and more involved in maintaining social relationships and traditions. This context is theorised to be conducive to a religious attitude (Trzebiatowska & Bruce, 2012). Gender role stereotypes also contribute to the association of womanhood with caring and community-oriented characteristics. However, as women's participation in the labour market progresses, the question arises why gender differences in religion and spirituality persist. It is conceivable that women will simply become affected by secularisation processes later, due to their still-lower presence in public life (Trzebiatowska & Bruce, 2012).

Further explanations of the gender difference in religiosity refer to psychological or physiological characteristics. Rodney Stark (2002) assumes that men tend to take risks because of their higher testosterone

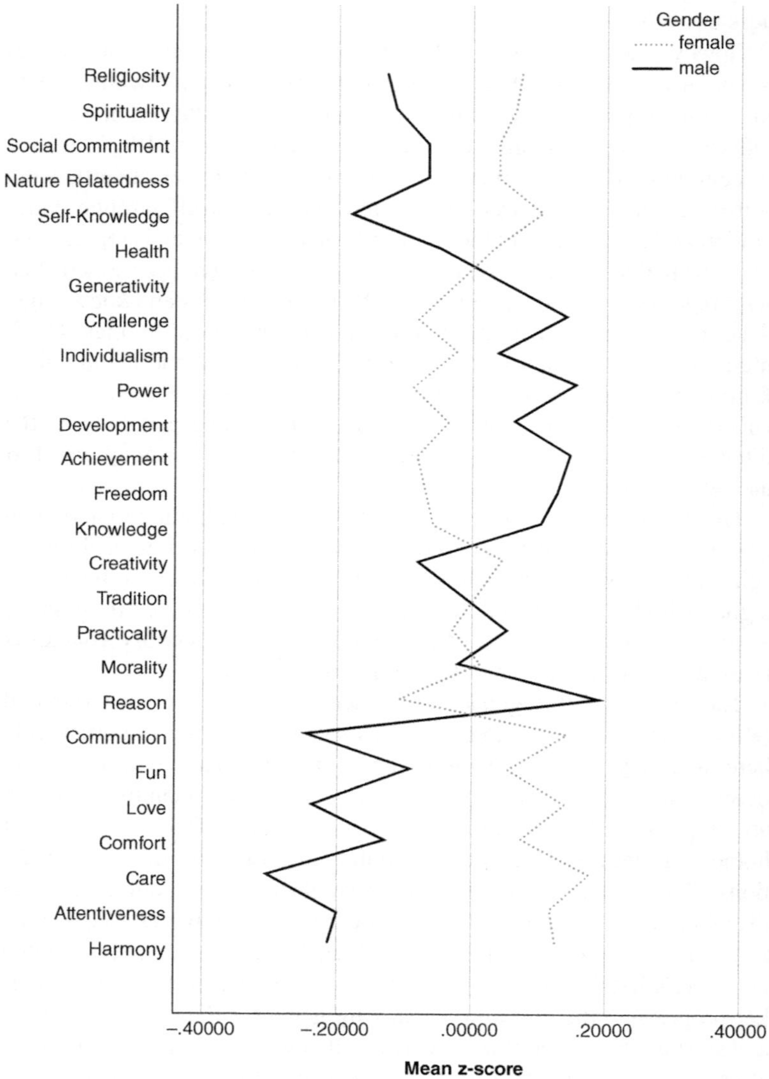

Figure 5.3 Different importance of sources of meaning for men and women (N = 1,123)

level – an aspect of agency/independence. Miller and Stark (2002) were able to show that women are more religious or have more supernatural beliefs than men do when deviations from these beliefs are accompanied by sanctions. In other words, men probably dare to question traditional beliefs because of their greater willingness to take risks.

Although this testosterone hypothesis is not regarded as the sole cause of gender differences in religion and spirituality, it has met with approval. It is also supported by the findings of our study on meaning in life in atheists (Schnell & Keenan, 2011). We compared sources of meaning of 61 female and 41 male convinced atheists. At first glance, the gender-specific pattern of agency and communion was also found here (Figure 5.4). Female atheists attached much more importance to well-being and relatedness than male atheists did. Selfactualisation was again more pronounced in male atheists – with one exception: challenge. Female atheists even reported an average value slightly higher than that of male atheists, although the difference was not statistically confirmed. This means that those women who turned away from supernatural beliefs were at least as interested in challenge as men. The operationalisation of challenge in the Sources of Meaning and Meaning in Life Questionnaire (SoMe) includes the active search for novelty, variety and risk.

In a follow-up study in Innsbruck, we investigated the direct connection between testosterone values and various dimensions of worldview (Scholz, 2019). Among the male study participants, a small positive correlation between testosterone and atheistic conviction was indeed found; this was not visible in women. Instead, they showed a positive correlation between testosterone levels and self-attributed religiosity. The results require further investigation, but there is an interesting agreement with current findings. High levels of testosterone in men are generally associated with an increased likelihood of aggressive or antisocial behaviour, which in turn is seen as intended to serve social status (see e.g. Hamilton, Carré, Mehta, Olmstead, & Whitaker, 2015). Casto and Edwards (2016) point out that prosocial behaviour can also serve social status. In an experimental study with a women's soccer team, they measured the players' testosterone levels before and after two games; in addition, they also measured their attitude towards their opponents. Regardless of whether it was victory or defeat, women with higher testosterone levels were more likely to reconcile with their opponents. According to the authors, this could indicate that high testosterone levels in women tend to inspire action that increases social status through social cohesion.

A parallel to our study can be seen in the fact that male participants with high testosterone levels leaned towards atheism. Atheism is characterised

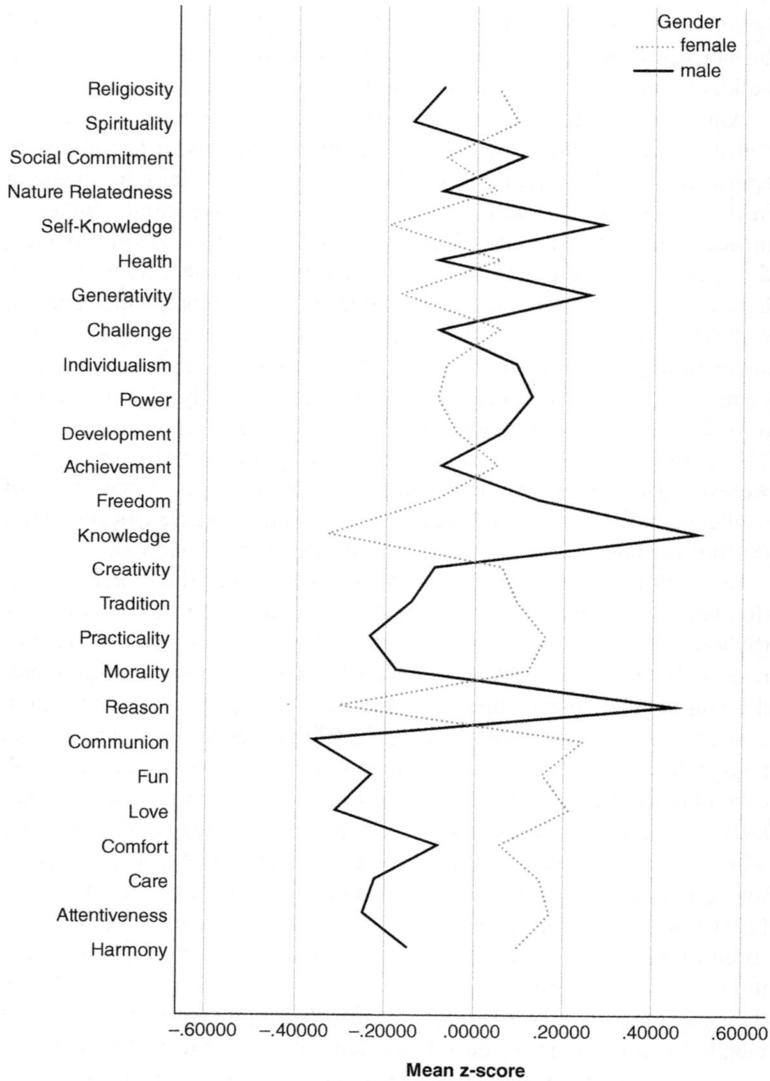

Figure 5.4 Different importance of sources of meaning for female and male convinced atheists (N = 102)

by a rejection of religion and belief in higher powers. Female participants with high testosterone levels, on the other hand, attributed higher religiousness to themselves, which has the claim of compassion and thus (at least theoretically) stands for cohesion rather than rejection.

If these findings can be further supported, they are of particular practical relevance to the widespread use of hormonal contraception. Our study clearly showed the expected relationship between the use of the birth control pill and testosterone levels. Among the 47 percent of women who took the birth control pill, testosterone levels were significantly lower. Should our attitudes and existential orientations indeed be related to hormonal characteristics, the use of hormonal contraception ought to be questioned in this respect too.

5.4 Meaning in life, education and intelligence

At the beginning of the millennium in Germany, the degree of perceived meaningfulness was independent of education: Values did not differ between those who had completed lower secondary school, secondary school or A levels (Schnell & Becker, 2007). When looking at more recent data, we see that this has changed. The results suggest a clear connection between education and meaning in life. Meaningfulness is least pronounced among people who have at most a lower secondary education certificate and continues to rise with intermediate education certificates, A levels and also graduation from university (Figure 5.5). People with a lower secondary school–leaving certificate and with a university degree differ from all other levels of education, while there is no significant difference in meaningfulness between people with a secondary school–leaving certificate and those with A levels.

These numbers are dramatic and demand interpretation. It should be considered, though, that participation in our surveys – like in most other surveys – may have been motivated by a specific interest in the topic, thus shaping the outcomes to a certain degree. However, this could hardly explain the present findings. Another possible explanation has to do with a change in our society's conceptualisation of education. In increasing distance from humanistic ideals, education has turned into a feature of individual employability: flexibility and adaptability in the face of global competition. In the neoliberal perspective that prevails today, it is every person's responsibility to upskill and improve throughout life. Failure or success in the modern lifeworld is thus traced back to the individual's (lack of) effort. With today's society being predominantly knowledge based, citizens with lower education might feel

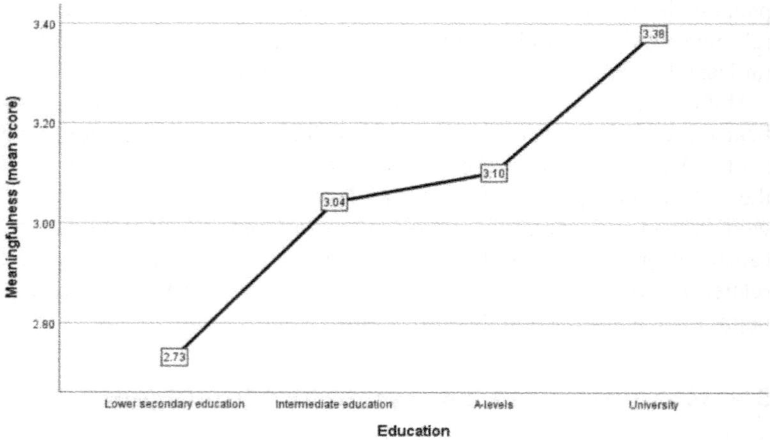

Figure 5.5 Degrees of meaningfulness in relation to education (N = 1,291)

disadvantaged from the start. This is enhanced by a societal disregard for (lower) secondary education, which has even turned into a stigma, often self-applied by those concerned (Völcker, 2016). Academic education is generally prioritised, although many jobs in the craft sector remain vacant. People with lower education are therefore subject to more or less implicit depreciation. On the other hand, they see themselves confronted with the imperative to continuously self-improve, albeit without access to the contexts that might cater to this – authentic or enforced – "need."

A surprising result which seems to contradict the findings I have just reported came up when we investigated the meaning in life of highly gifted individuals. We worked with two types of giftedness: high intellectual potential and high achievement. The first was represented by German and Austrian members of the high IQ society Mensa, who have a confirmed IQ of at least 130. The second was represented by graduates who received their PhD *sub auspiciis Praesidentis rei publicae* (under the auspices of the Austrian president). This is an Austrian award for outstanding school and study achievements for which the following criteria apply: All upper school classes, A levels, university exams and final degree, and the PhD must have been completed with excellent or very good results. The maximum duration of study may not exceed the average duration. Moreover, awardees should exhibit an exemplary way of life and thus prove worthy of distinction.

A total of 198 adult members of Mensa, 141 *sub auspiciis* awardees and, as a control group, 136 randomly selected citizens answered a series of questionnaires. We also conducted in-depth interviews with some of them. In line with the literature, we expected both highly gifted groups to lead meaningful and happy lives. This was suggested, for example, by the longitudinal Marburg Giftedness Project. Here, Detlef Rost and his team did not encounter any significant differences between gifted and not gifted participants. They thus concluded that highly gifted people are well integrated in the school system, successful at school, socially inconspicuous, psychologically stable and self-confident (Rost, 2009).

Therefore, we hypothesised that the highly intelligent (members of Mensa) and the high achievers (*sub auspiciis* awardees) would be as happy and fulfilled as the control group. When we compared the three groups empirically, our assumption was disproved. The highly intelligent and the high achievers differed substantially, where the highly intelligent were much worse off – both for happiness and, to a particularly great extent, for meaning in life (Pollet & Schnell, 2017). To gain insights into potential personal change, we analysed the two gifted groups a second time after four years. The highly intelligent still had lower values in their meaningfulness and subjective well-being (Vötter & Schnell, 2019a). What might be the reason for this finding?

Both gifted groups exhibited another noteworthy difference, which related to the retrospective evaluation of school experiences. Whereas the majority of the high achievers said they were challenged to an adequate degree, the majority of the highly intelligent said they were underchallenged. At the same time, 56 percent of them reported that their abilities had not been considered at all in school. Only 8 percent of the high achievers had had this experience. It is questionable how valid these assessments are, because they were made in retrospect and can be strongly coloured by the current situation. Nevertheless, they point to something important: A lot of highly intelligent people believe that they have not been valued, promoted and adequately challenged in school, and this perception goes hand in hand with a low sense of meaning.

Another difference between the highly intelligent and high achievers related to their intelligence, which was high in both, but even higher in the case of high intelligence than in the case of high performance. Could a very high level of intelligence have a negative effect on the experience of meaning in life? International analyses at country level showed a positive correlation between intelligence and suicide rates (Voracek,

2008): the higher the average national intelligence quotient, the higher the suicide rates. It is questionable, however, to generalise such data to the level of individuals. Here the findings are still thin. In a longitudinal study, Crandall and colleagues (2018) found that high verbal intelligence predicted suicidality in adolescents about six years later, but there was no correlation with suicides actually performed. The result suggests that a higher verbal ability can lead people in critical life situations to consider a variety of possible solutions – including considerations of suicide. At the same time, this ability might also help to find alternative solutions to suicide (Crandall, Allsop, & Hanson, 2018).

In addition, the authors discuss the possibility that highly intelligent people are more likely to experience crises of meaning. In crises of meaning, one's existence is called into question, which can also include considerations of suicide. We have demonstrated such a connection between a crisis of meaning and suicidal tendencies in adolescents (Schnell, Gerstner, & Krampe, 2018). A cautious conclusion might suggest that above-average intelligence goes hand in hand with a critical view of the self and the world. Accordingly, the highly intelligent would find it more difficult to cherish so-called positive illusions (Section 8.5), which are known for being conducive to self-esteem. Highly intelligent people might thus be more exposed to the injustice and potential absurdity of life, which could limit their sense of happiness and, above all, their experience of meaning in life.

Philosopher Iddo Landau's "Finding meaning in an imperfect world" (2017) offers another, rather different perspective on problems of meaninglessness, which he calls the perfectionist presupposition. According to this presupposition, life is meaningless if it does not show perfection, excellence or special achievements. Landau sees evidence for this assumption in everyday statements like "he is no Einstein" or "she is no Perlman," which are typically meant to imply that people are not just not a genius but even the opposite. Such devaluation is often self-applied, especially among people who have high expectations of themselves. This is likely the case for many of the highly gifted. A "diagnosis" of high giftedness evokes a culturally transmitted sense of responsibility to live up to one's talents, to multiply them and bring them to fruition by extraordinary achievements (Mofield & Parker Peters, 2018). If these expectations are internalised, perhaps creating narcissistic or particularly vulnerable personalities, a life that falls short of excellence is viewed as worthless, without meaning.

In Innsbruck, Bernadette Vötter and I then asked how gifted adults' meaning in life and subjective well-being might be enhanced (Vötter &

Schnell, 2019b). We concentrated on two psychological characteristics whose relevance has repeatedly been shown to apply to the general population: generativity and self-control. Generativity stands for the doing or creating of things with lasting value (Section 6.1) and is regarded as an excellent predictor of meaningfulness (Damásio & Koller, 2015; Pedersen et al., 2018; Schnell, 2011). Self-control is the ability to suppress or change inner impulses and thus control one's behaviour. Many studies have shown that high self-control goes hand in hand with higher subjective well-being (De Ridder & Gillebaart, 2017; Wiese et al., 2018).

As expected, a longitudinal design showed that both highly intelligent and high-performing adults who lived a generative attitude and subsequently regarded their life as meaningful reported high subjective well-being four years later. The two subgroups differed, however, with regard to the role played by self-control: Highly intelligent people felt happy and satisfied only when they had also exerted self-control. In summary, the results suggest that a generative orientation can help the gifted to develop both a sense of purpose and happiness over time. Highly intelligent people seem to benefit in particular from self-control. For those among them who were able to regulate and control their behaviour, the positive effect of generativity and meaningfulness on happiness was significantly increased. We could speculate that highly intelligent people are less forced to learn self-control than others, since a lot of skills come naturally to them. This might put them into a disadvantaged position, however, when professional life later demands high degrees of discipline and restraint.

Finally, it should be noted that by concentrating on members of Mensa, we examined a specific sample that does not represent all highly intelligent people. Further research is therefore needed to better understand the relationship between giftedness and meaning.

5.5 Meaning is dynamic: changes across activities and days

> And as with lifetimes, so it is with days. None of them really satisfies us, none is entirely pleasant, and each of them has, if not its worry, then its imperfection, but add them up, and a sum of joy and life will emerge.
>
> (Friedrich Hölderlin, 1799/1992, p. 797f., transl. TS)

When asked about meaning in our lives, about coherence, significance, orientation and belonging, we usually take a step back and apply a meta-perspective: All in all; given where we came from and what our goals were; with regard to the actual state and our ideals; from a god's eye point of view; and so on, our life is more or less meaningful. The criteria that we use for such an evaluation do not change all too often – which is why meaningfulness should be a relatively stable personality construct. The student data that we collected confirmed this assumption: There were hardly any changes over a period of two or four months (differential stability of $r = 0.84$ and 0.82). Even after half a year, people responded in a similar way ($r = 0.72$; Schnell & Becker, 2007). In our sample of highly gifted adults, the differential stability was still $r = 0.83$ after a period as long as four years (Vötter & Schnell, 2019a). Evaluations of life as meaningful – or meaningless – thus are not easily changed. Whether there is a genetic disposition for meaningfulness has not yet been sufficiently examined. First results indicated that this is either nonexistent (Güfel, 2010) or low (Steger, Hicks, Krueger, & Bouchard, 2011). Above all, meaning in life seems to develop from the experiences that this world confronts us with and the way we deal with them.

It is hard, however, to escape our moods. Assessments of meaning in life are tinted by tempers, as colleagues at the University of Missouri (Columbia) demonstrated: When we are in a good mood, we consider our life to be more meaningful than when we are in a bad mood (King, Hicks, Krull, & Del Gaiso, 2006). In addition, there are days that we (have to) spend mostly on activities that seem meaningless to us. One can therefore assume that meaningfulness varies depending on the day and the activity. This has been confirmed by experience-sampling studies: Everyday experiences are recorded as promptly as possible and in a natural environment, either through daily diary entries or through mobile devices that report several times a day and ask for answers to specific questions in situ.

Such experience-sampling studies have shown that meaningfulness fluctuates more between different days than between different people (King et al., 2006). It fluctuates even more between individual activities, as our study has shown (Schnell, 2015b):

Sixty-two students from the University of Innsbruck agreed to carry a mobile device (a palmtop) for one week. Five times a day, it called for a response, by means of vibration and sound. This happened at five randomly generated times within five time spans. No matter what our participants were doing, they had the task to pause briefly and answer the following questions on the palmtop within about a minute:

- Are you on your own, with friends, with family, with a partner, or with others?

- What are you doing right now? (studying/working/housekeeping/eating/resting/television/sports/reading/communication/culture/music/intimacy/on the way/other)

Please evaluate your current activity (using a scale from 0, for disagree completely, to 5, for agree completely):

A I experience it as meaningful.
B It fits my life's task.
C It fulfils me.
D It gives me the feeling of being part of something bigger.
E It has a deeper meaning.
F It is pleasant.

That's it, thank you. See you later.

The listed activities were the result of a previous diary study that we had conducted. Would you like to know what Innsbruck students are doing in a typical week between 9 am and 11 pm? In fact, they are most often occupied with studying (25 percent of the activities), followed by social exchange/communication (12 percent), resting (12 percent) and eating (10 percent).

How much meaning did the students attribute to their activities? To answer this question, the items from A to E were averaged, as one would do with a questionnaire scale. Like that, we did not measure random conceptions of meaning that our participants had in mind but instead a specific construct. The responses to the five items were highly correlated (Cronbach's Alpha = 0.87), so that this procedure was justified. Figure 5.6 shows how often activities were perceived as meaningful and – in comparison – as pleasant (item F).

Figure 5.6 can tell us various things. First of all, it confirms our expectation that some activities are perceived as more meaningful than others are. Meaningfulness is experienced most frequently in intimacy, culture/music, sports and communication. These activities are also perceived as pleasant. The least meaning is attributed to television and housekeeping, followed by locomotion, resting, eating and work. The latter finding should probably be annotated, since work, in this case, is mostly any type of spare-time activity that offers necessary financial support. Accordingly, such jobs are not expected to be especially meaningful or pleasant.

The data also show that it is much *easier* to experience activities as pleasant than as meaningful. As explained in Section 2.4, it can be challenging to experience meaning; in many situations, it is not easy to achieve. The biggest differences between *pleasant* and *meaningful* can be found when watching TV (usually pleasant, rarely meaningful), resting or eating. The only activity that is more often rated as meaningful than pleasant is studying.

Multilevel analyses have demonstrated that the evaluation of activities' meaningfulness does not depend solely on the type of activity involved (Schnell, 2015b). Rather, the evaluation is influenced by our mood, and by the pleasantness that we ascribe to an activity. It also depends on our general sense of meaningfulness: Those of us who assume that our life is meaningful will also attribute meaning to individual activities more frequently. Empirical data thus confirm the assumptions made by the hierarchic model of meaning (Section 4.1). In addition, another personality variable has proven to be relevant: autonomy, or self-determination. Those who reported a high degree of self-determination also perceived their everyday activities as more meaningful. This can probably be explained by the fact that people with a high degree of autonomy select their actions according to intrinsic criteria and perform them voluntarily – which increases the experience of meaningfulness (Ryan & Deci, 2001; Schnell, 2015b).

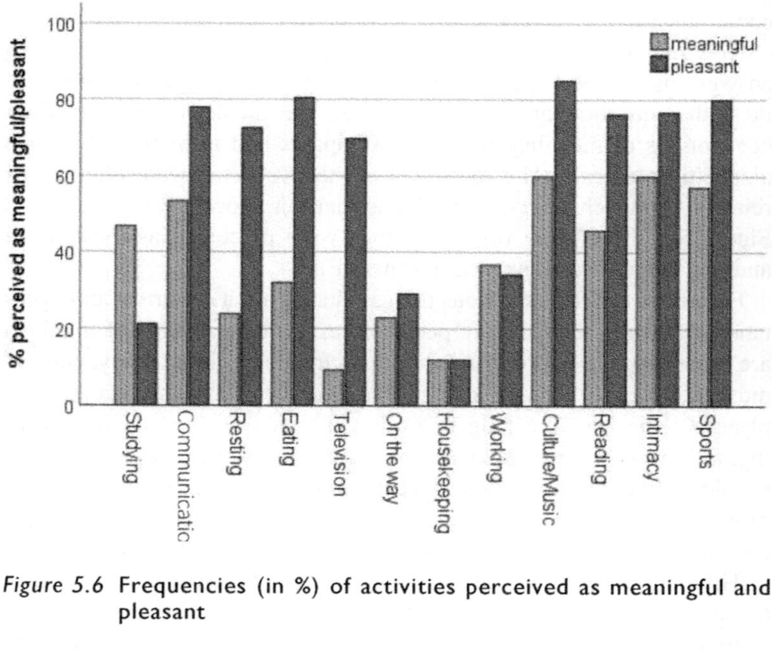

Figure 5.6 Frequencies (in %) of activities perceived as meaningful and pleasant

5.6 A brief discourse: studying – often pointless, usually no fun?

The students' evaluations of their study experiences are alarming. Only about half of the activities associated with studying are perceived as meaningful, only one-fifth of the activities as pleasant. From my teaching experience, I wonder whether the absence of meaning in so many study-related activities might be due to a lot of topics being presented and memorised without clarifying the relationships between them. The meaning and purpose of studying all these isolated details opens up only with a deeper understanding of the field. Most of our study participants were second-year psychology students, so there is hope that insight and a sense of purpose might increase with the progress of their studies. However, the strong specialisation and differentiation of course content continues to contribute to students perceiving the subject matter as disjointed information.

That studying is also largely experienced as unpleasant can be attributed, among other things, to high time pressure, pressure to perform and a school-like organisation of the study programme. Students in Austria, for example, must take examinations in several subjects at the end of each term. This system promotes a learning behaviour known as binge learning, which is accompanied by relatively little learning effort during term and excessive learning effort in the days before the exam (Cilliers, Schuwirth, Herman, Adendorff, & van der Vleuten, 2012). Such behaviour is enforced by time pressure and pressure to achieve, which elicits a prioritisation of good grades but which offers little space and incentive for continuous and experiential insight learning.

A similar pattern can already be seen in school. A recent study among six-year-olds to 13-year-olds confirmed what previous studies had already claimed: The vast majority of children who start school are motivated and interested – but their enjoyment of learning decreases with school years (Zeit Leo & Scoyo, 2013). Out of 860 children, 53 percent of six-year-olds stated that they always enjoyed school. Among ten-year-olds, 32 percent said that they always enjoyed school. Among 13-year-olds, it was only 6 percent. Eight percent of six-year-olds, 18 percent of ten-year-olds and 35 percent of 13-year-olds rarely or never enjoyed school. This trend seems to continue into higher education and underlines the need for new forms of teaching and learning (see e.g. Caspary, Spitzer, Hüther, & Roth, 2012).

5.7 Know thyself!

SELF-EXPLORATION: A MEANING DIARY

For one week, take a few minutes every evening and make a note:

> What have I done today that I would view as meaningful? What have I done that I experienced as pleasant?
>
> At the end of the week, you can reflect:

MEANINGFUL AND MEANINGLESS ACTIVITIES

- What is the ratio of meaningful to meaningless activities?
- Am I satisfied with this ratio?

If you find the meaningful activities were too rare, ask yourself the following:

- Why did I spend so much time on activities that are meaningless to me?
- What can I do to deal more frequently with things that are meaningful to me?

PLEASANT AND UNPLEASANT ACTIVITIES

- What is the ratio of pleasant to unpleasant activities?
- Am I satisfied with this ratio?

If you find the pleasant activities were too rare, ask yourself the following:

- Why did I spend so much time on unpleasant activities?
- What can I do to spend more time on things that I find pleasant?

5.8 Literature

Bakan, D. (1966). *The duality of human existence: Isolation and communion in Western man*. Boston, MA: Beacon Press.

Caspary, R., Spitzer, M., Hüther, G., & Roth, G. (Hrsg.). (2012). *Lernen und Gehirn: Der Weg zu einer neuen Pädagogik*. Hamburg: Nikol.

Casto, K. V., & Edwards, D. A. (2016). Testosterone and reconciliation among women: After-competition testosterone predicts prosocial attitudes towards opponents. *Adaptive Human Behavior and Physiology*, *2*(3), 220–233.

Cilliers, F. J., Schuwirth, L. W., Herman, N., Adendorff, H. J., & van der Vleuten, C. P. (2012). A model of the pre-assessment learning effects of summative assessment in medical education. *Advances in Health Sciences Education, 17*(1), 39–53.

Crandall, A., Allsop, Y., & Hanson, C. L. (2018). The longitudinal association between cognitive control capacities, suicidality, and depression during late adolescence and young adulthood. *Journal of Adolescence, 65*, 167–176.

Damásio, B. F., & Koller, S. H. (2015). Complex experiences of meaning in life: Individual differences among sociodemographic variables, sources of meaning and psychological functioning. *Social Indicators Research, 123*(1), 161–181.

Damásio, B. F., Koller, S. H., & Schnell, T. (2013). Sources of meaning and meaning in life questionnaire (SoMe): Psychometric properties and sociodemographic findings in a large Brazilian sample. *Acta de Investigación Psicológica, 3*(3), 1205–1227.

De Ridder, D., & Gillebaart, M. (2017). Lessons learned from trait self-control in well-being: Making the case for routines and initiation as important components of trait self-control. *Health Psychology Review, 11*(1), 89–99.

Erikson, E. H. (1988). *Der vollständige Lebenszyklus*. Frankfurt am Main: Suhrkamp.

Güfel, B. (2010). *Lebensbedeutungen bei Zwillingen* (Unveröffentlichte Diplomarbeit), Universität Innsbruck.

Halama, P., & Dedova, M. (2007). Meaning in life and hope as predictors of positive mental health: Do they explain residual variance not predicted by personality traits? *Studia Psychologica, 49*(3), 191–200.

Hamilton, L. D., Carré, J. M., Mehta, P. H., Olmstead, N., & Whitaker, J. D. (2015). Social neuroendocrinology of status: A review and future directions. *Adaptive Human Behavior and Physiology, 1*, 202–230.

Hölderlin, F. (1799/1992). *Sämtliche Werke und Briefe, Band 2* (M. Franz & M. Knaupp, Eds.). München: Carl Hanser.

Keysar, A., & Navarro-Rivera, J. (2013). A world of atheism: Global demographics. In S. Bullivant & M. Ruse (Eds.), *The Oxford handbook of atheism* (pp. 553–586). Oxford: Oxford University Press.

King, L. A., Hicks, J. A., Krull, J. L., & Del Gaiso, A. K. (2006). Positive affect and the experience of meaning in life. *Journal of Personality and Social Psychology, 90*(1), 179.

Klein, C. (2012). Fromme Frau, agnostischer Mann – sind Frauen grundsätzlich religiöser/spiritueller als Männer? *Spiritual Care, 1*(2), 6–22.

Landau, I. (2017). *Finding meaning in an imperfect world*. Oxford: Oxford University Press.

Matthews, G., Deary, I. J., & Whiteman, M. C. (2003). *Personality traits*. Cambridge: Cambridge University Press.

Miller, A., & Stark, R. (2002). Gender and religiousness: Can socialization explanations be saved? *American Journal of Sociology, 107*(6), 1399–1423.

Mofield, E. L., & Parker Peters, M. (2018). Mindset misconception? Comparing mindsets, perfectionism, and attitudes of achievement in gifted, advanced, and typical students. *Gifted Child Qarterly, 62*, 327–349.

Pedersen, H. F., Handegard Birkeland, M., Søndergaard Jensen, J., Schnell, T., Hvidt, N. C., Sørensen, T., & la Cour, P. (2018). What brings meaning to life in a highly secular society? A study on sources of meaning among Danes. *Scandinavian Journal of Psychology, 59*(6), 678–690.

Pollet, E., & Schnell, T. (2017). Brilliant: But what for? Meaning and subjective well-being in the lives of intellectually gifted and academically high-achieving adults. *Journal of Happiness Studies, 18*(5), 1459–1484.

Reker, G. T., Peacock, E. J., & Wong, P. T. (1987). Meaning and purpose in life and well-being: A life-span perspective. *Journal of Gerontology, 42*(1), 44–49.

Rost, D. H. (Hrsg.). (2009). *Hochbegabte und hochleistende Jugendliche. Befunde aus dem Marburger Hochbegabtenprojekt*. Münster: Waxmann.

Ryan, R. M., & Deci, E. L. (2001). On happiness and human potentials: A review of research on hedonic and eudaimonic well-being. *Annual Review of Psychology, 52*(1), 141–166.

Schnell, T. (2011). Individual differences in meaning-making: Considering the variety of sources of meaning, their density and diversity. *Personality and Individual Differences, 51*(5), 667–673.

Schnell, T. (2015a). Dimensions of secularity (DoS): An open inventory to measure facets of secular identities. *International Journal for the Psychology of Religion, 25*(4), 272–292.

Schnell, T. (2015b, March). *Predicting meaningful and pleasurable daily activities: Findings from an experience sampling study*. Presentation, Inaugural International Convention of Psychological Science, Amsterdam, Netherlands.

Schnell, T., & Becker, P. (2006). Personality and meaning in life. *Personality and Individual Differences, 41*(1), 117–129.

Schnell, T., & Becker, P. (2007). *Der Fragebogen zu Lebensbedeutungen und Lebenssinn (LeBe)*. Göttingen: Hogrefe.

Schnell, T., Gerstner, R., & Krampe, H. (2018). Crisis of meaning predicts suicidality in youth independently of depression. *Crisis–The Journal of Crisis Intervention and Suicide Prevention, 39*, 294–303.

Schnell, T., & Keenan, W. J. F. (2011). Meaning-making in an atheist world. *Archive for the Psychology of Religion, 33*(1), 55–78.

Scholz, C. (2019). *Eine geschlechtergetrennte Betrachtung des Zusammenhangs von Testosteronwerten mit Religiosität, Spiritualität und Atheismus* (Unveröffentlichte Masterarbeit), Universität Innsbruck.

Schweizer Bundesamt für Statistik (2019, June 27). *Lebensgeburten nach Alter des Vaters, 2016–2018*. Retrieved from www.bfs.admin.ch/bfs/de/home/statistiken/bevoelkerung/geburten-todesfaelle/geburten.html

Stark, R. (2002). Physiology and faith: Addressing the 'universal' gender difference in religious commitment. *Journal for the Scientific Study of Religion, 41*(3), 495–507.

Steger, M. F., Frazier, P., Oishi, S., & Kaler, M. (2006). The meaning in life questionnaire: Assessing the presence of and search for meaning in life. *Journal of Counseling Psychology, 53*(1), 80–93.

Steger, M. F., Hicks, B. M., Krueger, R. F., & Bouchard, T. J. (2011). Genetic and environmental influences and covariance among meaning in life, religiousness, and spirituality. *The Journal of Positive Psychology*, *6*(3), 181–191.

Steger, M. F., Kashdan, T. B., Sullivan, B. A., & Lorentz, D. (2008). Understanding the search for meaning in life: Personality, cognitive style, and the dynamic between seeking and experiencing meaning. *Journal of Personality*, *76*(2), 199–228.

Sullins, D. P. (2006). Gender and deconstructing universality, constructing complexity. *American Journal of Sociology*, *112*(3), 838–880.

Trzebiatowska, M., & Bruce, S. (2012). *Why are women more religious than men?* Oxford: Oxford University Press.

Völcker, M. (2016). Zwischen sozialer Verachtung und der individuellen Suche nach Anerkennung: Eckpunkte der Hauptschulsozialisation. *Zeitschrift für Qualitative Forschung*, *17*(1–2), 237–257.

Voracek, M. (2008). Cross-national social ecology of intelligence and suicide prevalence: Integration, refinement, and update of studies. *Perceptual and Motor Skills*, *106*(2), 550–556.

Vötter, B., & Schnell, T. (2019a). Cross-lagged analyses between life meaning, self-compassion, and subjective well-being among gifted adults. *Mindfulness*, *10*(7), 1294–1303.

Vötter, B., & Schnell, T. (2019b). Bringing giftedness to bear: Generativity, meaningfulness, and self-control as resources for a happy life among gifted adults. *Frontiers in Psychology*, *10*, Article 1972.

Wiese, C. W., Tay, L., Duckworth, A. L., D'Mello, S., Kuykendall, L., Hofmann, W., . . . Vohs, K. D. (2018). Too much of a good thing? Exploring the inverted-u relationship between self-control and happiness. *Journal of Personality*, *86*(3), 380–396.

Zeit Leo, & Scoyo. (2013). *Lernen mit Spaß. Studie, durchgeführt durch Marktforschungsinstitut FACT*. Retrieved from http://www-de.scoyo.com/dam/ratgeber-downloads/studie-lernen-mit-spass-booklet/booklet-lernen-mit-spass.pdf

Chapter 6

Sources of meaning

As described in Section 3.1, the sources of meaning were identified in a qualitative research programme. They are orientations that our interviewees identified as underlying their actions, convictions and experiences. They are thus not merely theoretical constructs but *meaning in action.* In several cycles of consensual validation, the large number of qualitatively identified sources of meaning was summarised until we finally arrived at 26 sources of meaning, which in turn can be grouped into five dimensions of meaning. Table 6.1 gives an annotated overview.

6.1 The strongest predictors of meaning

Due to the availability of the Sources of Meaning and Meaning in Life Questionnaire (SoMe), we were able to ask a large number of people about their sources of meaning. The results confirmed that these indeed were meaningful orientations: All sources of meaning correlated positively with meaningfulness (Schnell & Becker, 2007). Some had a closer association with meaningfulness than others did, however. They obviously have a stronger potential to create meaning. When ranking sources of meaning according to the strength of their connections with meaningfulness, the following top ten result:

1 Generativity.
2 Care.
3 Religiosity.
4 Harmony.
5 Development.
6 Social commitment.
7 Attentiveness.

Table 6.1 Sources and dimensions of meaning, with annotations

Scale//Dimension	*Content Description*
Selftranscendence	**Relating to something that is greater than the self**
Selftranscendence, Vertical	***Orientation towards transcendence***
Religiosity	Religious life and personal relationship with God
Spirituality	Subjective approach to a higher reality
Selftranscendence, Horizontal	***Commitment to concerns beyond immediate self-interest***
Social Commitment	Active advocacy for the common good or human rights
Nature Relatedness	Harmony and connectedness with nature
Self-Knowledge	Search for and confrontation with the "true" self
Health	Preservation and promotion of health
Generativity	Doing or creating things of lasting value
Selfactualisation	**Self-determination and self-optimisation**
Challenge	Search for new things, variety and risk
Individualism	Individuality and living out potentials
Power	Fight and dominance
Development	Goal-orientation and growth
Achievement	Competence and success
Freedom	Unconstraint and independence
Knowledge	Questioning, informing and understanding
Creativity	Fantasy and creative design
Order	**Conservative-preserving value orientation and pragmatism**
Tradition	Holding on to the proven and the familiar
Practicality	Applicability and practical relevance
Morality	Morality and clear guidelines
Reason	Prudence, consideration and rationality
Well-Being and Relatedness	**Promotion of own and shared well-being**
Communion	Closeness and friendship
Fun	Humour and pleasure
Love	Romanticism and intimacy
Comfort	Well-being and leisure
Care	Caring and helpfulness
Attentiveness	Mindfulness and rituals
Harmony	Balance and harmony with oneself and others

Source: Courtesy of Tatjana Schnell 2020.

8 Nature relatedness.
9 Creativity.
10 Communion.

Generativity, which is mentioned at the top of the list, has turned out to be a particularly potent predictor of meaningfulness. In most samples – of all ages, from the most diverse countries, among participants with psychological problems and participants without – it had the greatest connection to meaningfulness.

Generativity is a way of life committed to doing or creating something of lasting value. In the words of Erik H. Erikson, who coined the term, it is about "carrying love into the future" by making a contribution to society, the greater whole, the generations to come (Erikson, 1988). This can be done in various ways, including procreating, giving birth to and bringing up children; educating future generations; and political, artistic and cultural engagement. While Erikson assumed that generativity occurs above all in middle age, when developmental tasks of finding identity and intimacy have been completed, our studies show that generativity is possible from youth onwards and makes sense at any age.

6.2 Breadth, balance and depth of sources of meaning

Would it now be desirable to orient one's whole life towards generativity? Our study results show that it makes more sense to realise several sources of meaning – and they should be as different as possible.

6.2.1 Breadth

Paula is known as a good consultant. She is attentive and present in her encounters with clients. They can even contact her outside working hours, if necessary. In her spare time, Paula continues her education and reads topical literature. On several weekends a year, she travels to further training courses that are of particular interest to her.

Paul is also a good consultant: attentive and present. As often as possible, he spends his free time with his partner and their child, or with mutual friends. From time to time, Paul also needs to be alone, preferably outdoors in nature. Here he is entirely at one with himself but also opens up to what surrounds him, what he perceives as a larger whole encompassing him.

Both Paul and Paula are absorbed in their activity, perceiving it as meaningful and important. Nevertheless, our data show that Paul will most likely attribute more meaning to his life than Paula will. For a certain period of time, it may be fulfilling to set ambitious goals, to challenge oneself and to give everything for it. Once the goals have been reached, however, we might find ourselves glancing around, asking "And now?" Many know this experience as the famous "black hole" that opens after graduation, the end of education, studies or other goal markers.

A versatile involvement can prevent such experiences, as our studies show. The more sources of meaning are realised (breadth), the higher the meaningfulness is (Schnell, 2011a); the threshold value is at least four sources of meaning. Peggy Thoits came to similar conclusions in her research. She proposes: The greater number of identities a person realises, the more meaning they experience (Thoits, 2003) – as long as these identities do not contradict each other (Thoits & Evenson, 2008). We can add that with the number of relevant orientations also the amount of committed actions increases, which can contribute to self-confidence, self-efficacy and sense of significance.

6.2.2 *Balance*

In further analyses, the diversity of the realised sources of meaning turned out to be even more relevant than their pure number (Schnell, 2011a) – we are talking about balance here. Of course, both are connected: The more areas of life a person is meaningfully involved in, the more different they will be. But it makes a big difference whether someone concentrates on five sources of meaning all in the area of selfactualisation or whether they are spread over three, four or five dimensions.

In other words, not only is it important to pay attention to so-called work–life balance, but all areas of life should be balanced in their significance. A high diversity or balance means that a person experiences themselves as active, committed and involved in different respects. They thus have access to different sources from which they can draw personal meaning. This might be particularly helpful when an important source of meaning breaks away as shown by Heine, Proulx, and Vohs (2006), who found that when an important source of meaning is threatened, people tend to compensate for the loss by strengthening other sources of meaning. Zhang, Sang, Chan, and Schlegel (2019) further demonstrated this by using the example of threatened social belonging. In an experiment, they brought about an experience of social exclusion. As a consequence, the participants devalued social relationships in their relevance as a source of meaning, while they rated autonomy more positively. In reality, however, such attempts at compensation are successful only if other sources of meaning are available – in other words, if they were cultivated even in "uncritical" times. If this is not the case, the failure of a single, central source of meaning will likely result in a crisis of meaning. This has often been reported in the transition to retirement age, if retirees had previously self-defined solely through their occupation. It is also common among parents experiencing empty nest syndrome – that is, a lack of meaning experienced when meaning was predominantly derived through their caring role as mothers or fathers.

On the basis of empirical findings (Schnell, 2011a), we can speak of *balanced meaning* when sources of meaning from at least three of the five dimensions of meaning (vertical selftranscendence, horizontal selftranscendence, selfactualisation, order and well-being and relatedness) are being realised. A chair needs at least three legs to stand stable.

6.2.3 Depth

Two early researchers of meaning, Gary Reker and Paul Wong (1988), suggested that sources of meaning differ in their existential depth: They can be more or less profound. They defined this concept of depth, with reference to Maslow and Frankl, as the degree of realised selftranscendence.

In Abraham Maslow's later years, he supplemented his well-known hierarchy of needs (1943) with the concept of selftranscendence (1969), which he understood as overcoming egocentricity, egoism and self-centredness while opening up to a reality beyond the self (Ruschmann, 2011). Although this conceptual modification is of far-reaching significance, it has not been acknowledged in psychology. With the addition of selftranscendence to the top level of the pyramid of needs, the human image associated with the older model is radically questioned. The latter assumed that "the highest form of human motivational development is a well-adjusted, differentiated, fulfilled individual self or ego" (Koltko-Rivera, 2006, p. 306). The later model, on the other hand, postulates a highest stage of development characterised by transcending the self and its needs:

> This represents a monumental shift in the conceptualization of human personality and its development. At the level of selfactualization, the individual works to actualize the individual's own potential; there is thus, at least potentially, a certain self-aggrandizing aspect to this motivational stage, as there is with all the stages below it in

> Maslow's hierarchy. At the level of selftranscendence, the individual's own needs are put aside, to a great extent, in favor of service to others and to some higher force or cause conceived as being outside the personal self.
>
> (Koltko-Rivera, 2006, p. 306f.)

For Viktor Frankl, selftranscendence was a central feature of meaningfulness. He understood it to mean

> that being human always points, and is directed, to something, or someone, other than oneself – be it a meaning to fulfil or another human being to encounter. The more one forgets himself – by giving himself to a cause to serve or another person to love – the more human he is and the more he actualises himself.
>
> (Frankl, 2006, p. 1110f.)

Following on from Maslow and Frankl, Reker and Wong (1988) expected that the extent of selftranscendence – and thus of depth – is reflected in the experience of meaning. Our data confirmed this expectation. As soon as horizontal or vertical selftranscendence assumed a significant role in a person's life – independently of other sources of meaning – meaningfulness increased significantly (Schnell, 2008).

According to Frankl, we become fully human only once we overlook and forget ourselves. This seems to be a paradoxical call in our highly individualised society, in which everything is *personalised*, adapted to individual preferences, interests and needs: mobile phones, home furnishings, lifestyles, and so on. Self-tracking and self-optimisation increasingly determine both our professional life and leisure time. Our attention is drawn to ourselves, to what we do and how we do it. Little time, however, is spent on the question of why. Answering it would require a change of perspective: away from the self, considering our embeddedness in a social and natural environment and the consequences our individual acts have on them.

Recently, critical voices have registered the disciplining and controlling function that contemporary self-observation can have (e.g., Lupton, 2016). Self-tracking devices are widely accepted, and there is evidence that they might induce persistent pressure to improve in certain aspects of life (while other – less-quantifiable – aspects fade into the background). Moreover, while using such devices, we (unwillingly) provide various agents with insights into our most intimate lifeworlds, the use of which we are not yet fully aware of.

Whereas the strongly enforced focus on ourselves has the power to actually estrange us from ourselves even more, by demanding "effective" self-management and "presentable" improvement, it does not seem to leave much energy for resistance or dissent. Instead, the option chosen by a large majority is distraction. With television, radio, the Internet and other mass media, culturally sanctioned forms of diversion are available and used persistently. In 2018, Germans spent 10.5 hours a day with media, of which more than 9.0 hours were with audiovisual media (Vaunet, 2019).

Although we can easily forget ourselves in such activities, this form of self-forgetfulness has nothing in common with the selftranscendence just described. Meaningful selftranscendence is not obliviousness but instead actual engagement for concerns beyond the self.

6.3 Many roads to meaning

To get a better understanding of how people put sources of meaning into action in their daily lives, we have conducted further interviews. We asked individuals with a particularly high score in specific sources of meaning to tell us more about how this affects their everyday lives, their actions, thoughts and experiences. Next you will find some concise excerpts from these interviews.

Religiosity

- "My religion gives me a certain calmness."
- "When I am in need, I pray. But I also pray when I am not in need. To pray means to speak with God. Not really formal prayers, but to be with God in thought."
- "I believe, I am helpful, I care for other people. Willingness to help and love."
- "I go to church regularly. With my religiosity, I associate feelings like contentment, calmness and thoughtfulness."

Spirituality

- "For me, spirituality means being on my way. It denotes self-knowledge, development, change, pain, happiness, contact with life."
- "I have a deep feeling that things are not arbitrary, that things do not happen by chance. There are energies, forces beyond human power, perhaps simply a 'life energy.' I think this is something that cannot be understood but can only be sensed and felt."

- "I regularly practise yoga and reiki, make music and go to women's evenings."
- "I find sacred places in nature, especially old places of worship. Or also churches, which are basically also Christian places of worship, or temples and the like of other religions. I think the decisive thing is that in such places, people have come together or are still coming together who have a special consciousness, a certain energy level, who deal with the essential at that moment, who come with a certain reverence, for whatever. . . . And it works; it animates the place, so to speak."

Social commitment

- "There are three different levels. First, towards poor people whom I don't know at all, second at work and lastly social commitment towards friends and family."
- "Social commitment is important because everyone needs others. But there are people who make a show out of it, they get involved just for the sake of selfactualisation. I don't really like that. In general, you should always make sure that socially disadvantaged people are helped."
- "Social commitment ensures that social exchange takes place. This is important for everyone. Also for the rich."
- "I try to make sure that everyone gets something out of prosperity."
- "It can be accompanied by sadness, but I am also satisfied, motivated, helpful, strong."

Nature relatedness

- "I must say, I just feel very comfortable in the open countryside. I search for natural surroundings. And the protection of nature is also important to me. It ranges from turning out the lights or separating waste to buying things which I think are beneficial to the environment, or recreational activities (trying to spend time outdoors every now and then)."
- "Just as it is important to know oneself, it is essential to realise that we live in nature, that nature is a part of us, that humankind is nature. We must attach importance to this cycle."
- "I like to look at herbal books or a booklet like 'What's blooming here' I just like to see it."
- "It gives me the feeling of being part of a larger whole. Satisfaction, joy, happiness and peace."

Self-knowledge

- "Self-knowledge means that you question yourself again and again, or think about who you are, what you want or where you want to go, and in doing so you simply keep developing yourself."
- "Self-knowledge should ideally lead to being at peace with oneself. With your inner being, with your character. How you behave towards yourself, but also how you behave towards others. That you don't have to play a role that you don't like yourself. Rather, that you are at peace with the image you show to the outside world and how you feel. That is the goal of self-knowledge for me."
- "To me personally, it is reflected in the fact that I am sometimes so very glad if I manage to have half an hour without anything to do. When I can't hear a car, there's no TV, there's no radio, there's just silence. I don't consciously seek out such free time, but when it comes, I'm quite happy about it, because it's often the brightest moments."
- "This goes hand in hand with doubt. That's logical. When you think about yourself, you also doubt yourself. And it's also a bit of uncertainty, because you can try to change yourself, but in the end you don't know if you can achieve it. So there is no real reward for striving for self-knowledge."
- "Self-knowledge often has to do with grief or feelings of guilt. I think if everything runs like a charm, you will think less about yourself than if everything is not going so well. You will ask yourself, why did I act like this and not differently? In that case, you often have bursts of growth. With regard to others and also regarding yourself."
- "It's just an uncomfortable process and not something you enjoy. It's a process in which you learn to deal with yourself. The way you are. Sometimes, when something becomes clear to you, then you are at peace with yourself, for the moment. In that moment I am happy."

Health

- "For me, health means taking care in everyday life that I do something good for myself and my body, that I take care of what I take in and what I don't; it's both emotional and physical."
- "Living healthily means a lot of sleep, fresh air every day. Eat lots of fruit and little fat, little meat, lots of salads."

- "I don't have to make sacrifices for it. I don't have to abstain from anything. I am simply much more satisfied when I know that I have taken my walk again today. More self-confident. Sport is good for my self-confidence. But I also often have concerns about environmental pollution, am restless and worried."

Generativity

- "Generativity for me means not only to live for myself but to do things that have positive consequences for others – and perhaps being able to thus improve the lives of other people, especially those who suffer."
- "There are a thousand ways of being generative, and everyone can be generative in a different way. For example, in volunteering, or in work, when you're not just thinking about a career, but about the intrinsic value of the work and the consequences it has for others. Not always acting according to your feeling, but according to what you think is right."
- "I think it takes a certain satisfaction with yourself to do something for others."
- "It is about giving something back for what I have received. To do things differently, more humanely. Actually, I find the world very cruel and absurd. Generativity is for me a possibility to live humanity, to bring it to life. This also gives me a feeling of being alive."

Challenge

- "Seeking challenges means gaining experience – this is how people learn. You want to achieve something, get to know your own limits."
- "Challenge makes your life and your character more interesting. If you don't even try something, you'll regret it."
- "I spend energy and time on it. I feel dogged, cramped, focused, concentrated and tense. Challenges are accompanied by stress, palpitations, nervousness – and the drive is positive."

Individualism

- "Individualism for me means going your own way and not being influenced by others. It also means an evaluation from outside, from others. But also to do things in one's own way."

- "It shows in how I travel, what music I like, in my ways of thinking and how I discuss with others."
- "It's about trying to live up to your character: Live your preferences, do what you enjoy, don't listen too much to the opinions of others, don't let yourself be suppressed and always say what you think!"
- "I think that the more individual a person is, the more interesting someone is. I look for such friends, too."
- "I am not always compliant, I scandalise. I don't always please others with that. But I feel comfortable with it, satisfied, balanced, special."

Power

- "In my view, power means having a position where others look up to you and value your opinion. Now, without wanting to be conceited, it honours me when someone thinks a lot of my opinion or asks me for advice. That may be a strange kind of power, but that's how I understand it. Manipulation would be the negative example of power; I would never do that. That you don't totally take command and ride roughshod over others, but deal with power in such a way that you make a profit for yourself and others. Achieve something good for a whole team."
- "You should say what you want and push it through. Only then will you get what you want. You always stay insignificant and have to put your own needs aside if you don't try to be a bit dominant. Because dominance is something that goes hand in hand with self-confidence – and that's a good thing. That's something that makes you look at yourself."
- "In my everyday life, I don't let myself be quickly distracted from what I have set out to do. Often, however, I feel guilty when I take command because I then think that I am pushing others aside."
- "Power makes me feel self-confident, organised, satisfied, but sometimes intrusive."

Development

- "Development is something that never ends and always goes on. In the best case, you will continue to develop your whole life and not stop. The development is a result and a process of life somehow."
- "Normally I set myself goals through which I develop myself. I believe that if you have no tasks and no goals, life becomes quite

boring. And if you don't have that, then you don't develop either. Development is not only the goal in itself, but also the way. If you have things that interest you in life, then development usually comes automatically."

- "I sacrifice time for it, a massive amount of time. I just need time to learn and to develop and study, for example. That's a full-time job, I'd say."
- "The feelings associated with it are effort and work, a flow state when things are going well. Also overstraining, tiredness, euphoria. The pride and euphoria of having made it is much stronger when you have overcome resistance."

Achievement

- "Nothing works without achievement. In everything there is performance, no matter what it is – whether at work, in sports, in games, in encounters – without performance it does not work. For me, achievement is the top priority."
- "Without achievement our life means nothing, without achievement we cannot achieve anything, without achievement we are not accepted in society."
- "I show achievement through commitment, through punctuality, through precise targets. It is also an achievement to help someone."
- "When I see that something has become extraordinarily beautiful through my achievement, then it makes me happy, then I am proud. It's all about recognition. The confirmation that I have performed well must also come from others. Then I experience joy and satisfaction with myself."
- "Before that there is a certain pressure: tenseness, anxiety as to whether it is enough, the willingness to give everything. . . . It is also about overcoming oneself. If I don't feel like doing anything at all and still perform. . . . That's sometimes worth more than simply doing it."

Freedom

- "Freedom means feeling that I can do what I want to do. I do adhere to certain social rules and don't behave totally off-key, but freedom is that I can definitely live my life according to a structure I have chosen."
- "I often think about what norms and rules you have to follow in life. All the things you are deprived of, with regard to leisure and how you organise your time."

- "As long as you don't have the feeling that freedom is important, you let yourself be restricted quickly. Then one simply lives according to prescribed norms and is too uncritical in one's life."
- "I live the way I want to live. Sometimes it is complicated when you have to assert yourself or have to justify yourself for how you live and how you think."
- "Sometimes you can feel free and content, but on the other hand, if you feel totally free and not tied to anything, you can be completely dissatisfied. With me it varies a lot."

Knowledge

- "Knowledge is not purely factual knowledge for me, but knowledge is also to question underlying assumptions, to understand things, and not only 'know that,' but also 'know why.'"
- "Knowledge is important because it makes you understand how other people tick, and why something happens. It gives you the opportunity to make better decisions. The more you know, the more you have the chance to survive in society. The more you know, the more you see injustice – or you see injustice where others do not see it. And the more you know yourself, the more you can live in harmony with yourself."
- "I gain knowledge by reading newspapers, watching television, listening to the radio. Probably 90 percent of what I do every day I do out of thirst for knowledge. I want to know how my friends are doing. I want to know what the world is like. I want to know what the athlete did in any competition."
- "This is accompanied by feelings of relief and understanding. That I start to understand how all this is connected, how all this is coordinated with each other. How the cogwheel meshes. I feel relieved, but also slain in certain moments. When you recognise things and think, oh shit, I wouldn't have thought so. And I feel powerful. That's what I have to say. Power is something I only feel when I know. If I'm not sure, I don't feel the power."

Creativity

- "I think that creativity has a lot to do with being open and going through life with open eyes. That's something that certainly helps everyone in life."
- "I think you can be creative in many ways. I would say that it is important to go through life with your eyes open. That practically

promotes creativity, and that's also very good for yourself, because you reflect a lot yourself."

- "In many different ways I make sure that my everyday life is geared towards creativity, for example by going out for coffee and observing people. Or by going to unknown places. Or looking through magazines and getting impressions from them. I also photograph and paint and always keep my eyes open in everyday life and look what I like or what I could make of it, like a cool photo."
- "Before my creative phase I am often dissatisfied. When I'm dissatisfied and have more negative emotions and less fun, I'm more creative. But when I draw something or have a great idea, I feel very good, almost euphoric. That's such a high because you have cool ideas."

Tradition

- "Tradition is what your parents pass on to you, most people pass that on to their children, and that is also important to the children. Every person needs the basics of tradition. You have to remember them, otherwise you have no roots."
- "Tradition are the celebrations, Christmas, Easter. You go to church and try to make it beautiful and then it shapes the whole family. With a special meal, intensive conversations, conveying feelings, showing others that you like them, or whatever. Our parents did it that way, and we had to take part in it, but it shaped me so much that I still practise it today as if I were a Christian who regularly goes to church. To me, that is tradition."
- "Without community there is no tradition. Traditions have always connected me with everything."
- "Tradition also forms a certain security. A certainty of ideas. They have done that before, and you can still do that now. Such customs give a lot of support."
- "It's a wonderful feeling, you can't describe it. Warm, it warms your heart. It's just warmth, and you always have to think that you're doing so well and that you're healthy. It is joy, enthusiasm, sometimes sadness. And helpfulness is also very important."

Practicality

- "Practicality means that I'm both feet on the ground, that I know what I want, and that I keep it like that, as long as I'm happy with it."

- "I always say, as long as a person is satisfied with the way life is going, then that is enough. The most important thing in life is the job, prudence and being down to earth."
- "I live practicality by keeping my family's back free. Always, every day, all year round, so that everyone can do their part without additional burdens."
- "For me this means satisfaction at the end of the day, that you're mentally well, that you're happy, that you feel good."

Morality

- "Decency and morality, that's the whole character to me. It's about keeping promises."
- "I am honest and conscientious. When I act, I think about it. I always try to behave right, to do the right thing. So that my fellow travellers are satisfied, and that I don't hurt anyone."
- "Then I am satisfied. When I do the right thing, I feel good."

Reason

- "I always try to do behave sensibly. It shouldn't result from emotions but from considerations."
- "I am a very precise person. If the bookkeeping isn't right, then I'm desperate. I think that is a predisposition, it's personality. I am an exact person. Also when doing handicrafts. Everything must fit one hundred percent, otherwise I'm not satisfied."
- "Experience shows that one regrets it afterwards, if one decides emotionally and not rationally. That's why it's better to think before you do something."
- "In my life, reason shows in the way I shop, drive a car, make decisions. I don't do that 'ad hoc,' I think before I do something."
- "This is accompanied by satisfaction, perhaps also pride."

Communion

- "To feel like you're connected to someone. It might even go on hiatus for a while, but you simply know that you can always depend on someone, that you actually live in community with others."
- "I think communion is very important because you get new influences, impressions and opinions from others."

- "I need the feeling that I am doing something for someone, but that something is also being done for me. That you have regular contact with people and exchange ideas and are also asked for advice. That someone wants to know my opinion."
- "Fun and humour I experience only in community with others. When you're alone, it's completely different. You can't laugh like you do with friends, but that's obvious."

Fun

- "By fun I mean a lot of humour, going through life with humour, being positive and cheerful."
- "Fun has always been at the top of my list. It's easier to go through life with fun. The ideal would be to have fun all day long."
- "I laugh a lot during the day and can thus show my fun to the outside world."
- "Fun makes me feel happy, cheerful, satisfied and balanced."

Love

- "Love means respecting each other, compromising, sharing."
- "When I do something with love, it's very different than when I do it without love."
- "I think a lot about the beloved person and the love for her. I want to be completely there for her."
- "Love is important for personal development and stability. It goes along with security, harmony and joy. It feels calming and frightening at the same time."

Comfort

- "For me, comfort means doing something good for myself. It has nothing to do with my job, it has nothing to do with my private life. It simply has to do with the fact that it is time for me to switch off. Where it doesn't matter what I do; the main thing is that I'm fine."
- "Relax, be pampered, eat healthy food. Do something good for the body, mind and soul."
- "Once a week I make a face mask at home. I use certain products that are good for the body. In the morning I drink a healthy juice and every evening I drink a large glass of tomato juice, and I think that's

good for the immune system. I also go to a wellness hotel every other year for a few days. Financially, you just have to back off a bit."

- "There are situations where I know exactly that I need it, where I simply ignore my obligations. I sacrifice time that I could also use 'productively.' It takes a certain balance between what you have to do, what you should do and what I want to do."
- "I feel calm, content, healthy and happy. And the more relaxed I am, the less rational I am – which is very pleasant."

Care

- "I, as a mother, consider as care that I am always there for my husband and my children. I do everything for them, so that their everyday life runs as usual, that I fix everything at home, that the food is on the table. Talk to them when they're not in shape."
- "For me, caring is a self-evident duty. I think it is part of life to be there for one's family and for one's people."
- "Care goes hand in hand with feelings of happiness, but also with fear. You feel good and satisfied, but sometimes anxious and restless."

Attentiveness

- "For me, it means experiencing intensely. To be in the here and now, not being unaware. To see as clearly as possible what I am doing, what is happening around me. Intense 'being in the moment.'"
- "There are certain ritual actions that I do in the morning. It also has to do with how I design the room. It is actually completely integrated into my everyday life. Simply the point of view on how to deal with things. For example, knowing what I've done: whether the cup is now to the left or right of the computer, whether my bag is in front of the door or behind it. Whether the computer is off or on. Those are things that have to do with attentiveness for me."
- "It goes hand in hand with joy. With clarity, in the sense of transparency. It even is a body feeling; presence, to feel present."

Harmony

- "Harmony means to understand each other well and to have a good relationship with each other, not to be tense. That you talk to each other, that you are relaxed and easy-going with each other and that you react positively to each other."

- "I just don't like arguments or tensions. That does exist, but I try to bypass them or clear them out."
- "You work better in a harmonious environment; things just work better. For me, harmony also has something to do with order, i.e. practical order in the household. I'm terribly upset if it's messy, then I'm somehow out of balance myself."
- "When I clean up, I feel a little better and that has a calming influence on me. I actually do sports, too, so I can be in balance with myself. If I don't do sports, the inner harmony is lost."
- "In harmony I feel good and balanced. That's something that drives you. If you are in a harmonious environment, then you are more efficient and more interested in things. When I'm in a non-harmonious environment, it paralyses me."

6.4 Brief discourse: on worldview and meaning

The results on the *depth* of sources of meaning have shown that selftranscendence – and in particular vertical selftranscendence (religiosity and spirituality) – is closely related to the experience of meaningfulness. Why might this be the case? And what does this say for secular people?

6.4.1 Religion, spirituality and meaning

For a long time, meaning in and of life were associated primarily with religion: If there is a God who created the world, then this God probably also has a plan for the world and its inhabitants. The meaningfulness of life is thus implied – even if it may remain hidden from the individual. Today religion has lost its "monopoly on meaning." In Central, Western and Northern Europe, not many people draw their meaning from religious sources. For these few, however, meaningfulness is particularly high, as described in Section 6.2.3. Also spirituality is a strong predictor of meaning. What might be the cause for religion's and sprituality's extraordinary potential to create meaning? A review of the four criteria of meaningfulness – belonging, significance, orientation and coherence – can provide further insight here (Schnell, 2010).

Both religiosity and spirituality refer to the existence of a higher reality to which we can relate. Such affiliation offers a strong sense of *belonging*, even on a cosmic scale. Believing in the existence of a higher power further serves as a relief: Meaning is not bound to our human abilities. It does not have to be created by us – it *is*. Moreover, religiosity and spirituality also support a this-worldly social sense of belonging. Religiosity alludes to a centuries-old tradition, to a "community of saints" whom we can identify with or feel at home with. Albeit less structured, since it mostly is not institutionalised, spirituality too can go hand in hand with a sense of belonging and connectedness. This often refers to nature, humanity in general or the whole cosmos.

Moreover, the *significance* of our being and acting is strengthened by religiousness and spirituality. Those who believe in a higher power that observes all our steps – and possibly judges them in an afterlife – will assume that their actions are significant and have consequences. However, it is not guaranteed that faith will then also produce righteous action. Here, for example, denominational differences seem to play a role. For example, in a Belgian-Dutch study, Protestants had a higher morality than Catholics; the latter did not differ from atheists (Rassin & Koster, 2003). This may have to do with the Roman Catholic ritual of confession, which absolves people of their guilt. In Protestantism, private confession was practically abolished. Sola fide applies: the justification solely by faith, not by good works. A personal assurance of justification or forgiveness of guilt, however, does not take place, which might be the reason for a more strongly perceived responsibility for one's own actions, as has been found among Protestants. Comparisons between secular and religious people further show that the latter do not act more morally in principle. A study by Schroeder, Broadus, and Bradley (2018) found comparable criminal offence rates among religious, atheistic and agnostic students in North America. DeCamp and Smith (2019) showed that religious and nonreligious people were equally involved in crimes and offences on the basis of a sample of over 10,000 American youths.

Religious and many spiritual traditions claim to explain the world and give ethical instruction. They are linked to values and norms that serve as a direction for personal life and thus provide *orientation* (Pargament, 1997). Stories and guidelines illustrate what constitutes a good life and how suffering can be overcome. In the case of historically grown and culturally recognised traditions, such as Christian churches, there are strong plausibility structures (Berger, 1967): The environment – or a large part of it – supports and confirms the assumptions made. This strengthens the perceived validity and protects it from relativisation. By referring to irrevocable truth and ultimate values, religion seems to offer orientation, especially when one's life is marked by fear and insecurity (Emmons, Colby, & Kaiser, 1998).

Last but not least, religiosity and spirituality are particularly suited to creating *coherence*. They offer a unifying philosophy of life and are able to meaningfully integrate even painful experiences. As Robert Emmons (2005) was able to show, North American people with religious goals in life report few goal conflicts. Their different goals fit together; they are vertically coherent with the overarching religious orientation. Emmons concluded that "religion invests human existence with meaning by establishing goals and value systems that potentially pertain to all aspects of a person's life. A *goals* approach provides a general unifying framework to capture the dynamic aspect of *religion* in people's lives" (Emmons, 2005, p. 731).

In less-religious countries than the US, however, establishing coherence between one's own religious or spiritual belief system and the prevailing cultural worldview remains a challenge. Gebauer, Sedikides and Neberich (2012) found that religious people exhibit a higher sense of well-being than nonreligious people *only* if they live in countries in which religion is highly valued. In Sweden, Germany and France, which the authors classified as less-religious countries, there was no correlation between religiousness and well-being. It is thus to be expected that the integrative effect of religious life goals is also lower here than in Emmons's sample.

Although religiosity and spirituality have a similar potential for creating meaning, they differ considerably. This is also reflected in people's self-description. In 2018, the General Population Survey of the Social Sciences (ALLBUS; GESIS – Leibniz Institute for Social Sciences) asked Germans whether they saw themselves as religious and/or spiritual. Thirteen percent saw themselves as religious and spiritual, 22 percent as religious but not spiritual, 16 percent as spiritual but not religious, and 49 percent as neither. In part, religiosity and spirituality are based on different ideological assumptions. In practice, too, they are often linked to diverse actions and orientations. For example, in one of my studies (Schnell, 2012), highly religious people attached particular importance to health, nature relatedness and generativity. Highly spiritual people did not take their health that seriously but invested in social commitment, self-knowledge, attentiveness, harmony and creativity in addition to nature relatedness and generativity. Furthermore, it turned out that the more religious a person was, the higher their (vertical and horizontal) selftranscendence, and the lower their selfactualisation. This self-relativising effect did not apply to spirituality.

When further distinguishing between a spirituality that rejects religion and a spirituality that integrates religion, a surprising gap opened up: Those who were spiritual but not religious were significantly more neurotic. They reported above-average hostility, inhibition, depression and anxiety (Schnell, 2012). A similar finding was reported by Michael King and colleagues (King et al., 2013): English adults who described themselves as spiritual but not religious were more likely to be drug addicts, and they more frequently had anxiety disorders, eating disorders, phobias and other neurotic disorders than did religious adults. While we are still a long way from understanding these findings, some first considerations relate to the idiosyncratic character of nonreligious spirituality. Elements (beliefs and rituals) from different traditions are assembled; it is up to the individual to connect them in a coherent and meaningful way. Instead of resorting to strong plausibility structures and communities, such as those offered by churches, the nonreligious spiritual person relies on personal experience to assert their convictions' validity ("experiential validity"; Schnell, 2008, 2011b). However, if one's own experience is the sole yardstick, this can easily lead to strain and uncertainty. Worldview uncertainty, again, can impair resilience and health, as we demonstrated in an experimental study of cardiovascular and cortisol stress responses (Schnell, Fuchs & Hefti, 2020). A study by Jeffrey Vittengl (2018) also pointed in this direction. He examined connections between religious and nonreligious spirituality and later depression. His hypothesis was based on the observation that spiritual people who do not resort to religious structures refer primarily to inner processes and experiences. Vittengl saw an equivalent in depressive thinking and behaviour, which is characterised by rumination and social withdrawal. He thus assumed that nonreligious spirituality would go hand in hand with depression. In fact, he was able to prove through a longitudinal study that Americans who were very spiritual but little religious were significantly more likely to have depression in the subsequent survey (approximately nine years later) than religious people were.

Another explanation for the mental instability apparently connected with spirituality might be that especially in times of crisis, people turn to spirituality or to religion, but this does not (or not directly) have a healing effect. With regard to religiosity, Peter la Cour found that among male (but not female) hospital patients, religious beliefs and practice increased with illness severity (la Cour, 2008). More recently, a Danish research group around Niels Christian Hvidt conducted a large-scale twin study on religion and health (Hvidt, Hvidtjørn, Christensen, Nielsen, & Søndergaard, 2017). The data confirmed that the sicker the participants were (with regard to subjective health assessment, chronic illnesses and life-threatening illnesses), the more they believed in God, prayed and attended church services. After analysing longitudinal data from several European countries, Ahrenfeldt and colleagues (2017) concluded that associations between religion and health depend on the way religiosity is lived: Religiousness characterised by praying, being religiously educated and being an active member of a religious organisation was associated with good health, whereas praying without other religious characteristics was associated with poor health. The authors propose to call this crisis religiosity (Ahrenfeldt et al., 2017). It might be conceivable that many people today also turn to spirituality as an attempt to overcome a crisis and that this explains the lower average mental health of spiritual people.

6.4.2 Meaning without religion

Not so long ago, atheism was regarded as "something obscene and blasphemous going on under cover of night" (cf. Becker, 1932/2003, p. 75). Today, it is assumed that there are between 450 and 500 million people worldwide who identify as atheist or agnostic – 7 percent of the world's population (Keysar & Navarro-Rivera, 2013). Nonbelievers are increasingly self-confident and organise themselves, such as in the International Humanist and Ethical Union (IHEU), The Brights' Net and various international and national atheist or secular alliances and societies. They advocate equal treatment of the nonreligious in state and society and argue for a stronger presence of nonreligious people in public debates and ideological neutrality of the state.

With a bus campaign, atheists have also become active in missionary work: In Great Britain, the journalist Ariane Sherine launched an advertising campaign for a fulfilled life without religion. She reacted to a Christian advertising campaign in which non-Christians were "informed" that they would spend "all eternity in torment in hell," burning "in a lake of fire" (Sherine, 2008). Sherine felt compelled to counter this campaign with something corresponding to her own view of the world. Many sympathisers supported her idea with generous donations, and soon London buses spread the news: "There's probably no god. Now stop worrying and enjoy your life."

Atheists from other countries were also enthusiastic about the idea of this bus campaign, but in most cases, the transport companies were not willing to accept the content of the advertisement. In Germany, therefore, several individuals decided to rent a bus and print the message "There is (almost certainly) no God" on it. Accompanied by teams of volunteers, the bus then traversed Germany. In some of the 23 cities they visited, the volunteers offered free "atheist city tours." In Austria, too, the transport companies rejected the application. As an alternative, posters were put up in Vienna's largest shopping street, saying, "There is no God. Doing good is human. It depends on us" and "God is almost certainly a Czech pop singer [referring to pop singer Karel *Gott*]. Relax. He won't hurt you."

In addition to advocating equality and participation, the majority of initiatives are concerned with raising awareness that meaning, joy and morality are not necessarily linked to religion. Especially atheists in the US endure strong prejudices. Many of the (typically very religious) US citizens assume that atheists see no meaning in life, reject spiritual experiences and have no foundation for moral action (Harris, 2006). Indeed, Americans would rather vote for a presidential candidate who is a Muslim or a homosexual than for an atheist (Edgell, Gerteis, & Hartmann, 2006).

Do these prejudices have any empirical basis? Research on atheism, agnosticism and other forms of nonreligiousness is still in the early stages of development. Until recently, religion and increasingly also spirituality were the main foci of researchers interested in attitudes towards transcendence. Nonbelief was not seen as a characteristic but rather as an "absence," and thus, it was not considered worth researching. One of the first psychological studies to explicitly deal with atheists was carried out by Bob Altemeyer and Bruce Hunsberger (2006). They found relatively highly dogmatic values and slight signs of fanaticism among members of atheist associations in the US. A few years later, the British sociologist William Keenan and I conducted a study among German and Austrian atheists in which we examined their meaning in life (Schnell & Keenan, 2011). We started from the assumption that atheists experience a similarly strong sense of meaningfulness as the rest of the population. However, the data contradicted our hypothesis. Atheists reported lower meaningfulness than religious participants; their scores were also lower than those of nonreligious participants who did not call themselves atheists. But this was no reason for atheists to experience crises of meaning: Like in the other subsamples, only 4 percent reported experiencing a crisis of meaning.

We did not want to stop at this result, however, because legitimate questions arose: Can all those who call themselves atheists be lumped together? Does the absence of a belief in a God or higher power suggest the presence of other unifying characteristics? Using cluster analyses, we searched for possible subgroups on the basis of the participating atheists' sources of meaning. We were able to identify three subgroups, and they differed significantly in their experienced meaningfulness. First of all, there were those who were not committed to any source of meaning. They reported low meaningfulness, and 30 percent of them experienced a crisis of meaning. We assumed that these might be people in transition who have turned away from faith but have not yet found any compensation from other sources of meaning. A second subgroup was characterised by a strong emphasis on selfactualisation. Their dominant sources of meaning were knowledge, freedom, self-knowledge, individualism and comfort. Other dimensions of meaning were not represented, so that we can speak of narrow breadth, balance and depth here. Their meaningfulness scores were not as low as those in the first cluster but were still below average. In contrast, crises of meaning did not occur at all in this group (0 percent). The third subgroup showed a broad profile of sources of meaning. The dimensions of horizontal selftranscendence and of well-being and relatedness were prominent. In this cluster, meaningfulness scores were the highest. They did not differ significantly from that of the general population.

The results substantiate the assumption that atheism can indeed go hand in hand with a sense of meaningfulness in life. They also demonstrate that atheists can have widely divergent convictions. When expanding the scope to include secular individuals identifying as agnostic or indifferent, the diversity is bound to increase further. But let's turn to an equally interesting perspective, which is that of similarities between different secular positions. In one of my recent studies, I compared atheist, agnostic, indifferent, spiritual and religious people on their ontological and ideological beliefs. Atheists and agnostics were in no way lagging behind the spiritual and religious participants in terms of agreement with an ethical, value-oriented attitude to life. Moreover, all respondents were equally ready and willing to take responsibility for their own lives (Schnell, 2015). Elpine de Boer, Hans Alma and I found similar results in a large-scale transnational study on secular identities, which I carried out in Germany, Austria and Switzerland, and Alma and de Boer in the Netherlands. The study targeted individuals who saw themselves as decidedly nonreligious. In Germany, Austria and Switzerland, study participants reported a high average humanistic value orientation with regard to tolerance, social justice and mindful interaction with other people. They further assumed responsibility for their own life and attached little importance to material possessions as a foundation for their well-being (Schnell, 2019).

6.5 Know thyself!

SELF-EXPLORATION: BREADTH, BALANCE AND DEPTH IN YOUR AUTHENTICITY PROFILE

- Take another look at your authenticity profile, from Section 3.2.2. The number of sources of meaning that you marked as realised

(4 or 5) is the breadth of your meaning in life. Are you concentrated on a few sources of meaning, or are you set up "broadly" (at least four life meanings)?

- If your realised sources of meaning are distributed over at least three of the five dimensions, then you can assume a balanced meaning in life.
- If you have high realised values in the dimensions of vertical or horizontal selftranscendence, you can speak of depth in the sense described earlier.

FOR CONTEMPLATION

> And if that word [God] has not much meaning for you, translate it, and speak of the depth of your life, of the source of your being, of your ultimate concern, of what you take seriously without any reservation. Perhaps in order to do so, you must forget everything traditional that you have learned about God, perhaps even that word itself.
>
> (Paul Tillich, 1948, p. 59)

What does "depth" mean to you? What is your absolute concern, and what do you take seriously without reservation?

6.6 Literature

Ahrenfeldt, L. J., Möller, S., Andersen-Ranberg, K., Vitved, A. R., Lindahl-Jacobsen, R., & Hvidt, N. C. (2017). Religiousness and health in Europe. *European Journal of Epidemiology*, *32*(10), 921–929.

Altemeyer, B., & Hunsberger, B. (2006). *Atheists: A groundbreaking study of America's nonbelievers*. Amherst, NY: Prometheus.

Becker, C. L. (1932/2003). *The heavenly city of the eighteenth-century philosophers*. New Haven, CT: Yale University Press.

Berger, P. L. (1967). *The sacred canopy: Elements of a sociological theory of religion*. New York: Anchor Books.

DeCamp, W., & Smith, J. M. (2019). Religion, nonreligion, and deviance: Comparing faith's and family's relative strength in promoting social conformity. *Journal of Religion and Health*, *58*(1), 206–220.

Edgell, P., Gerteis, J., & Hartmann, D. (2006). Atheists as "other": Moral boundaries and cultural membership in American society. *American Sociological Review*, *71*(2), 211–234.

Emmons, R. A. (2005). Striving for the sacred: Personal goals, life meaning, and religion. *Journal of Social Issues*, *61*, 731–745.

Emmons, R. A., Colby, P. M., & Kaiser, H. A. (1998). When lossses lead to gains: Personal goals and the recovery of meaning. In P. T. P. Wong & P. S. Fry (Eds.), *The human quest for meaning* (pp. 163–178). Mahwah, NJ: Erlbaum.

Erikson, E. H. (1988). *Der vollständige Lebenszyklus*. Frankfurt am Main: Suhrkamp.

Frankl, V. (2006). *Man's search for meaning*. Boston, MA: Beacon Press.

Gebauer, J. E., Sedikides, C., & Neberich, W. (2012). Religiosity, social self-esteem, and psychological adjustment on the cross-cultural specificity of the psychological benefits of religiosity. *Psychological Science*, *23*(2), 158–160.

GESIS – Leibniz-Institut für Sozialwissenschaften (2019). *ZA5270: Allgemeine Bevölkerungsumfrage der Sozialwissenschaften ALLBUS 2018*. Retrieved from https://zacat.gesis.org/webview/index.jsp

Harris, S. (2006, December 24). 10 myths – and 10 truths – about atheism. *Los Angeles Times*.

Heine, S. J., Proulx, T., & Vohs, K. D. (2006). The meaning maintenance model: On the coherence of social motivations. *Personality and Social Psychology Review*, *10*(2), 88–110.

Hvidt, N. C., Hvidtjørn, D., Christensen, K., Nielsen, J. B., & Søndergaard, J. (2017). Faith moves mountains – mountains move faith: Two opposite epidemiological forces in research on religion and health. *Journal of Religion and Health*, *56*(1), 294–304.

Keysar, A., & Navarro-Rivera, J. (2013). A world of atheism: Global demographics. In S. Bullivant & M. Ruse (Eds.), *The Oxford handbook of atheism* (pp. 553–586). Oxford: Oxford University Press.

King, M., Marston, L., McManus, S., Brugha, T., Meltzer, H., & Bebbington, P. (2013). Religion, spirituality and mental health: Results from a national study of English households. *The British Journal of Psychiatry*, *202*(1), 68–73.

Koltko-Rivera, M. E. (2006). Rediscovering the later version of Maslow's hierarchy of needs: Selftranscendence and opportunities for theory, research, and unification. *Review of General Psychology*, *10*(4), 302–317.

la Cour, P. (2008). Existential and religious issues when admitted to hospital in a secular society: Patterns of change. *Mental Health, Religion & Culture*, *11*(8), 769–782.

Lupton, D. (2016). *The quantified self*. Cambridge: Polity Press.

Maslow, A. H. (1943). A theory of human motivation. *Psychological Review*, *50*, 370–396.

Maslow, A. H. (1969). The farther reaches of human nature. *Journal of Transpersonal Psychology*, *1*(1), 1–9.

Pargament, K. I. (1997). *The psychology of religion and coping*. New York: Guilford.

Rassin, E., & Koster, E. (2003). The correlation between thought – action fusion and religiosity in a normal sample. *Behaviour Research and Therapy*, *41*(3), 361–368.

Reker, G. T., & Wong, P. P. (1988). Aging as an individual process: Toward a theory of personal meaning. In J. E. Birren & V. L. Bengston (Eds.), *Emergent theories of aging* (pp. 214–246). New York: Springer.

Ruschmann, E. (2011). Transcending towards transcendence. *Implicit Religion, 14*(4), 421–432.

Schnell, T. (2008). Deutsche in der Sinnkrise? Ein Einblick in die Sinnforschung mit Daten einer repräsentativen Stichprobe. *Journal für Psychologie, 16*(3), Article 9.

Schnell, T. (2010). Religiosität und Spiritualität als Quellen der Sinnerfüllung. In C. Klein, H. Berth, & F. Balck (Eds.), *Gesundheit–Religion–Spiritualität. Konzepte, Befunde und Erklärungsansätze* (pp. 259–271). Weinheim: Juventa.

Schnell, T. (2011a). Individual differences in meaning-making: Considering the variety of sources of meaning, their density and diversity. *Personality and Individual Differences, 51*(5), 667–673.

Schnell, T. (2011b). Experiential validity: Psychological approaches to the sacred. Position paper. *Implicit Religion, 14*(4), 387–404.

Schnell, T. (2012). Spirituality with and without religion – differential relationships with personality. *Archive for the Psychology of Religion, 34*, 33–61.

Schnell, T. (2015). Dimensions of secularity (DoS): An open inventory to measure facets of secular identities. *International Journal for the Psychology of Religion, 25*(4), 272–292.

Schnell, T. (2019). Säulen des Humanismus in der Studie zu Konfessionsfreien Identitäten. In R. Schöppner (Ed.), *Humanistische Identität heute* (pp. 167–182). Aschaffenburg: Alibri Verlag.

Schnell, T., & Becker, P. (2007). *Der Fragebogen zu Lebensbedeutungen und Lebenssinn (LeBe)*. Göttingen: Hogrefe.

Schnell, T., Fuchs, D., & Hefti, R. (2020). Worldview under stress: Preliminary findings on cardiovascular and cortisol stress responses predicted by secularity, religiosity/spirituality, and existential search. *Journal of Religion and Health.* Advance online publication. https://doi.org/10.1007/s10943-020-01008-5.

Schnell, T., & Keenan, W. J. F. (2011). Meaning-making in an atheist world. *Archive for the Psychology of Religion, 33*(1), 55–78.

Schroeder, R. D., Broadus, E. J., & Bradley, C. (2018). Religiosity and crime revisited: Accounting for non-believers. *Deviant Behavior, 39*(5), 632–647.

Sherine, A. (2008, October 21). All aboard the atheist bus campaign. *The Guardian.* Retrieved from www.theguardian.com/commentisfree/2008/oct/21/religion-advertising

Thoits, P. A. (2003). Personal agency in the accumulation of multiple role-identities. In P. J. Burke, T. J. Owens, R. Serpe, & P. A. Thoits (Eds.), *Advances in identity theory and research* (pp. 179–194). New York: Kluwer Academic, Plenum.

Thoits, P. A., & Evenson, R. J. (2008). Differential labeling of mental illness revisited: Patterns before and after the rise of managed care. *Sociological Forum, 23*(1), 28–52.

Tillich, P. (1948). *The shaking of the foundations*. New York: C. Scribner's Sons.

Vaunet. (2019, January 21). *Mediennutzung in Deutschland 2018*. Retrieved from www.vau.net/system/files/documents/vaunet_mediennutzung-2018-publikation.pdf

Vittengl, J. R. (2018). A lonely search? Risk for depression when spirituality exceeds religiosity. *The Journal of Nervous and Mental Disease*, *206*(5), 386–389.

Zhang, H., Sang, Z., Chan, D. K. S., & Schlegel, R. (2019). Threats to belongingness and meaning in life: A test of the compensation among sources of meaning. *Motivation and Emotion*, *43*(2), 242–254.

Chapter 7

The social dimension of meaning in life

In an existential context, "belonging" is understood as the experience of having a place in this world, of being part of something that goes beyond the self (Schnell, Höge, & Weber, 2019). As such, it is a response to the fundamental experience of separation between self and world that Irvin Yalom (1980) calls existential isolation. In a psychological context, belonging stands for social inclusion. Thus, Baumeister and Leary (1995, p. 497) define belonging as "strong desire to form and maintain enduring interpersonal attachments." Such bonds manifest themselves in the form of family and friendship or in belonging to different collectives. Meaning deriving from the social dimension is at the forefront of this chapter.

7.1 Asked directly: social relationships as primary sources of meaning

Whenever researchers ask the direct question of what gives meaning to people's lives, social relationships come up first, with particular emphasis on the family. Let me summarise the corresponding studies in chronological order – even if this may be a little monotonous, given that the findings have repeatedly been confirmed. In 1981, Karen de Vogler and Peter Ebersole reported that relationships were most frequently mentioned when they asked 96 US citizens about their most important sources of meaning. In a study by Steven Baum and Robert Stewart (1990), who interviewed 185 Americans of different ages, two sources of meaning, specifically love/marriage and work/career/education, took the first two places, with apparently no gender or age effects. Kay O'Connor and Kerry Chamberlain (1996) interviewed 38 middle-aged New Zealanders about their purpose in life. All (100 percent) mentioned social relationships. Dominique Debats (1999) asked 732 Dutch students (321 of whom were in psychological treatment) to name their current most important sources of meaning. Relationships were by far the most frequently mentioned by patients and non-patients.

Antonella delle Fave and her colleagues conducted a particularly extensive study (2013): They interviewed 666 adults in Australia, Germany, Croatia, Italy, Portugal, Spain and South Africa. Participants were asked to indicate "the three most important things in their lives (sources of meaning)" (p. 520). After coding the open answers, family proved to be the most frequently cited source of meaning (84 percent); as much as 40 percent of the answers referred to it. Work followed by a large margin (44 percent of the people, 15 percent of the answers). This strong prioritisation of family and the ranking of work in second place was found among respondents from all cultures surveyed.

Melissa Grouden and Paul Jose (2014) asked their 247 middle-aged New Zealand study participants to describe their sources of meaning. Again, relationships were the most frequently cited: In first place (36 percent) was family, followed by social relationships (14 percent). Only just under 9 percent of the surveyed New Zealanders cited work as a source of meaning, which could indicate a cultural peculiarity. In addition, participants were asked to rate to which extent a list of sources of meaning contributed to their personal meaning in life. Again, family achieved the highest rating. The important role of family and other social relationships applied to both sexes and all ages.

Paul Wong developed the Personal Meaning Profile, which defines eight sources of meaning and measures their personal relevance. In the presentation of the instrument (Wong, 1998), relationships were rated the highest of all eight sources of meaning. In a study by Liora Bar-Tur and colleagues (2001), 362 Jewish and Arab Israelis were asked to assess the importance of 11 given sources of meaning; family relationships were given the highest rating. A group of American authors (Lambert et al., 2010) conducted a series of successive studies to explore the role of the family in young adulthood. The studies confirmed the assumption that when asking an open question about personal sources of meaning, family would be mentioned most frequently by young adults. Family also came first in a ranking of given sources of meaning. As expected, the perceived closeness to the family and support by the family correlated with meaningfulness. Another of their studies suggested that these results had nothing to do with social desirability. The authors concluded that "for young adults, family relationships are a primary source of meaning in life and they contribute to their sense of meaning" (p. 517).

Through in-depth interviews, I have researched interpersonal sources of meaning in young adults in Germany (Schnell, 2012). Ten men and ten women aged between 19 and 26 were interviewed about their personal myths, rituals and experiences of transcending (Schnell, 2003, 2009). The importance of peers and family was evident in all three dimensions, although in contrast to the American study just described, friendship was mentioned even more often than family was.

When asked what they would put on a "personal altar," what they "considered sacred or inviolable," 55 percent of the participants named "friends" and 40 percent "family." These are three examples:

Male, 19 years old: "Music, parents and brother, guitar, openness, friends."

Female, 20 years: "My parents, the family itself, tolerance, reliability, loyalty, honesty, love, children, consideration, happiness, my friend."

Female, 21 years: "Family, plants, books, candles, studying, astrology, bed, boyfriend, photos, plush toys, friends."

We also asked our interviewees about past key experiences. In the majority of cases, they mentioned interpersonal experiences such as moments of solidarity, closeness, or first love. Also, when asked about a life motto or life task, responses revolved around social concerns. Many participants referred to "being able to be the way you are" in relationships, to "being able to let your feelings run free," thereby receiving strength, encouragement and support. Mutuality, the willingness not only to take but also to give, was emphasised again and again. A 20-year-old man expressed it succinctly: "If I am friends with someone, I can do anything. I could die for my friends. If someone is a friend of mine, that's not so easy. That is friendship" (Schnell, 2012, p. 18; transl. TS).

Such commitment to social relationships was also reflected in personal rituals reported by respondents. They were about special forms of greeting or communication, gifts and regular shared activities. They were the space for experienced closeness and belonging, for helpfulness and expression of appreciation. They thus also created a medium for significant experiences of selftranscendence. As an example for many others, a 17-year-old recounted the following self-transcending experience:

> When I'm with friends; that you can really do any nonsense and then not be portrayed as stupid or so, but that you have fun together and everyone can do something that is not considered normal. For

> example, if you say something stupid and just spin a stupid idea and get into it. That everyone says something about it and that it's only funny afterwards. For me that signifies stability, to have fun, to enjoy life and to see the beauty in life.
>
> (Schnell, 2012, p. 21; transl. TS)

Several people shared that in caring and active listening, they forgot everything around them. A 25-year-old man recounted the following:

> It means that I give someone my attention and of course he also gives me recognition because he tells me something. And then I am not interested in the fact that a nuclear bomb might fall next door, but at that moment it is crucial to me that I am there for this person, that I can perhaps help him.
>
> (Schnell, 2012, p. 21; transl. TS)

Experiences of transcending are extraordinary states of consciousness characterised by the deactivation of standard cognitive control mechanisms (Schnell, 2009, 2011a). Those who self-transcend are temporarily helpless, vulnerable, childlike. Trustworthy interpersonal relationships seem to represent a shelter in which an unconditional acceptance applies. The experience of being recognised and held despite unmasking and being "stupid" is an important contribution to a person's experience of meaningfulness, probably by strengthening the sense of belonging and significance (Schnell, 2012).

7.2 Family and friendship as sources of meaning?

When there is no reason for explication, sources of our meaning are not part of our working memory but stored as implicit knowledge. They are part of our worldview, along with other fundamental (ideological, ontological, epistemological, etc.) assumptions. "Worldviews are not products of thought," Dilthey (1960, p. 86, transl. TS) wrote: "They emerge from life behaviour, life experience, the structure of our mental totality" and are therefore not easily accessible through cognition.

Anyone who thinks they can access this hidden structure with a simple, direct question could end up with all-too-simple, obvious answers. Family and friends always take top positions when people are confronted with the direct question of what gives meaning to their lives. Nevertheless, they do not number among the sources of meaning assessed by the Sources of Meaning and Meaning in Life questionnaire (SoMe; Schnell & Becker, 2007; Section 3.2.1). This is because sources of meaning are understood as part of our worldview, as fundamental orientations guiding thinking, acting and experiences in different areas of life. Sources of meaning are the ultimate concerns mentioned when we are asked about the meaning of our values, assumptions and action. Of course, the terms "family" and "friends" often appeared in the qualitative studies that preceded the development of the SoMe. But underlying them were many – highly individual – ultimate concerns.

Consider the following responses of a young man to the following question: "Are there any celebrations or ceremonies that are particularly important to you?" obtained with the laddering technique Section 3.1.1).

Answer 1: Family celebrations
Interviewer: What do these celebrations mean for you?
Answer 2: I like being with my family. They are very funny; we can laugh a lot.
Interviewer: What does that mean for you?
Answer 3: To relax, unwind, compete a little with the others, a few challenges!

We have summarised the meanings that the young man finally came up with by the terms "comfort," "fun" and "challenge." They represent what family celebrations meant to him and thus reflect a personal experience of family. Other meanings that our interviewees associated with family were communion, care, tradition or generativity. Concepts such as family or friends are too superficial, too generic, to inform us about actual personal meanings. For this reason, the SoMe does not include family or friendship as a source of meaning.

7.3 Meaning and marital status

The significance that family has for meaning in life can also be captured via demographic variables. For example, we know that meaningfulness is closely associated with marital status (Damásio, Koller, & Schnell, 2013; Schnell, 2009). The institution of marriage seems to play a special role here: Married people, for example, report higher meaningfulness than singles but also than cohabitants. Perhaps people with a higher sense of meaning are more willing to enter into marriage. On the other hand, marriage might also strengthen meaningfulness. Although the number of people living in a non-marital partnership is increasing, for many, there seems to be a significant difference between a partnership per se and its being sealed by marriage.

However, this does not mean that unmarried people more often experience crises of meaning than married people do. With an existing partnership – whether officially confirmed or not – crises of meaning are significantly less frequent than among single people. This suggests that the possibility of loving a partner and being loved by this person might constitute a protection against a crisis of meaning.

7.4 Children as a source of meaning

And what about children? In the literature, we can read about the paradox of parenthood: Many people regard children as a goal in life, as positive and desirable. At the same time, the social discourse on children and parenthood revolves largely around problematic aspects. The low birth rate is criticised with the primary reason that too few workers "grow up." Parenthood focuses on the (expected) burdens associated with children. A study by the German Federal Institute for Population Research stated that a culture of concern, doubt and worry dominates parenthood (Schneider, Diabaté, & Ruckdeschel, 2015). Potential parents assume that their own needs will become less important with the birth of a child; that the mother's employment in particular might be impeded; and that the parents' participation in social life will be hampered. Financial insecurity and fear of educational errors further prevent or delay the practical implementation of a widespread desire to have children.

In fact, these concerns are not entirely unfounded. A meta-analysis showed that both life satisfaction and partnership satisfaction decline continuously after the birth of a child and that they do not increase again (Luhmann, Hofmann, Eid, & Lucas, 2012). But the limitation of this hedonic aspect of well-being (Section 10.1) is – according to one theory – compensated for by an increase of eudaimonic well-being: Parents' sense of meaning is significantly higher than that of childless adults, as Baumeister and colleagues demonstrated (2013).

We continued to investigate the issue and came up with some surprising results (in preparation): In fact, at first glance, parents' sense of meaning is higher than that of childless adults. If, however, parenthood and marital status are considered at the same time, parenthood does not additionally contribute to the explanation of meaningfulness. In other words, married parents' sense of meaning is no higher than that of childless married couples.

Further information was provided by gender-specific analyses. In principle, meaningfulness is somewhat *higher* among mothers than among childless women, whereas it is *lower* among fathers than among childless men – irrespective of age and marital status. On the other hand, men report significantly higher meaningfulness in marriage, compared with single men or cohabiting men. There are no differences among women in this respect.

Are there any insights into the paradox of parenthood that the available data can provide? According to Baumeister, Vohs, Aaker, and Garbinsky (2013), a loss of happiness after parenthood should be compensated for by an increased sense of meaning. This seems to be the case with the women in our sample, but not with the men. A possible explanation can be found in Trivers's parental investment theory (1972). It assumes that investment by mothers is far higher than investment by fathers. Consequently, motherhood should be more important for female identity (and female meaning in life) than fatherhood for male identity and meaning in life.

For the average man in our study, paternity is not a strong source of meaning, but marriage appears to be. How is this to be understood? Here too, evolutionary psychology could provide an explanation. It has shown that women are selective in their choice of partners in order to ensure that their offspring grow up optimally. Accordingly, women attach importance to the dedication and commitment of their partners, especially when it comes to a long-term partnership (Buss & Schmitt, 1993). The subgroup of married men in our study represents those who were "chosen" as husbands – perhaps because of their strong sense of meaning. On the other hand, there is also evidence that people with a high sense of meaning are more willing to marry than people with a lower sense of meaning (Stavrova & Luhmann, 2016).

Marriage is accompanied by expectations, rights and duties that can strengthen all four aspects of meaningfulness. Marriage implies a special *significance*: In Germany, for example, it is still subject to special state protection (see Article 6 of the German Constitution). It is also regarded as a particularly stable form of *belonging*, which is publicly affirmed and legally protected (which, of course, can be questioned in view of high divorce rates). Furthermore, married life is associated with a number of codes of conduct (Waite & Gallagher, 2002), which, if followed, strengthen *coherence* in behaviour and self-perception. Last but not least, marriage is associated with a generative *orientation* since it is still regarded (by the state as well as many contemporaries) as the ideal environment for children to grow up in. Generativity (Erikson, 1980; Section 6.1) has repeatedly been identified as the strongest predictor of meaningfulness (Damásio, Koller, & Schnell, 2013; Pedersen et al., 2018; Schnell, 2011b; Schnell & Hoof, 2012).

The fact that today every third marriage in Germany fails and more and more children are born without prior marriage announces a change in our understanding of possible forms of relationships. Nevertheless, marriage still appears to remain attractive, as evidenced by the fact that in 2018 one-third of marriages were performed by couples of which at least one partner had previously been divorced or widowed (DESTATIS, 2019).

7.5 Social inclusion

Our need for social inclusion is not limited to family and friends. According to Maslow (1943), social needs such as group membership, communication, social exchange, mutual recognition and support are human deficit needs: as long as they are not satisfied, they are salient (accessible to consciousness) and urge us to fulfil them. Edward Deci and Richard Ryan (2008) consider social inclusion, autonomy and competence to be the three basic psychological needs.

Impressively, Jean Twenge and colleagues (2003) showed the importance of social inclusion through the consequences of social rejection: In experiments, they brought about the experience of social rejection by first letting the participants talk to each other in small groups and then asking them to write down the names of the two with whom they would like to work. Half of the (randomly selected) participants were then told that no one wanted to work with them; the other half learned that they had been named by all. This information had nothing to do with reality but was intended to create a feeling of social exclusion in some and a feeling of social acceptance in others. The study participants then worked on several tasks and questionnaires. As the authors had hypothesised, the socially rejected had entered a state of cognitive deconstruction (Baumeister, 1990): They had the feeling that "time was dragging on" – they estimated time intervals to be significantly longer than they actually were. They avoided thinking about the future. Compared to the socially accepted, they opted more often for momentary advantages than for the option of later but farther-reaching advantages (which is considered an indicator of low self-control). Regardless of which decision they made, they were not very convinced of it. Further experiments in this study showed that social rejection was associated with slower response times, emotional flattening and the avoidance of self-attention. Last but not least, socially excluded people were much more likely to agree that life was meaningless.

Tyler Stillman and colleagues (2009) also confirmed the hypothesis that social exclusion and loneliness affect meaning in life. In another series of studies, Lambert, Stillman and colleagues (2013) focused on the positive experience of social belonging. Both in a cross-sectional and in a three-week longitudinal study, social belonging correlated with meaningfulness. In a subsequent experiment, various forms of belonging were evoked: feeling belonging, experiencing support and receiving compliments. Participants were prompted to recall the people whom they linked to these experiences and then to describe the people and the situation. Those who had evoked a sense of belonging reported higher meaningfulness than the other two groups did (although the initial values were not given, and it is therefore unclear whether the groups differed from the start or whether this was attributable to an actual increase in meaning through the experimental induction). In a replication of the experiment with Indian students, the evocation of social support was accompanied by a similar increase in meaningfulness as the evocation of felt belonging.

In a longitudinal study with older Americans, Neil Krause (2007) has demonstrated that social support can indeed increase a person's sense of meaning. The study showed that the type of support plays an important role: Meaningfulness was most influenced by anticipated social support: trusting that you will receive help when you need it. This finding recalls the importance of manageability that Antonovsky (1997) postulated in his sense of coherence. He assumed that health is promoted by the following:

1 We experience our life as meaningful (meaningfulness).
2 We have sufficient resources available to master life (manageability).
3 We perceive the world as comprehensible and coherent (comprehensibility).

The three aspects of the sense of coherence are closely related, and anticipated social support can be viewed as an aspect of manageability.

Krause also found that emotional support from family and friends played an important role in meaning in life in old age. Interestingly, this did not apply to active or informational support – at least not per se. Perhaps these types of support – so the author muses – put age-related functional limitations too much into the foreground, thus exposing older people in their need of help. But they were still important, as further analyses showed: The more tangible help or information the study participants received, the higher they rated their emotional support – which in turn increased their sense of meaning.

7.6 From social inclusion to meaning – or vice versa?

Olga Stavrova and Maike Luhmann (2016) used data from American and British long-term studies to examine the effects of social inclusion on meaning in life but also in the opposite direction – the influence of meaningfulness on social inclusion. They distinguished three forms of social connectedness: intimate, relational and collective. The analyses showed that collective involvement predicted meaningfulness ten years later. However, this effect was not found for connectedness with partners, family and friends. The authors speculate that more than spouses, friends and family, the experience of involvement in a collective community contributes to strengthening self-esteem and self-efficacy and thus also to meaningfulness.

In a further step, the other possible direction of influence was analysed: Does meaningfulness contribute to people feeling connected to their partners, friends, family or the social community? Here effects were observed with regard to all three forms of social integration: Ten years later, those who had perceived their lives as meaningful at the time of the first study reported a stronger sense of partnership, family, friendship and social solidarity. Stavrova and Luhmann substantiated this finding on the basis of British survey data: Here it became apparent that a high level of meaningfulness at the time of the first study predicted higher levels of social solidarity and voluntary activity two years later. In addition, the rate of marriages contracted within these two years was significantly higher among those who had reported a high level of meaningfulness two years earlier.

We can thus conclude that being integrated into a larger social whole strengthens meaningfulness to a particular degree. More than partnership, family or friendship, feeling attached to a community seems to promote belonging in an existential sense. We might argue that it also offers more possibilities for experiencing personal significance, such as through various forms of generativity (Section 6.1). Finally, this study shows that a sense of meaning in life can motivate people to take an active and responsible approach to life – demonstrated here by the respondents' willingness to enter into long-term relationships and become socially involved (see also Chapter 14).

7.7 Social inclusion at work

For Aristotle, a human being is a social being (*zoon politicon*). Only in community – according to the Greek philosopher – can we realise our potentials. States and regional collectives have thus emerged. The world of work, too, is organised in the form of collectives: companies, organisations and institutions. Here, people work as experts but always also as social beings (Schnell et al., 2019). Therefore, belonging also represents a central criterion for meaningful work (Schnell, 2019; Chapter 13).

Relations between employers and employees are characterised by different types of give and take. Individuals who feel a sense of belonging are motivated to commit to a common goal, a shared task. Identification with a team or an organisation supports processes of self-investment (Leach et al., 2008), which in turn increase the satisfaction of being part of the group and the importance of the group for one's self-concept. Employees who offer commitment and identification expect loyalty from their employers as well (Rousseau, 1995; Schnell, Höge, & Pollet, 2013). They hope for recognition, appreciation and social support from colleagues and superiors (Siegrist, 1996).

Successful social inclusion in the workplace is associated with increased occupational and general well-being, whereas a lack of belonging has been associated with depression (Cockshaw, Shochet, & Obst, 2014; Somoray, Shakespeare-Finch, & Armstrong, 2017; Shakespeare-Finch & Daley, 2017). Some psychological constructs therefore explicitly address this important aspect. Early on, Allen and Meyer (1990) emphasised the importance of affective commitment for an organisation, rooted in positive emotions towards it. The concept of organisational identification takes this one step further. It describes a psychological fusion of self and organisation with regard to organisational norms, values and interests (van Knippenberg & Sleebos, 2006). Empirical studies have shown that the experience of work as meaningful predicts both affective commitment (e.g. Geldenhuys, Laba, & Venter, 2014; Milliman, Czaplewski, & Ferguson, 2003; Steger, Dik, & Duffy, 2012) and organisational identification (Demirtas, Hannah, Gok, Arslan, & Capar, 2017). Likewise, it can be assumed that organisational identification and affective commitment contribute to a sense of meaningfulness at work (Ashforth, Harrison, & Corley, 2008).

The concept of psychological ownership also addresses employees' connectedness with the organisation. It describes the experience of being a (co-)owner of a material or non-material object – in this case, the organisation, or a part (project, area of work, tool, idea, etc.) thereof. The experience of ownership is perceived as an extension of the self (Pierce, Kostova, & Dirks, 2001). Pierce and Jussila (2010) define jointly experienced psychological ownership as "a collective understanding that we are one, bound and interdependent on one another for some purpose that is larger than the self" (p. 817).

While the previously mentioned concepts describe individuals' attitudes, the socio-moral atmosphere is a characteristic (perceived by individuals) of the organisation (Weber, Unterrainer, & Höge, 2008). It is characterised by trusting and respectful relationships; participative cooperation; an atmosphere open to diversity and criticism; mutual support between colleagues, employees and superiors; and the transfer of responsibility for the well-being of others. Studies have shown the socio-moral atmosphere to be associated with prosocial work behaviour, solidarity in the workplace and democratic orientation (Weber et al., 2008; Pircher Verdorfer, Weber, Unterrainer, & Seyr, 2013) and to contribute to meaningful work (Höge & Weber, 2018; Schnell et al., 2013).

Time and again, social and economic developments in recent decades have jeopardised experiences of belonging to the workplace. Organisations have responded to intensified global competition and structural change with deregulation and restructuring strategies. These include unconventional, precarious working conditions and high flexibility requirements for employees. For temporary workers, part-time workers, teleworkers and outsourced self-employed people, it is difficult to impossible to develop affiliation with an organisation (Cartwright & Holmes, 2006; Schnell et al., 2013). The experience of alienation is a possible consequence (Rosa, 2014; Schnell et al., 2013; Yeoman, 2014).

Yet a strong sense of belonging in the workplace cannot be regarded as unreservedly positive. It raises the question whether merging with the organisation (see organisational identification) is desirable and mentally healthy. Anyone who derives identity and meaning solely from their professional affiliation has little balance in their life and runs the risk of losing autonomy and becoming dependent (Mael & Ashforth, 2001; Schnell, 2011b, 2016). Dave Eggers's *The Circle* (2014) offers great literary insight into such processes. Further potential disadvantages of a strong identification with the profession are described in Chapter 13, which deals more generally with meaningful work.

7.8 Know thyself!

SELF-EXPLORATION: SOCIAL BELONGING

In some of the experiments described earlier, social belonging was evoked via *priming*. This process produces a vivid memory, allowing for further introspection. Use it to explore your personal social involvement:

Think of two people or a group to whom you feel closely connected. Describe these people or this group in writing. Describe your relationship with them. Outline an experience you had with these people or group that you remember as particularly strong social inclusion and belonging.

Reflect: How often do I experience myself as socially well integrated? What characterises such situations? With which people or groups is this possible? Am I satisfied with the social integration I experience? If not, how could I strengthen it, and what can I personally contribute to it?

FOR CONTEMPLATION

> No relationship can eliminate isolation. Each of us is alone in existence. Yet aloneness can be shared in such a way that love compensates for the pain of isolation.
>
> (Yalom, 1980, p. 363)

7.9 Literature

Allen, N. J., & Meyer, J. P. (1990). The measurement and antecedents of affective, continuance and normative commitment to the organization. *Journal of Occupational and Organizational Psychology*, *63*(1), 1–18.

Antonovsky, A. (1979). *Health, stress and coping*. San Francisco: Jossey-Bass.

Ashforth, B. E., Harrison, S. H., & Corley, K. G. (2008). Identification in organizations: An examination of four fundamental questions. *Journal of Management*, *34*(3), 325–374.

Bar-Tur, L., Savaya, R., & Prager, E. (2001). Sources of meaning in life for young and old Israeli Jews and Arabs. *Journal of Aging Studies*, *15*(3), 253–269.

Baum, S. K., & Stewart Jr, R. B. (1990). Sources of meaning through the lifespan. *Psychological Reports*, *67*(1), 3–14.

Baumeister, R. F. (1990). Suicide as escape from self. *Psychological Review*, *97*(1), 90–113.

Baumeister, R. F., & Leary, M. R. (1995). The need to belong: Desire for interpersonal attachments as a fundamental human motivation. *Psychological Bulletin*, *117*(3), 497.

Baumeister, R. F., Vohs, K. D., Aaker, J. L., & Garbinsky, E. N. (2013). Some key differences between a happy life and a meaningful life. *The Journal of Positive Psychology*, *8*, 505–516.

Buss, D. M., & Schmitt, D. P. (1993). Sexual strategies theory: An evolutionary perspective on human mating. *Psychological Review*, *100*, 204–232.

Cartwright, S., & Holmes, N. (2006). The meaning of work: The challenge of regaining employee engagement and reducing cynicism. *Human Resource Management Review*, *16*(2), 199–208.

Cockshaw, W. D., Shochet, I. M., & Obst, P. L. (2014). Depression and belongingness in general and workplace contexts: A cross-lagged longitudinal investigation. *Journal of Social and Clinical Psychology*, *33*(5), 448–462.

Damásio, B. F., Koller, S. H., & Schnell, T. (2013). Sources of meaning and meaning in life questionnaire (SoMe): Psychometric properties and sociodemographic findings in a large Brazilian sample. *Acta de Investigación Psicológica*, *3*(3), 1205–1227.

De Vogler, K. L., & Ebersole, P. (1981). Adults' meaning in life. *Psychological Reports*, *49*(1), 87–90.

Debats, D. L. (1999). Sources of meaning: An investigation of significant commitments in life. *Journal of Humanistic Psychology*, *39*(4), 30–57.

Deci, E. L., & Ryan, R. M. (2008). Self-Determination theory: A macrotheory of human motivation, development, and health. *Canadian Psychology*, *49*, 182–185.

Delle Fave, A., Brdar, I., Wissing, M. P., & Vella-Brodrick, D. A. (2013). Sources and motives for personal meaning in adulthood. *The Journal of Positive Psychology*, *8*(6), 517–529.

Demirtas, O., Hannah, S. T., Gok, K., Arslan, A., & Capar, N. (2017). The moderated influence of ethical leadership, via meaningful work, on followers' engagement, organizational identification, and envy. *Journal of Business Ethics*, *145*(1), 183–199.

DESTATIS. (2019, August 14). *Erst-Ehen und Wiederverheiratungen bei Eheschließungen zwischen Mann und Frau*. Retrieved from www.destatis.de/DE/Themen/Gesellschaft-Umwelt/Bevoelkerung/Eheschliessungen-Ehescheidungen-Lebenspartnerschaften/Tabellen/erstehen-wiederverheiratung.html

Dilthey, W. (1960). *Gesammelte Schriften. 8. Weltanschauungslehre: Abhandlungen zur Philosophie der Philosophie*. Göttingen: Vandenhoeck & Ruprecht.

Eggers, D. (2014). *The Circle*. London: Penguin.

Erikson, E. H. (1980). *Identity and the Life Cycle*. New York: W W Norton & Company.

Geldenhuys, M., Laba, K., & Venter, C. M. (2014). Meaningful work, work engagement and organisational commitment. *SA Journal of Industrial Psychology*, *40*(1), 1–10.

Grouden, M. E., & Jose, P. E. (2014). How do sources of meaning in life vary according to demographic factors? *New Zealand Journal of Psychology*, *43*(3), 29–38.

Höge, T., & Weber, W. G. (2018). Das soziomoralische Organisationsklima und Sinnerfüllung in der Arbeit: Erkenntnisse über zwei Gesundheitsressourcen. In B. Badura, A. Ducki, H. Schörder, J. Klose, & M. Meyer (Eds.), *Fehlzeiten-Report 2018. Sinn erleben–Arbeit und Gesundheit* (pp. 225–233). Berlin: Springer.

Krause, N. (2007). Longitudinal study of social support and meaning in life. *Psychology and Aging, 22*(3), 456–469.

Lambert, N. M., Stillman, T. F., Baumeister, R. F., Fincham, F. D., Hicks, J. A., & Graham, S. M. (2010). Family as a salient source of meaning in young adulthood. *The Journal of Positive Psychology, 5*(5), 367–376.

Lambert, N. M., Stillman, T. F., Hicks, J. A., Kamble, S., Baumeister, R. F., & Fincham, F. D. (2013). To belong is to matter: Sense of belonging enhances meaning in life. *Personality and Social Psychology Bulletin, 39*(11), 1418–1427.

Leach, C. W., van Zomeren, M., Zebel, S., Vliek, M. L., Pennekamp, S. F., Doosje, B., Ouwerkerk, J. W., & Spears, R. (2008). Group-level self-definition and self-investment: A hierarchical (multicomponent) model of in-group identification. *Journal of Personality and Social Psychology, 95*(1), 144–165.

Luhmann, M., Hofmann, W., Eid, M., & Lucas, R. E. (2012). Subjective well-being and adaptation to life events: A meta-analysis. *Journal of Personality and Social Psychology, 102*(3), 592–615.

Mael, F. A., & Ashforth, B. E. (2001). Identification in work, war, sports, and religion: Contrasting the benefits and risks. *Journal for the Theory of Social Behaviour, 31*(2), 197–222.

Maslow, A. H. (1943). A theory of human motivation. *Psychological Review, 50*(4), 370–396.

Milliman, J., Czaplewski, A. J., & Ferguson, J. (2003). Workplace spirituality and employee work attitudes: An exploratory empirical assessment. *Journal of Organizational Change Management, 16*(4), 426–447.

O'Connor, K., & Chamberlain, K. (1996). Dimensions of life meaning: A qualitative investigation at mid-life. *British Journal of Psychology, 87*(3), 461–477.

Pedersen, H. F., Handegard Birkeland, M., Søndergaard Jensen, J., Schnell, T., Hvidt, N. C., Sørensen, T., & la Cour, P. (2018). What brings meaning to life in a highly secular society? A study on sources of meaning among Danes. *Scandinavian Journal of Psychology, 59*(6), 678–690.

Pierce, J. L., & Jussila, I. (2010). Collective psychological ownership within the work and organizational context: Construct introduction and elaboration. *Journal of Organizational Behavior, 31*(6), 810–834.

Pierce, J. L., Kostova, T., & Dirks, K. T. (2001). Toward a theory of psychological ownership in organizations. *Academy of Management Review, 26*, 298–310.

Pircher Verdorfer, A., Weber, W. G., Unterrainer, C., & Seyr, S. (2013). The relationship between organizational democracy and socio-moral climate: Exploring effects of the ethical context in organizations. *Economic and Industrial Democracy, 34*(3), 423–449.

Rosa, H. (2014). *Beschleunigung und Entfremdung*. Berlin: Suhrkamp.

Rousseau, D. M. (1995). *Psychological contracts in organizations: Understanding written and unwritten agreements*. Thousand Oaks, CA: Sage.

Schneider, N. F., Diabaté, S., & Ruckdeschel, K. (Eds.). (2015). *Familienleitbilder in Deutschland. Kulturelle Vorstellungen zu Partnerschaft, Elternschaft und Familienleben. Beiträge zur Bevölkerungswissenschaft* (Bd. 48). Opladen: Barbara Budrich.

Schnell, T. (2003). A framework for the study of implicit religion: The psychological theory of implicit religiosity. *Implicit Religion, 6*(2–3), 86–104.

Schnell, T. (2009). *Implizite Religiosität–Zur Psychologie des Lebenssinns* (2nd ed.). Lengerich: Pabst.

Schnell, T. (2011a). Experiential validity: Psychological approaches to the sacred. Position Paper. *Implicit Religion, 14*(4), 387–404.

Schnell, T. (2011b). Individual differences in meaning-making: Considering the variety of sources of meaning, their density and diversity. *Personality and Individual Differences, 51*(5), 667–673.

Schnell, T. (2012). "Für meine Freunde könnte ich sterben" – Implizite Religiosität und die Sehnsucht nach Transzendenz. In U. Kropac, U. Meier, & K. König (Eds.), *Jugend–Religion–Religiosität. Resultate, Probleme und Perspektiven der aktuellen Religiositätsforschung* (pp. 87–108). Regensburg: Pustet.

Schnell, T. (2016). Die Arbeit und wir – eine Beziehungsanalyse. *Sucht, 99*, 8–11.

Schnell, T. (2018). Von Lebenssinn und Sinn in der Arbeit. Warum es sich bei beruflicher Sinnerfüllung nicht um ein nettes Extra handelt. In B. Badura, A. Ducki, H. Schröder, J. Klose, & M. Meyer (Eds.), *Fehlzeiten-Report 2018* (pp. 11–21). Berlin and Heidelberg: Springer Verlag.

Schnell, T., & Becker, P. (2007). *Der Fragebogen zu Lebensbedeutungen und Lebenssinn (LeBe)*. Göttingen: Hogrefe.

Schnell, T., Höge, T., & Pollet, E. (2013). Predicting meaning in work: Theory, data, implications. *The Journal of Positive Psychology, 8*(6), 543–554.

Schnell, T., Höge, T., & Weber, W. G. (2019). 'Belonging' and its relationship to the experience of meaningful work. In R. Yeoman, K. Bailey, A. Madden, & M. Thompson (Eds.), *The Oxford handbook of meaningful work* (pp. 165–185). Oxford: Oxford University Press.

Schnell, T., & Hoof, M. (2012). Meaningful commitment: Finding meaning in volunteer work. *Journal of Beliefs & Values, 33*(1), 35–53.

Shakespeare-Finch, J., & Daley, E. (2017). Workplace belongingness, distress, and resilience in emergency service workers. *Psychological Trauma: Theory, Research, Practice, and Policy, 9*(1), 32–35.

Siegrist, J. (1996). Adverse health effects of high-effort/low-reward conditions. *Journal of Occupational Health Psychology, 1*(1), 27–41.

Somoray, K., Shakespeare-Finch, J., & Armstrong, D. (2017). The impact of personality and workplace belongingness on mental health workers' professional quality of life. *Australian Psychologist, 52*(1), 52–60.

Stavrova, O., & Luhmann, M. (2016). Social connectedness as a source and consequence of meaning in life. *The Journal of Positive Psychology*, *11*(5), 470–479.

Steger, M. F., Dik, B. J., & Duffy, R. D. (2012). Measuring meaningful work: The work and meaning inventory (WAMI). *Journal of Career Assessment*, *20*(3), 322–337.

Stillman, T. F., Baumeister, R. F., Lambert, N. M., Crescioni, A. W., DeWall, C. N., & Fincham, F. D. (2009). Alone and without purpose: Life loses meaning following social exclusion. *Journal of Experimental Social Psychology*, *45*(4), 686–694.

Trivers, R. L. (1972). Parental investment and sexual selection. In B. G. Campbell (Ed.), *Sexual selection and the descent of man 1871–1971* (pp. 136–179). Chicago, IL: Aldine Publishing Company.

Twenge, J. M., Catanese, K. R., & Baumeister, R. F. (2003). Social exclusion and the deconstructed state: Time perception, mean-inglessness, lethargy, lack of emotion, and self-awareness. *Journal of Personality and Social Psychology*, *85*, 409–423.

van Knippenberg, D., & Sleebos, E. (2006). Organizational identification versus organizational commitment: Self-definition, social exchange, and job attitudes. *Journal of Organizational Behavior*, *27*(5), 571–584.

Waite, L., & Gallagher, M. (2002). *The case for marriage: Why married people are happier, healthier and better off financially*. New York: Broadway Books.

Weber, W. G., Unterrainer, C., & Höge, T. (2008). Socio-moral atmosphere and prosocial and democratic value orientations in enterprises with different levels of anchored participation. *Zeitschrift für Personalforschung*, *22*, 171–194.

Wong, P. T. P. (1998). Implicit theories of meaningful life and the development of the personal meaning profile. In P. T. P. Wong & P. S. Fry (Eds.), *The human quest for meaning: A handbook of psychological research and clinical applications* (pp. 111–140). Mahwah, NJ: Erlbaum.

Yalom, I. (1980). *Existential psychotherapy*. New York: Basic Books.

Yeoman, R. (2014). Conceptualizing meaningful work as a fundamental human need. *Journal of Business Ethics*, *125*(2), 235–251.

Chapter 8

Crises of meaning – when foundations shake

In most cases, crises of meaning occur when external events rupture the experience of continuity or when internal contradictions exceed a critical level. They are accompanied by a realisation that things are not as assumed, as expected or hoped for. Crises of meaning are painful but can be viewed as constructive because they motivate us to develop a different – usually more realistic – view of the world. One of our interviewees described the experience as follows: "Behavioural patterns that no longer fit, an idea of life that was abruptly abandoned. Yes, and having to realise that preconceived opinions or castles built . . . that reality was different and that it just didn't fit" (quoted from Tobias, 2010).

8.1 A lack of meaning

Crises of meaning are painful. They are typically associated with depression, anxiety, pessimism and negative mood (Damásio, Koller, & Schnell, 2013; Pedersen et al., 2018; Schnell, 2009; Sørensen et al., 2019). At the same time, positive affect, life satisfaction, hope and self-efficacy are greatly reduced (Damásio et al., 2013; Pedersen et al., 2018; Schnell, 2009). Resilience is also significantly diminished, and self-regulation processes such as self-determination, self-motivation, self-calming, self-perception and coping with failure are limited (Hanfstingl, 2013; Sørensen et al., 2019). Accordingly, people in such a phase tend to withdraw; they find it almost impossible to describe their situation or explain it to others (Tobias, 2010). Moreover, a study with Peruvian pupils has shown that crises of meaning are a strong predictor of suicidality. In male students, crises of meaning even predicted suicidal tendencies better than depression and highly stressful events (Schnell, Gerstner, & Krampe, 2018).

Time and again, there are cases in which an unresolved crisis of meaning has dramatic consequences for others as well. This is how the student Bastian B., who ran amok at his school in Emsdetten in 2006, described his desperation in a suicide note (Bastian, 2006; transl. TS):

> What's all this for? Why should I work? To bust a gut in order to retire at the age of 65 and die 5 years later? Why should I try hard to achieve anything if it does not matter a damn anyway because I'm going to die sooner or later?
>
> I can build a house, have children and what not. But what for? The house will be demolished at some point, and the children will die, too. So please, what is the meaning of life?

Nevertheless, existentialist philosophers emphasise the necessity of such critical confrontations on the way to an authentic life. Heidegger argues to admit the angst that makes us ask about the meaning of being (Heidegger, 2008). Angst arises when familiar convictions and illusions are questioned, when it is only a matter of me and the world. In this situation, existence acquires an alienated quality: We become aware of our isolation, finiteness, meaninglessness and of the freedom from which the responsibility for our action arises. As another of our interviewees explained, "It is a feeling of simply not having any hold, of being truly alone. And it was in this sense that the thought occurred to me that life actually has no meaning, that nothing has meaning" (quoted from Tobias, 2010).

Whether we arrive there as a result of intellectual courage or because we were struck by an external event, this angst has great potential. It shows us the possibilities of our potentiality for being which lie beyond routine and superficiality. Accordingly, crises of meaning are motivating; they lead to an active and illusionless search for meaning (Klinger, 1998; Skaggs & Barron, 2006; Tobias, 2010). Another interviewee said, "I am definitely searching for a meaning in my life, even if this search should result in the fact that there does not necessarily have to be a meaning of life" (quoted from Tobias, 2010).

8.2 Are Western societies in a crisis of meaning?

Based on the results of our 2006 representative survey in Germany (Schnell & Becker, 2007), I wrote an article in which I questioned the epidemic of crises of meaning (midlife crisis, quarterlife crisis, crises at work, etc.) as repeatedly proclaimed by the media (Schnell, 2008). In our sample, which represented an average of the population, only 4 percent had reported a crisis of meaning. Since then, however, things have obviously changed.

Data from the past five years substantiate that the number of crises of meaning has risen significantly. Since we did not have the opportunity to conduct another representative survey, the following results come from various data sets, collected from 2015 to 2018 and with a total of more than 8,000 German-speaking participants. From these, stratified random samples were drawn to obtain a demographic approximation to the general population. The resulting sample contains data from 1,291 people. The average age of the group is 45 years; in it, men and women are equally represented. The level of education for the younger participants and those of middle age reflects that of society, whereas participants aged 60 and over have a slightly higher level of education than the general population. In this sample, the point prevalence of crisis of meaning amounts to 14 percent.

Whereas previously the peak value was in midlife, we now see that crises of meaning occur most frequently among young people (Figure 8.1). As many as 27 percent of those aged 16 to 29 experience a crisis of meaning. Even in middle age, the prevalence is still high: 15–17 percent. People over 60 are least likely to report crises of meaning (4–5 percent). This suggests that the transition from working life to retirement is

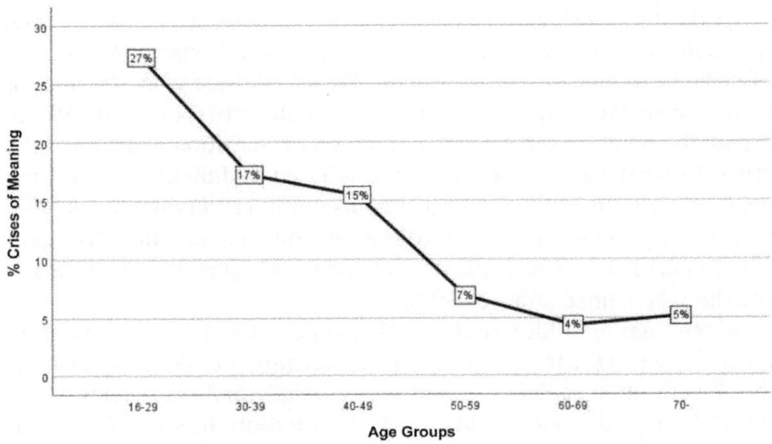

Figure 8.1 Crises of meaning (%) in six age groups (N = 1,291)

rarely a traumatic experience today. Perhaps the relief of having escaped the pressures of working life outweighs the trauma.

But for some, life still holds one last difficult challenge in store – as might be indicated by the slightly renewed increase of crises of meaning at the age of 70 and above (Figure 8.1). Rudolf Vogel visited and interviewed 36 people with an average age of 85 in nursing homes (Vogel, 2010). They completed the SoMe and various open interview questions. More than half of them said they were experiencing a crisis of meaning. Statements like "Every day is a good day for me to die" and "I would rather die today than tomorrow" were frequent. Vogel attributes these crises of meaning to a prevailing lack of perspective among those affected. As the respondents explained, they experienced "no longer being needed" and "not having any responsibility." They were afraid of losing control and thus coming under the control of others. It was not death itself that caused fear and suffering but the living conditions until then.

Restrictions, discomfort and loneliness can severely affect the quality of life in old age. This is also reflected in national surveys on subjective well-being. A longitudinal study examined well-being in old age in Germany, Great Britain and the United States (Gerstorf et al., 2010). Their conclusion was reflected in the title: "Something is seriously wrong at the end of life." In all three countries, the well-being of the population declined rapidly three to five years before death. We apparently have a problem dealing with age-related decline and dying in general (see also Schnell, 2018).

We recently conducted a study on the prevalence of crises of meaning, in which we also asked whether the participants had experienced a crisis of meaning at any point in their lives. We asked those who affirmed for their assessment of what may have triggered the crisis. In the 16–39 age group, the majority indicated that a period of transition had caused the crisis. In most cases, the explanations referred to difficulties in making decisions with regard to the further course of life ("simply not knowing what exactly should come next, where I should go in my life"; "compulsion to decide between unpleasant alternatives"; and "no idea how my life should continue after school").

In the case of older study participants, critical life events were mostly cited as the trigger for crises of meaning. For 40–50-year-olds, these were often separations and professional conflicts ("being abandoned by my girlfriend at the time"; "separation, loss of job"; "feeling of meaninglessness at work"), while for those over 50, illnesses and family conflicts played a greater role ("being caught in the middle between husband and parents, cancer"; "death of brother, dementia of mother, burnout"; "the insight that I had to let go of my three adult children").

8.3 Overcoming crises of meaning

Crises of meaning are often part of depression. In this case, it is advisable to seek professional advice, to start therapeutic and perhaps psychopharmacological treatment. The risk of suicide must also be clarified. However, a crisis of meaning can also stand for itself, as an existential problem, independent of a mental disorder. Thoughts of death, even of suicide, are not necessarily indicators of suicidal tendencies. Rather, they are close to the question of meaning: "Judging whether life is or is not worth living amounts to answering the fundamental question of philosophy" (Camus, 2018, p. 3). The explicit confrontation with one's own mortality might be necessary on the way to authenticity. One may come to the conclusion with Sartre that death robs life of all meaning (Sartre, 2000) and that it is precisely for this reason that humans must give meaning to their own lives. Or perhaps Frankl is right that our mortality can motivate us to take responsibility for our actions in the present to "rescue" them into the reality of the past (Frankl, 2014). Yalom (1980) puts it like this: "Although the physicality of death destroys man, the idea of death saves him" (p. 30).

Due to the strong mental impairment during a crisis of meaning, people usually experience it as difficult to cope with everyday life, to "function." A confrontation with experienced meaninglessness needs space and time. It is advantageous, if not indispensable, therefore, to take time out. Furthermore, it is helpful to be close to a person who is available as a companion, either privately or professionally (e.g. existential psychotherapy, logotherapy, pastoral care, philosophical practice). A retreat from the familiar environment and a visit to a place of silence and shelter (monastery, retreat, etc.) can also be valuable.

Similar to anxiety disorders, a crisis of meaning – with a predominant feeling of existential angst – requires an active approach to anxiety and anxiety-inducing issues. This confrontation may be painful, but it can save us, as Yalom assures us. In contrast to anxiety disorders, the angst that accompanies a crisis of meaning usually is not catastrophic or irrational. It is real, arises from the impositions of the factuality of one's own death, the freedom of choice and the resulting responsibility, from the absurdity of the world or, in the case of believers, from God being concealed (*deus absconditus*).

Existential philosophers such as Kierkegaard, Jaspers and Tillich speak of the need to admit the burden of the crisis, to allow suffering to take place in order to experience its transformative power (Schnell, 2018). It is on this basis that clarification of the mind can take place. The crisis challenges previous beliefs. In due course, we either regain them or replace them with new insights. The cornerstones of existence are thus redefined. Successful reorientation provides a direction that motivates meaningful action by pursuing goals and intermediary steps.

In this context, it seems less productive to explicitly search for meaning (Steger, Kashdan, Sullivan, & Lorentz, 2008). Meaning cannot be found in thought. Rather, it requires the willingness to trust in the possibility of the meaningfulness of one's life – in the sense of a "leap of faith." Such trust often grows when despair is great. Paul Tillich (2015) describes despair as an experience that nothing or nobody holds or helps. But it is also a situation in which a person can realise that they experience meaninglessness only because they have an understanding of meaning; that their despair is possible only because they *are*; and that they continue to be, even if everything that was previously valid is obviously no longer valid. This experience, which is difficult to communicate, is described as an experience of being accepted (Tillich, 2014) or as a transformation of heaviness and strangeness into familiarity and loyalty (Rilke, 1904/2002). So Rilke writes,

> And if only we regulate our life according to that principle which advises us always to hold to the difficult, what even now appears most alien to us will become most familiar and loyal. How could we forget those old myths which are to be found in the beginnings of every people; the myths of the dragons which are transformed, at the last moment, into princesses; perhaps all the dragons of our life are princesses, who are only waiting to see us once beautiful and brave. Perhaps everything terrifying is at bottom the helplessness that seeks our help.
>
> (Rilke, 1904/2002, p. 39)

Such an experience of alienation or fright can give rise to trust in the meaning of one's life, which in turn motivates one to discover personal sources of meaning and put them into practice, according to a top-down interpretation of the hierarchic model of meaning (Section 4.1). Laddered conversations or the SoMe-Card Method (la Cour & Schnell, 2019, 2020; Schnell & la Cour, 2018) open up possibilities for remembering or identifying sources of meaning that are of actual relevance.

The questions can be used to reveal what shapes and controls our lives. They assist in evaluating and identifying practical options for action or in searching for alternatives.

If it does not seem possible for a person to grant life such an "advance of trust," another possibility is to evoke experiences of meaningfulness through concrete actions, in the sense of a bottom-up reading of the model of meaning. Here generative actions have proven to be effective, especially when they tie in with the individual's personal lifeworld. For example, Steven Southwick and his colleagues have encouraged their patients – war veterans with posttraumatic stress disorder – to develop and implement voluntary projects as part of their therapy. As a result, patients experienced an increase in self-efficacy, their sense of responsibility and purpose (Southwick, Gilmartin, McDonough, & Morrissey, 2006). Their view of themselves and their lives changed fundamentally as a result of this generative action: They realised that they meant something to others.

Specific interventions developed to support meaning in life are presented in Chapter 11.

8.4 A brief discourse: pilgrimage – on the way to meaning

Pilgrimage is an archaic religious ritual – and it enjoys great popularity. Over the past five years, approximately 281,300 people have set out each year to follow the pilgrims' trail to Santiago de Compostela (Oficina de Acogida al Peregrino, 2019); the trend is rising. They travel for many weeks, covering hundreds of kilometres on foot. Why do people make such an effort? In early Christianity, pilgrimages were made in the hope of purification, repentance or healing (Haab, 1998). Today, only a minority of (German-speaking) pilgrims are religiously motivated – and yet their expectations do not seem so dissimilar to those of their predecessors.

Sarah Pali and I conducted a longitudinal study with people who walked the Way of St. James to Santiago de Compostela. A total of 85 people aged 16 to 70, 72 percent of whom were women, answered our questionnaire before their departure. When asked about the motives for their trip, 66 percent said they "wanted to gain clarity." Athletic (44 percent), spiritual (39 percent), religious (31 percent) and cultural (26 percent) motives followed at a clear distance (multiple answers were possible). The pilgrims who hoped for clarification also showed high scores in crisis of meaning.

On the basis of our follow-up surveys one week later and four months later, we can say that still today a pilgrimage appears to be an extremely efficient way of purification – in the sense of mental or spiritual clarification. After the pilgrimage, all signs of a crisis of meaning had disappeared, while meaningfulness had clearly increased – both immediately after the journey and four months later. In addition, in both follow-up surveys, pilgrims reported increased selftranscendence (both vertical and horizontal) and selfactualisation.

What happens during a pilgrimage, and what is its transformative and meaningful potential? Pilgrimage on the Way of St. James is a formalised event structured like a ritual (Schnell & Pali, 2013). All three phases of a rite of passage can be discerned (van Gennep, 1960): In the phase of detachment, the pilgrims separate from their everyday lives, which can amount to a complex undertaking. In our study, the average distance travelled was 646 km, which takes about four to five weeks. Such a long absence from work and social connections demands careful preparation. At the moment of departure, all identity-establishing roles and insignia are left behind.

Thus "disrobed," the travellers enter the second phase, the so-called liminal phase. Here, they assume their new role as pilgrims – symbolised by the pilgrim's identity card and perhaps a scallop attached to their backpack. In the liminal phase, pilgrims expose themselves to transformative events. They are particularly receptive and vulnerable then, as the ritual theorists Victor and Edith Turner (1969, 1978) describe. Although the pilgrims' way to Santiago is known for its strong pilgrim traffic, large parts of the journey are covered alone and in silence. A stimulus deprivation occurs, which directs the attention of the walkers to internal processes. Conflicts, which until then had been ignored or repressed by the hectic pace of everyday life, are now pushing their way into consciousness. At the same time, the rhythm and monotony of walking induces a kind of trance. As d'Aquili, Laughlin and McManus reported back in 1979, evenly repeated movements support the synchronisation of perception, cognition and action. Experiences of selftranscendence are thereby facilitated, such as the loss of self, space and time; experiences of unity; increased awareness; sudden insights or cognitions. Walking in silence thus provides a framework that promotes conscious self-exploration and unconscious forms of reordering priorities. Alternative perspectives on the world and the self open up; one's view widens; and from a kind of meta-perspective, contexts of meaning become (newly) apparent. "Clarification" occurs (Schnell & Pali, 2013).

The third and last phase marks the end of the ritual, the return and reintegration into everyday life – but as a different person. The task here is to take on the newly acquired identity in a familiar environment. This is often perceived as difficult: The transformed person returns to an everyday life that is still the same. It is almost impossible for pilgrims to share the profound experiences that they had during their journey (Pali, 2010). Our data reflect this process: Meaningfulness scores reached a high peak immediately after the return but fell slightly over the next few months (yet remained significantly above the baseline). Rigid social, professional and economic structures can hinder the implementation of new insights and dampen enthusiasm. On the other hand, the newly acquired sources of meaning proved to be more stable. After four months, vertical and horizontal selftranscendence as well as selfactualisation scores were still higher than before departure.

8.5 Know thyself!

SELF-EXPLORATION: POSITIVE ILLUSIONS – BECAUSE THEY'RE GOOD FOR YOU (PERHAPS)

> With great and varied skills we create a delusion that enables us to coexist serenely with the most monstrous things, simply because we recognize these frozen grimaces of the universe as a table or a chair, a shout or an outstretched arm, a speed or a roast chicken. We are capable of living between one open chasm of sky above our heads and another, slightly camouflaged chasm of sky beneath our feet, feeling as untroubled on earth as if we were in a room with the door closed.
>
> (Musil, 2011, p. 574)

Crises of meaning are characterised by the fact that some positive assumptions about the world are exposed as illusions. In psychology, we know about the concept of positive illusions. Everyday processes of perception are characterised by three kinds of distortions of reality: self-aggrandisement, unrealistic optimism and exaggerated notions of control (Taylor & Brown, 1988). Several studies conclude that such illusions are positive because they increase well-being and have a psychologically protective effect. Some examples of positive illusions are listed next. Do you recognise yourself in them? What do you think of such distortions of reality?

JUST-WORLD BELIEF

The belief that we generally get what we deserve and that the world is orderly and just. ("There will be a reason for this if he is bullied by his colleagues. He has always been such a strange guy.")

ABOVE-AVERAGE ILLUSION

The belief that we are more intelligent, more attractive, more interesting, more just or more organised than average people. ("I do my job better than my colleagues.")

OPTIMISTIC FALLACY

We estimate our health risks to be lower than those of others. ("I know about the dangers of alcohol, but I have my drinking under control; the two or three glasses of wine in the evening are rather good for my health.")

LEARNED OPTIMISM

Success is attributed to our motivation and competence, whereas failure is attributed to external disturbing events. ("I received the funding because I wrote a brilliant proposal." "I didn't get the funding because too many people applied for it this time.")

ILLUSION OF IMMORTALITY

Generally behaving as if we are going to live forever, perceiving death as so distant that it has no relevance to the present. ("Others die, but I am far from it!")

"THAT'S HOW YOU DO IT"

As long as we do what "one" does, we do not have to assume responsibility; conformity replaces the necessity of our own decisions of conscience. ("I acted only according to the guidelines!" "My colleagues do the same.")

When in a crisis of meaning, previously viable positive illusions are destroyed: Should they be rebuilt as part of overcoming the crisis of meaning, or does this contradict an honest confrontation with reality?

8.6 Literature

Bastian, B. (2006, November 21). *Suicide note*. Retrieved from www.heise.de/tp/artikel/24/24032/1.html

Camus, A. (2018). *The myth of Sisyphos*. New York: Vintage.

Damásio, B. F., Koller, S. H., & Schnell, T. (2013). Sources of meaning and meaning in life questionnaire (SoMe): Psychometric properties and sociodemographic findings in a large Brazilian sample. *Acta de Investigación Psicológica, 3*(3), 1205–1227.

D'Aquili, E. G., Laughlin, C. D., & McManus, J. (1979). *The spectrum of ritual: A biogenetic structural analysis*. New York: Columbia University Press.

Frankl, V. E. (2014). *The will to meaning*. London: Penguin.

Gerstorf, D., Ram, N., Mayraz, G., Hidajat, M., Lindenberger, U., Wagner, G. G., & Schupp, J. (2010). Late-life decline in well-being across adulthood in Germany, the United Kingdom, and the United States: Something is seriously wrong at the end of life. *Psychology and Aging, 25*(2), 477–485.

Haab, B. (1998). *Weg und Wandlung: zur Spiritualität heutiger Jakobspilger und -pilgerinnen*. Freiburg, CH: Academic Press.

Hanfstingl, B. (2013). Ego- and spiritual transcendence: Relevancies for psychological resilience and the role of age. *Evidence-Based Complementary and Alternative Medicine*, 9 pages.

Heidegger, M. (2008). *Being and time*. New York: Harper Perennial.

Klinger, E. (1998). The search for meaning in evolutionary perspective and its clinical implications. In P. T. P. Wong & P. S. Fry (Eds.), *The human quest for meaning* (pp. 27–50). Mahwah, NJ: Erlbaum.

la Cour, P., & Schnell, T. (2019). *The sources of meaning card method*. Innsbruck: Studia.

la Cour, P., & Schnell, T. (2020). Presentation of the sources of meaning card method: The SoMeCaM. *Journal of Humanistic Psychology, 60*(1), 20–42.

Musil, R. (2011). *The man without qualities*. London: Picador.

Oficina de Acogida al Peregrino. (2019). *Informes Estadisticos*. Retrieved from http://peregrinossantiago.es/esp/servicios-al-peregrino/informes-estadisticos/

Pali, S. (2010). *Ein Pilger ist der, welcher geht, und der, welcher sucht. Eine Längsschnittstudie zu Lebenssinn und Lebensbedeutungen bei Pilgern des Jakobswegs* (Unveröffentlichte Diplomarbeit), Universität Innsbruck.

Pedersen, H. F., Handegard Birkeland, M., Søndergaard Jensen, J., Schnell, T., Hvidt, N. C., Sørensen, T., & la Cour, P. (2018). What brings meaning to life in a highly secular society? A study on sources of meaning among Danes. *Scandinavian Journal of Psychology, 59*(6), 678–690.

Rilke, R. M. (1904/2002). *Letters to a young poet*. New York: Dover Publications.

Safranski, R. (1999). *Martin Heidegger: Between good and evil*. Cambridge, MA: Harvard University Press.

Sartre, J.-P. (2000). *Being and nothingness*. New York: Citadel Press.

Schnell, T. (2008). Deutsche in der Sinnkrise? Ein Einblick in die Sinnforschung mit Daten einer repräsentativen Stichprobe. *Journal für Psychologie, 16*(3), Article 9.

Schnell, T. (2009). The sources of meaning and meaning in life questionnaire (SoMe): Relations to demographics and well-being. *The Journal of Positive Psychology, 4*(6), 483–499.

Schnell, T. (2018). Einlassen, Zulassen, Loslassen. Ein philosophisch-psychologischer Zugang zu einem aktiven Leidensbegriff. *Zeitschrift für Palliativmedizin, 19*, 249–255.

Schnell, T., & Becker, P. (2007). *Der Fragebogen zu Lebensbedeutungen und Lebenssinn (LeBe)*. Göttingen: Hogrefe.

Schnell, T., Gerstner, R., & Krampe, H. (2018). Crisis of meaning predicts suicidality in youth independently of depression. *Crisis–The Journal of Crisis Intervention and Suicide Prevention, 39*, 294–303.

Schnell, T., & la Cour, P. (2018). Von der Tiefe im Leben sprechen. Erkenntnisse der empirischen Sinnforschung und Exploration von Lebensbedeutungen mit der LeBe-Kartenmethode. *Wege zum Menschen, 70*(1), 33–47.

Schnell, T., & Pali, S. (2013). Pilgrimage today: The meaning-making potential of ritual. *Mental Health, Religion & Culture, 16*(9), 887–902.

Schnell, T., & Vötter, B. (2019). Crises of meaning: Prevalence, causes, consequences. In *European federation of psychologists' associations, book of abstracts: XVI European Congress of Psychology (ECP 2019)* (pp. 192–193). Moscow: Moscow University Press.

Skaggs, B. G., & Barron, C. R. (2006). Searching for meaning in negative events: Concept analysis. *Journal of Advanced Nursing, 53*(5), 559–570.

Sørensen, T., Stifoss-Hansen, H., Lien, L., Pedersen, H. F., la Cour, P., DeMarinis, V., Danbolt, L. J., & Schnell, T. (2019). The sources of meaning and meaning in life questionnaire (SoMe) in the Norwegian context: Relations to mental health, quality of life and self-efficacy. *International Journal for the Psychology of Religion, 29*(1), 32–45.

Southwick, S. M., Gilmartin, R., McDonough, P., & Morrissey, P. (2006). Logotherapy as an adjunctive treatment for chronic combat-related PTSD: A meaning-based intervention. *American Journal of Psychotherapy, 60*(2), 161–174.

Steger, M. F., Kashdan, T. B., Sullivan, B. A., & Lorentz, D. (2008). Understanding the search for meaning in life: Personality, cognitive style, and the dynamic between seeking and experiencing meaning. *Journal of Personality, 76*(2), 199–228.

Taylor, S. E., & Brown, J. D. (1988). Illusion and well-being: A social psychological perspective on mental health. *Psychological Bulletin, 103*(2), 193–210.

Tillich, P. (2014). *The courage to be*. New Haven, CT: Yale University Press.

Tobias, T. (2010). *Die Sinnkrise–Auslöser, Erleben, Bewältigung und die gewonnene Einsicht*. [Crisis of meaning – triggers, experience, coping] (Unpublished Master thesis), University of Innsbruck.

Turner, V., & Turner, E. (1969). *The ritual process*. London: Routledge.

Turner, V., & Turner, E. (1978). *Image and pilgrimage in Christian culture*. New York: Columbia University Press.

Van Gennep, A. (1960). *The rites of passage*. Chicago, IL: University of Chicago Press.

Vogel, R. (2010). *Lebenssinn in schweren Erkrankungen älterer Menschen* (Doctoral dissertation), Heidelberg University, Heidelberg.

Yalom, I. D. (1980). *Existential psychotherapy*. New York: Basic Books.

Chapter 9

Existential indifference

Not every absence of meaning is reflected in a crisis of meaning, causes irritation and motivates us to search. Indifference is much more frequent. About one-fourth of all Germans experience their lives as meaningless but have no problem with it. They neither search for meaning nor experience a lack of meaning or a crisis of meaning. I have therefore called them existentially indifferent (Schnell, 2010). While Viktor Frankl assumed that human beings have an inherent need for meaning, which if not fulfilled leads to an "existential vacuum" and subsequently to a "noogenic neurosis" (Frankl, 2014, p. 14), today we have to say that a lot of people do not care if their life has meaning. They are not particularly happy with this attitude, but they do not suffer from it either.

9.1 Whatever!

In 1964, psychologist Abraham Maslow lamented a widespread loss of values in Western societies. He then stated that this was followed by a joyless, dull, boring, passionless, indifferent attitude to life (Maslow, 1964). In psychology, this thesis has not yet been investigated further. The presumed attitude might simply be too inconspicuous, since it is not subject to psychological stress: If you don't care, you don't seek support.

From a humanist or existentialist perspective, however, we should be worried if it is indeed the case that large sections of society retreat into indifference. Several philosophers and psychologists (Martin Heidegger, Viktor Frankl, Rollo May, Irvin Yalom and Kirk Schneider) have provided important theoretical insights into the difference between an active, committed and authentic life and a shallow, superficial mode of existence. Heidegger (2008), to whom subsequent authors repeatedly refer, contrasted authentic ("owned") with inauthentic ("unowned") being. He understood the inauthentic as the original mode of being. It is ordinary behaviour, what "one" does – and thus the environment in which we all find ourselves – which constitutes our conditions of existence. To turn our lives into authentic being, we have to come "to our own."

The mode of being that we have empirically identified as existential indifference is characterised by a lack of owning the self. Most likely, people who are existentially indifferent have not (yet) exposed themselves to the angst described in Chapter 8, have not (yet) faced up to nothingness – at least this is suggested by our research findings, which are presented next.

9.2 How to assess existential indifference

Also for methodological reasons, empirical research on meaning has long overlooked existential indifference. Most researchers assumed that meaning in life was to be represented on a single continuum, with one pole reflecting meaningfulness and the other a crisis of meaning. This was based on Frankl's assumption that an absence of meaning amounts to a crisis. Only when the availability of the SoMe (Schnell & Becker, 2007; Schnell, 2014) allowed for a separate measurement of meaningfulness and crisis of meaning were we able to detect a state of low meaningfulness and, at the same time, low crisis of meaning. To identify existential indifference, the two scales are combined. Existential indifference occurs when the mean values of both scales are below 3 (values from 0 to 2 indicate rejection, whereas values 3 to 5 indicate affirmation). This kind of calculation allows for four types of meaning to be identified (Table 9.1).

9.3 Relationships and explanatory approaches

On the basis of our data, we can say who is more likely to be existentially indifferent in demographic terms. Correlations with sources of meaning

Table 9.1 Identification of four types of meaning (mean scores)

Meaningfulness	*Crisis of Meaning*	*Type of Meaning*
≥ 3	< 3	Meaningfulness
< 3	≥ 3	Crisis of meaning
< 3	< 3	Existential indifference
≥ 3	≥ 3	Conflicting

and personality traits contribute to a better understanding of the phenomenon, and intercultural comparisons provide further clues.

9.3.1 Correlations with demographics

Parallel to the reported changes regarding crises of meaning (Chapter 8), the frequency of existential indifference has decreased in recent years. Only 23 percent of our current sample account for this type of meaning. Also, the age distribution has changed. Whereas in 2006 almost half of all young people were existentially indifferent (Schnell, 2008, 2016), today this is only true for 23 percent (Figure 9.1). An existential mobilisation of youth seems to have taken place, for which phenomena such as Fridays for Future might be taken as evidence. At nearly one-third, most existentially indifferent people are to be found among the 30–39-year-olds. With progressing age, the numbers decrease continuously; the lowest figure, that of 9 percent, is found among people over 70.

Also in contrast to the earlier data, gender differences are now becoming apparent: More men report existential indifference than women do (26 percent vs 20 percent). Moreover, a correlation with the level of education has been established: People with higher education report less existential indifference (18 percent) than people with minimum compulsory schooling (31 percent). With regard to marital status, 30 percent

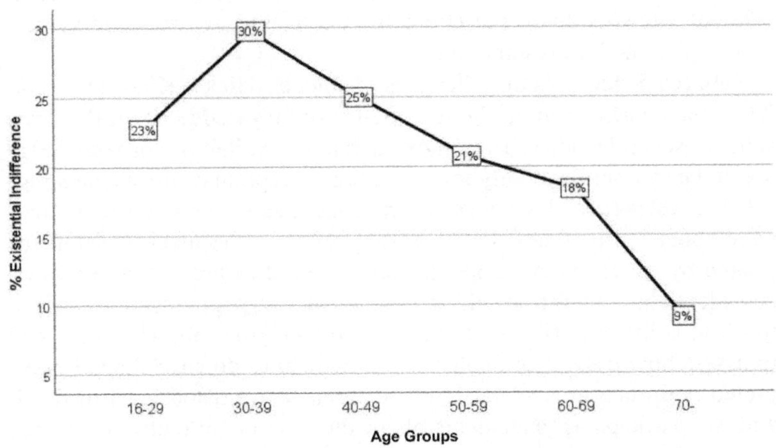

Figure 9.1 Existential indifference (in %) in six age groups (N = 1,291)

of unmarried cohabitants and over a quarter of singles (26 percent) are classified as indifferent, compared to just under a fifth of married people (19 percent).

9.3.2 (No) sources of meaning in existential indifference

Let us remember once again the hierarchic model of meaning (Section 4.1): It suggests that personally relevant sources of meaning, when put into action, support the perception of life as meaningful. If meaningfulness is low, as with existentially indifferent individuals, there should also be little commitment to sources of meaning. This assumption has been clearly confirmed. Existential indifference is related to very low general commitment. Religiosity, spirituality and generativity are particularly low, even to an extent that indicates rejection. When comparing the values of indifferent individuals with those who report meaningfulness, the largest differences can be found in generativity, religiosity, spirituality, care, harmony, communion and attentiveness.

Using Maslow's words, we can summarise as follows: Existentially indifferent "people have nothing to admire, to sacrifice themselves for, to surrender to, to die for" (Maslow, 1964, S. 42). They have no passions, no commitment. The idea of a supernatural reality is of no use to them; even in this world, they are not interested in leaving traces or making a contribution. At the same time, they avoid exploring themselves (self-knowledge). This again obstructs the way to a more authentic being. Without knowing about our strengths, weaknesses, desires and values, "owning" ourselves is impossible.

Rebecca Schlegel and colleagues (Schlegel, Hicks, King, & Arndt, 2011) have elaborated on the importance of knowledge about the "true self," in several studies. They showed that the availability of knowledge about the true self is closely related to the perception of life as meaningful. The researchers developed several approaches for measuring knowledge about the true self: One measure refers to the level of detail (as judged by experts) that people achieve when they are asked to write a short text about their true self. In another survey, people were requested to create a list of attributes that described their true self. They then had to assess how easy or difficult it was for them to do so. Schlegel interpreted both measures – that is, the externally evaluated level of detail and the participants' statements about the ease or difficulty in making the description of the true self – as personal accessibility of the true self; both went hand in hand with increased meaningfulness.

Nevertheless, as Schlegel notes, thinking about the true self is not always pleasant, because it can be accompanied by existential discomfort. This ambivalence of self-knowledge also shows up in our data. On the one hand, we see clear indications for the meaning-making potential of self-knowledge. On the other hand, self-knowledge is positively related to neuroticism (Section 5.1 and Schnell & Becker, 2007). From an existential perspective, these findings make sense. According to Heidegger, as described earlier, the confrontation with angst is a necessary prerequisite for authenticity. This experience of existential angst might well be reflected in increased neuroticism scores, indicating the occurrence of anxiety, worry, fear, frustration, loneliness and so on.

As existentially indifferent people reject a reflection on their actual or "true" self, this may prevent authenticity but at the same time avoid the state of angst. The low manifestation of development (as a source of meaning) also underlines the assumption that in existential indifference, people tend to avoid unpleasant states that arise when the actual state is questioned by the possibility of change. Furthermore, low mean scores in attentiveness indicate that awareness of the present, the actual state, is also suppressed or ignored. The low level of generativity, on the other hand, can be explained by the lack of a stable self-concept: As long as we do not know who we are, we will have difficulties to leave traces, to create something lasting.

9.3.3 Informative correlates of existential indifference

Various studies deal with potential predictors and consequences of existential indifference. Summarising the available results, the following picture emerges: With regard to the three basic psychological needs – autonomy, competence and psychological relatedness (Deci & Ryan, 2002) – existentially indifferent people have below-average values in competence (Schnell, 2013). Competence refers to the experience of behaviour as effectively enacted. Accordingly, also self-efficacy (Damásio & Koller, 2015; Hörmann, 2016) and internal locus of control are limited (Schnell, 2013). Self-efficacy stands for the personal judgement of one's ability to cope with difficulties and barriers in daily life (Schwarzer, 1992). An internal locus of control is present when a person is convinced that they can control events and thus experiences them as consequences of their own actions (Krampen, 1991). Existentially indifferent individuals therefore experience themselves neither as capable of coping with the problems of their everyday lives nor as capable of influencing the events in their lives. Their hope of success is also below average. Especially with regard to attractiveness and career, they expect fewer chances of success than others (Hörmann, 2016). Existentially indifferent people do not feel personally responsible for the course of their lives; instead, their trust in science and technology is above average (Schnell, 2015).

We can conclude from this that existentially indifferent people do not feel comfortable with the demands placed on them. They react by withdrawing into indifference, which is an act of resignation but one that does not reach the status of a crisis. Their self-perception is characterised by moderate self-esteem and moderate resilience (Damásio & Koller, 2015; Vötter & Schnell, in press). With regard to dealing with potential partners, data suggest that existentially indifferent people are characterised by attachment avoidance. They tend to distance themselves and avoid closeness and intimacy (Hörmann, 2016). Finally, they are neither pessimists nor optimists: Both values are in the middle range, as are the values for hope (Damásio & Koller, 2015).

How do the existentially indifferent fare? So-so. Life satisfaction and subjective well-being are neither highly developed nor in a critically low range. There is no psychological strain. Neither depression nor anxiety reach values that would indicate mental problems. In young adulthood, they do not smoke and drink more than those who find their lives meaningful, nor do they consume drugs more frequently (Schnell, 2013).

9.3.4 Cultural differences

When we compared data from different countries and cultures, we found differences that were revealing. Existential indifference was much more common in countries with high levels of prosperity than in countries with lower levels of prosperity. For an overview of the frequency of existential indifference in different countries, see Table 9.2. To ensure comparability, the table presents data from participants aged 16 to 25, all of whom were surveyed between 2010 and 2014. Existential indifference was most common in Germany, followed by Austria, Denmark and France. These countries also had high levels of prosperity in the Legatum Prosperity Index, 2014, which is calculated from eight subscales: economy, entrepreneurship, governance, education, health, security, personal freedom and social capital. By contrast, existential indifference was much rarer in Ecuador, Brazil and Bulgaria – countries that also show significantly lower levels of prosperity. Thus, there seems to be an inverse relationship between existential indifference and prosperity.

An interpretation of these results can only be speculative. High social prosperity might encourage some citizens to minimise their involvement and participation, as this will entail little or no material loss for them.

Table 9.2 Existential Indifference (%) – Legatum Prosperity Index (ages 16–25; data collection 2010–2014)

Countries	*Existential Indifference (%)*	*Prosperity Index** **(-5 to +5)**
Germany	51	> 2.5
Austria	39	> 2.5
Denmark	35	> 2.5
France	32	> 2
Ecuador	11	< 0
Bulgaria	9	< 0.5
Brazil	4	< 0.5

Note: * Legatum Prosperity Index for 2014

A desire for active and creative participation, on the other hand, has many barriers to overcome: Industrially highly developed societies are characterised by pressure to perform, competitive thinking, rivalry and economisation. The pursuit of higher goals is accompanied by a risk of failure that should not be underestimated (Anhut & Heitmeyer, 2007). The low expectation of self-efficacy and competence that we have observed in existentially indifferent people can explain their passive-negative attitude under such conditions. In addition, professional success and even social success require clear self-positioning. To increase career and partnership opportunities, personal strengths must be identified, promoted and optimised. On the part of existentially indifferent people, avoidance of self-knowledge and challenge constitutes a hindrance in this way.

Should this sociopolitical derivation of existential indifference apply, we should find evidence also for the alternative: for those who face social challenges with a clear self-image and without fear of failure. And we do find them, represented by the so-called Generation Y. Youth studies and generational analyses suggest that the following characteristics apply to Generation Y: They have a relatively high level of education and are technology oriented without being monopolised by technology. They are well aware of their values and orient their lives accordingly. The focus here is less on status and career than on meaningful action and a balanced life plan (Bund, 2014).

Our society thus elicits (at least) two kinds of approaches to the world: one that uses the existing demanding structures confidently and willingly (such as Generation Y) and another that is associated with feelings of overburdening, withdrawal and relinquishing claims to societal participation (such as existential indifference).

Various youth studies provide indications of this gap: In the 16th Shell Youth Study (Albert, Hurrelmann, Quenzel, & Schneekloth, 2011), 59 percent of young people stated that they were confident about their personal future. However, 35 percent said that they saw their future "sometimes up, sometimes down," and 6 percent expected a dark future. An Allensbach survey commissioned by the Vodafone Foundation and published in 2014 pointed out that almost half of young people found it difficult to choose a career after finishing school (Vodafone Foundation, 2014). The Sinus Institute has identified the following long-term trends of change in our society (Sinus, 2018, p. 17, transl. TS):

- Modernisation and individualisation: opening of the social space through higher educational qualifications, increasing mobility, communication and networking and thus a wider scope for development and choice.
- Excessive demands and regression: growing overextension and insecurity through technological, sociocultural and economic change, through the diversity of possibilities (multi-option paralysis) and the de-standardisation of life courses, with the consequence of disorientation and loss of meaning and a search for relief, support and certainty (regrounding).
- Dissolution of boundaries and segregation: drifting apart of life-worlds and values driven by globalisation and digitalisation, social-hierarchical differentiation and growing social declassification processes, erosion of the centre and the emergence of a cosmopolitan elite (one-world-consciousness).

The remarkable clarity of Generation Y – winner of the trend towards modernisation and individualisation – often hides those who find it difficult to orient and assert themselves and who experience a pressure to perform that is perceived as too strong (excessive demands and regression). These include the existentially indifferent. The British author Clive Martin (Martin, 2014) self-critically and revealingly gives a personal insight into this state:

> It's no longer just teenagers and students who seem to be running away from real life. It's people in their twenties and thirties, too – people who should really know better but don't seem to know how to do much else. . . . This is my generation, the generation with no real incentive to grow up. No kids to feel guilty about, just jobs that let them scrape the money they need to feed, house, and wash

> themselves. . . . In my parents' day, it was easier to grow up. It was borderline impossible not to; society dragged you up whether you wanted it or not. . . . We are the new aging Italian bachelors in our own mundane versions of The Great Beauty – the new-British professional wreckheads, the generation that doesn't know what to do with itself now that it's been forced to choose reality over the grand, overarching myths that steered our parents the way of relative peace and respectability. When you have no myth to guide you, what do you lock in on when the hangovers and comedowns demand some normalcy to return to? . . . We claim to hate the system that's made us like this, yet we're all so desperate to be a part of it.

The Japanese phenomenon of hikikomori can be regarded as an extreme example of withdrawal and indifference. Here, too, we find indications that existential indifference arises when a high level of prosperity, which guarantees the satisfaction of basic needs, meets high competition and pressure to perform. Hikikomori are young people, most of them male, who refuse to leave their home or even their room and withdraw from family and society for months or years. The psychologist Tamaki Saito was the first to draw attention to the rising numbers of withdrawing young people; he coined the term "hikikomori." He believes that the withdrawal is caused by two things: the strong pressure to achieve excellence in school, education and working life and close family ties that ensure that parents sustain their children even for decades, should they not move out – sometimes into the fourth decade of life (Jones, 2006).

Parents of hikikomori claim to have paid particular attention to the promotion of performance in their children, while other aspects have receded into the background. If achievement is the only source of meaning and identity, it is easy to understand the fear experienced by young people when they face the possibility of failure. Withdrawal can be understood as an attempt to avoid potential failure. "Better to stay in the room than to venture out into the world and fail" (Jones, 2006). Hikikomori spend most of their time watching television, playing video games or other distracting activities that do not pose mental challenges. They are convinced that they are not needed by society, that they have no place in it. A social worker describes how she asked a withdrawn person who spent most of his time building model cars for a sample to give to children in a day-care centre. "He seemed so pleased. . . . It was as if he'd never been asked to do something for someone else before. He was sitting in his room all day where nothing was expected of him, and he did nothing to show his value" (Jones, 2006). Those affected experience themselves as outsiders, as not belonging, as alienated and insignificant.

A large number of studies on hikikomori are now available (e.g. Harding, 2018; Li & Wong, 2015; Teo et al., 2015). They were mainly conducted in the Japanese context, but they repeatedly draw parallels to similar phenomena in countries such as Hong Kong ("Hidden Youth"), the United States ("adultolescent"), Spain ("Ni-ni") or the United Kingdom ("NEET" – Not in Education, Employment or Training). The OECD (Organisation for Economic Co-operation and Development) regularly publishes statistics on the frequency of NEETs in its member states, limited to 15–29-year-olds. In the United Kingdom, for example, the share of NEETs in this age group was 15 percent in 2006, 16 percent in 2012 and 13 percent in 2018 (OECD, 2019). Figures for Scandinavian countries are significantly lower, varying from 8 percent to 9 percent in Norway, from 9 percent to 10 percent in Sweden and from 7 percent to 12 percent in Denmark.

It is necessary for us to gain understanding for people who withdraw into indifference – with those who drop out of educational and professional paths being only the tip of the iceberg. In doing so, it is important to distinguish what might look the same on the surface. An increasing number of people are consciously leaving the dominant system and distancing themselves from it to varying degrees (e.g. downshifting, living off the grid, minimalism, anti-consumerism). Despite their withdrawal, their decisions are based on not indifference but clear convictions. As grassroots movements, such initiatives contribute to making alternative lifestyles more visible in our society (Chapter 14).

In the case of disengagement and withdrawal, as can be seen in existential indifference, social scientists and practitioners call for more vigilance, because such people easily disappear into invisibility ("invisible youth"). In contrast to those who express their displeasure through violence and antisocial behaviour, those who withdraw receive little attention; their needs remain hidden (Wong, Yuen, Su, & Yung, 2019).

9.4 Ways out of indifference?

What possibilities may we have to counteract the segregation observed by the Sinus Institute and other surveys? As long as it does not concern extreme phenomena like total withdrawal (à la hikikomori), existentially indifferent individuals do not perceive psychological strain. From the outside, therefore, there are hardly any starting points or justifications for intervention. Nevertheless, it seems necessary to think about possibilities of preventing and overcoming indifference and regression. Democracies depend on the participation of their citizens. If large sections of the people show no interest in participating, in shaping society, then the model of democracy is in danger. If social structures lead to the empowerment of one part of the population but to the alienation of the other, then criticism is appropriate.

The results of empirical studies on existential indifference demonstrate that indifference is accompanied by subjective helplessness and loss of control. It is not our autonomy that is limited; we are all aware that we have to make our own decisions about our lives. The question is whether we can. The low level of competence reported by existentially indifferent individuals shows that they feel overwhelmed by the demands they encounter. They experience themselves as ineffective, not as designers of their own lives. There is no hope for positive change and therefore no motivation to become active in this direction. Existentially indifferent people reject exploring themselves just as much as they reject committing to things that go beyond themselves.

Rahel Jaeggi (2014, p. 3) describes, in her socio-philosophical analysis, the phenomenon of alienation similarly to existential indifference:

> Alienation means indifference and internal division, but also powerlessness and relationlessness with respect to oneself and to a world experienced as indifferent and alien. Alienation is the inability to establish a relation to other human beings, to things, to social institutions and thereby also – so the fundamental intuition of the theory of alienation – to oneself. An alienated world presents itself to individuals as insignificant and meaningless, as rigidified or impoverished, as a world that is not one's own, which is to say, a world in which one is not "at home" and over which one can have no influence. The alienated subject becomes a stranger to itself; it no longer experiences itself as an "actively effective subject" but a "passive object" at the mercy of unknown forces.

According to Jaeggi, the solution lies in affectively identifying oneself with the world as a precondition and object of one's actions. The conditions for this, she claims, are openness to experience and vitality (Jaeggi, 2007). However, existentially indifferent people lack precisely this openness to experience. As one of our fundamental personality traits, openness is not easily attainable without a respective predisposition. And vitality arises from a will to live that is difficult to achieve without a sense of meaningfulness.

Let's think about more feasible approaches. We can assume, for example, that unnecessary competition and pressure to perform would decrease if successful curricula vitae were not made dependent on a high level of education. This would require a new appreciation of a wide variety of vocational activities, especially in the area of skilled trades. Moreover, we should increase opportunities to participate in the shaping of society. Such opportunities for getting involved beyond one's own affairs are actually diminishing. This fact is partly masked by the large amount of attention that we direct to the design of our own little world. The huge choice of mobile phone cases, TV stations, car tyres, study courses, face creams, sneakers, cereal brands, holiday resorts, websites and so on occupies our working memory. As a consequence, we perceive more-crucial or even existential decisions as overtaxing and gladly leave them to chance, algorithms, or others who apparently know better.

Self-efficacy and experiences of control arise, among other things, from responsible action. Our society is characterised by a high degree of individual freedom, which relieves us of role prescriptions and rigid moral norms. At the same time, however, the individual has also been "freed" from responsibilities that do concern not the self but concern others (Schnell, 2013). But experiences of self-efficacy and control are particularly evident when responsibility for others is assumed: Getting involved, standing up for others results in an immediate feeling of personal significance. Judith Rodin and Ellen Langer were able to prove this effect as early as 1977 with a simple intervention. They placed plants in the rooms of a retirement home. Half of the residents were able to choose "their" plant from among those available; they were also given the task of taking care of it. The other half of the residents were given a random plant; they were then told that the staff would take care of the plant. The first half of the residents, who had both control over the selection of the plant and responsibility for its welfare, were found to be more active, more positive and less depressed.

Similar interventions to make personal responsibility tangible have also been successfully employed with hikikomori in Hong Kong. In one study, young people were invited to visit neglected dogs in an animal shelter. They were asked to build trusting relationships with the dogs and to engage in joint activities. According to their own reports, the reclusive youngsters were able to offer the dogs love, care, camaraderie and a safe environment. The experience allowed them to believe in their ability to care for living beings. Moreover, the interaction was also beneficial for the dogs. They trusted the youngsters, became more affectionate and accepted human care – which in turn gave the youngsters a sense of significance (Wong et al., 2019).

To strengthen experiences of personal significance, it is necessary to replace our understanding of responsibility as a burden with one that sees responsibility as an opportunity for development. At the same time, we need opportunities to take on responsibility, regardless of our social background or educational level. When are the children of migrants involved in social decision-making processes? When do pensioners experience that they are needed? Where do trainees experience playing an important role in our society? What right to a say do unemployed people have?

9.5 Know thyself!

SELF-EXPLORATION: RESPONSIBILITY

Write down your connotations of the term "responsibility":

Are your connotations more positive or negative? Why?

SELF-EXPLORATION: "PUBLIC SELF" AND "TRUE SELF"

First, write down six characteristics or terms that describe your "public self":

Using a numerical scale from 0 to 10, rate how easy it was for you to create this list (0 = very easy; 10 = extremely difficult).

0-1-2-3-4-5-6-7-8-9-10

Now write down six characteristics or terms that describe your "true self":

Again, use a numerical scale from 0 to 10 to estimate how easy it was for you to create this list (0 = very easy; 10 = extremely difficult).

0-1-2-3-4-5-6-7-8-9-10

According to Rebecca Schlegel's results (Schlegel et al., 2011), there is a connection between meaningfulness and easy accessibility of the characteristics of the "true self." To increase meaningfulness, it might therefore be advisable to invest time in self-knowledge.

FOR CONTEMPLATION

For a substantial part of society, our data on existential indifference tie in with Maslow's lament that "people have nothing to admire, to sacrifice themselves for, to surrender to, to die for" (Maslow, 1964, S. 42). A collection of Theravada Buddhist writings contains the following words attributed to the Buddha (extracted from the Purabheda-Sutta of Sutra-Nipata; FWBO, undated; transl. TS):

> A peaceful man has left all his desires behind before his body even disintegrates. He does not wonder how it all began or how it will end, nor does he hang on to what happens in between. Such a person has no expectations and desires for the future. He feels no anger, no fear and no stress. Nothing disturbs his conscience and his peace of mind. He is a wise man who speaks calmly. He has no desire for the future, no regret for the present. Free from the confused world of the senses, no opinions or views guide him.

Should we imagine indifference as a desirable state? Does it not create less suffering than people who sacrifice themselves for, surrender to or die for their cause?

9.6 Literature

Albert, M., Hurrelmann, K., Quenzel, G., & Schneekloth, U. (2011). Jugend 2010: Die 16. Shell Jugendstudie. *Diskurs Kindheits- und Jugendforschung, 6*(2).

Anhut, R., & Heitmeyer, W. (2007). Desintegrationstheorie – ein Erklärungsansatz. *Universität Bielefeld, Forschungsmagazin, 30*(1), 55–58.

Bund, K. (2014). *Glück schlägt Geld. Generation Y: Was wir wirklich wollen.* Hamburg: Murmann Verlag.

Damásio, B. F., & Koller, S. H. (2015). Complex experiences of meaning in life: Individual differences among sociodemographic variables, sources of meaning and psychological functioning. *Social Indicators Research, 123*(1), 161–181.

Deci, E. L., & Ryan, R. M. (2002). *Handbook of self-determination research.* Rochester: University Rochester Press.

Frankl, V. E. (2014). *The will to meaning.* London: Penguin.

FWBO Freunde des Westlichen Buddhistischen Ordens (Eds.). (undated). *Excerpt from the Purabheda-Sutta of the Sutra-Nipata.* Retrieved from www.buddhanetz.org/dharma.htm

Harding, C. (2018). Hikikomori. *The Lancet Psychiatry, 5*(1), 28–29.

Heidegger, M. (2008). *Being and time.* New York: Harper Perennial.

Hörmann, C. (2016). *Bindung, Selbstkonzept und Lebenssinn* (Unpublished Master thesis), University of Innsbruck, Innsbruck.

Jaeggi, R. (2007, February 13). *Was ist Entfremdung? Was kann man dagegen tun?* Im Gespräch mit Robert Misik, Reihe Genial Dagegen. Retrieved from https://misik.at/2007/02/anders_leben/

Jaeggi, R. (2014). *Alienation.* New York: Columbia University Press.

Jones, M. (2006, January 15). Shutting themselves in. *New York Times.* Retrieved from www.nytimes.com/2006/01/15/magazine/15japanese.html?pagewanted=all&_r=0

Krampen, G. (1991). *Fragebogen zu Kompetenz- und Kontrollüberzeugungen (FKK).* Göttingen: Hogrefe.

Legatum Prosperity Index. (2014, November 4). *2014 Legatum Prosperity Index.* Retrieved from https://li.com/reports/2014-legatum-prosperity-index/

Li, T. M., & Wong, P. W. (2015). Youth social withdrawal behavior (hikikomori): A systematic review of qualitative and quantitative studies. *Australian & New Zealand Journal of Psychiatry, 49*(7), 595–609.

Martin, C. (2014, December 1). *This sad generation doesn't know when the party stops.* Retrieved from www.vice.com/en_au/article/3b7w79/when-does-the-party-stop

Maslow, A. H. (1964). *Religions, values, and peak-experiences.* Columbus: Ohio State University Press.

OECD. (2019). *Youth not in employment, education or training (NEET).* Retrieved from www.oecd-ilibrary.org/education/youth-not-in-employment-education-or-training-neet/indicator/english_72d1033a-en

Rodin, J., & Langer, E. J. (1977). Long-term effects of a control-relevant intervention with the institutionalized aged. *Journal of Personality and Social Psychology, 35*(12), 897–902.

Schlegel, R. J., Hicks, J. A., King, L. A., & Arndt, J. (2011). Feeling like you know who you are: Perceived true self-knowledge and meaning in life. *Personality and Social Psychology Bulletin, 37*(6), 745–756.

Schnell, T. (2008). Deutsche in der Sinnkrise? Ein Einblick in die Sinnforschung mit Daten einer repräsentativen Stichprobe. *Journal für Psychologie, 16*(3), Article 9.

Schnell, T. (2010). Existential indifference: Another quality of meaning in life. *Journal of Humanistic Psychology, 50*(3), 351–373.

Schnell, T. (2013, August). *Meaning in the making: Contemporary sources and types of meaning*. International Association for the Psychology of Religion (IAPR), Lausanne, Switzerland.

Schnell, T. (2014). An empirical approach to existential psychology: Meaning in life operationalized. In S. Kreitler & T. Urbanek (Eds.), *Conceptions of meaning* (pp. 173–194). New York: Nova Science.

Schnell, T. (2015). Dimensions of secularity (DoS): An open inventory to measure facets of secular identities. *International Journal for the Psychology of Religion, 25*(4), 272–292.

Schnell, T. (2016). *Psychologie des Lebenssinns*. Heidelberg, Berlin and New York: Springer.

Schnell, T., & Becker, P. (2007). *Der Fragebogen zu Lebensbedeutungen und Lebenssinn (LeBe)*. Göttingen: Hogrefe.

Schwarzer, R. (Hrsg.). (1992). *Self-efficacy: Thought control of action*. Washington, DC: Hemisphere.

Sinus (2018, September). *Informationen zu den Sinus-Milieus® 2018*. Retrieved from www.sinus-institut.de/veroeffentlichungen/downloads/download/informationen-zu-den-sinus-milieusR/download-file/2875/download-a/download/download-c/Category/

Teo, A. R., Fetters, M. D., Stufflebam, K., Tateno, M., Balhara, Y., Choi, T. Y., . . . Kato, T. A. (2015). Identification of the hikikomori syndrome of social withdrawal: Psychosocial features and treatment preferences in four countries. *International Journal of Social Psychiatry, 61*(1), 64–72.

Vodafone Stiftung. (2014). *Schule, und dann?* Retrieved from www.google.com/url?sa=t&rct=j&q=&esrc=s&source=web&cd=5&ved=2ahUKEwjpndS5_PbmAhVSkFwKHdP_D8cQFjAEegQIBRAC&url=https%3A%2F%2Fwww.schule-wirtschaft-hamburg.de%2Ffileadmin%2Fdownload%2FInfo%2FSchule__und_dann._Herausforderungen_bei_der_Berufsorientierung_von_Schuelern_in_Deutschland.pdf&usg=AOvVaw2TdiZbzKbMpIYQ81WfdgfG

Vötter, B., & Schnell, T. (in press). Life meaning versus intelligence? An analysis of three qualities of meaning among gifted adults. In A. Batthyany (Ed.), *Logotherapy and existential analysis: Proceedings of the Viktor Frankl institute Vienna* (Vol. 2). Berlin and Heidelberg: Springer.

Wong, V., Yuen, J., Su, X., & Yung, J. (2019, June 6). Social isolation experienced by youth in social withdrawal: Toward an interdisciplinary analysis and practice. *IntechOpen* [Online First]. Retrieved from www.intechopen.com/online-first/social-isolation-experienced-by-youth-in-social-withdrawal-toward-an-interdisciplinary-analysis-and-

Chapter 10

Meaning and happiness

Meaningfulness and happiness are the same thing, aren't they? At least that's what many people think. However, the closer you get to an understanding of both concepts, the clearer it becomes that neither are they synonyms nor does one inevitably emerge from the other. Happiness is a positive emotional state that can be more or less intense; it is a feeling. Meaningfulness is not a feeling. It is a cognition, resulting from implicit or explicit evaluation processes. But the differences go far beyond the conceptual level. Depending on whether we strive for happiness or meaning, quite different ways of life ensue.

10.1 Hedonic and eudaimonic well-being

When psychologists deal with happiness, they tend to call it subjective well-being. One of the pioneers of well-being research, Ed Diener, has defined "subjective well-being" as frequent positive affect, infrequent negative affect, and the cognitive evaluation of life as satisfactory. Due to the emphasis on pleasure and pain, subjective well-being has also been called hedonic well-being (Kahneman, Diener, & Schwarz, 1999). In the following subchapter, current findings on the development (and inhibition) of hedonic well-being are presented. Subsequently, the concept of eudaimonic well-being is introduced; here the focus is no longer on feeling good but on a good – and meaningful – life.

10.1.1 Happy ...

Who wouldn't want to be happy? Given the choice between pleasure and pain, probably all of us would choose pleasure. But we do not always have the choice. And if we do, then our decision has to take context into account. It is embedded in a specific situation; it will have consequences;

and it will open one way, while closing other ways. Happiness is complicated; and paradoxically, if you're searching for happiness, you most likely won't find it. Research findings show that the search for happiness can actually prevent the experience of happiness. Iris Mauss and her colleagues (2011) discovered that it is particularly dangerous to strive for happiness when, in principle, we are doing rather well. People who lived a stress-free life and were looking for happiness were unhappier and more depressed than those who did not value happiness so much. The researchers were also able to replicate these findings experimentally: High striving for happiness led to fewer feelings of happiness in a joyful situation. Those participants who were not so eager to be happy experienced significantly more joy in the happy situation.

How can we explain this? The authors suggest that we are disappointed by our own feelings when we consider happiness to be crucial and find ourselves in a situation that potentially promotes happiness. This is exactly the situation that describes Western societies: Happiness is important and feasible, as mass media and counsellors suggest. And many of us are doing well from a material and social point of view. Happiness should thus make its appearance, but somehow, we don't feel as good as we expect to.

The volatility of happiness is also evidenced by the adaptation effect known as the hedonic treadmill. Soon after a positive event, most people's state of well-being returns to the previous level. This phenomenon was first encountered by psychologists when they studied lottery winners. Compared to a control group, they did not report greater happiness. They also reported being similarly happy before and after winning the lottery (Brickman, Coates, & Janoff-Bulman, 1978). With regard to negative and traumatic events (e.g. an accident followed by paralysis), the phenomenon of hedonic adaptation holds a hopeful message: Even after painful events, it is possible to return to initial levels of happiness.

In a literature review, however, Ed Diener and colleagues (2006) found that in the event of the death of a partner, divorce or unemployment, adaptation processes do take place but that the previous level of well-being is not fully regained. Unfortunately, the effect of hedonic adjustment is much more reliable when it comes to the decline of happiness after positive events. After a marriage, a goal achievement, a salary increase, most of us are a little happier in the short term but soon afterwards are as happy as before the event. Therefore, it is useless to condition our happiness on the occurrence of certain events. This applies in particular to the availability of financial resources. For a long time, our society propagated a development model in which an increase in available financial resources was regarded as a measure of personal success. More money was equated with more well-being. Economic happiness research has refuted this general assumption. The so-called Easterlin paradox proves that in nations in which the gross domestic product increases, the average expressed happiness remains the same (Easterlin, 1974; Easterlin, McVey, Switek, Sawangfa, & Zweig, 2010).

On an individual level, however, there is a positive correlation between income and happiness – but it only applies up to a certain income level. This is slightly above the average annual income (Kahneman & Deaton, 2010). A sufficient availability of material goods is therefore necessary for a high sense of happiness, since it allows for the satisfaction of needs like security, nutrition, health, education and participation in society. The fact that a position slightly above the average is also conducive to happiness once again proves the all-too-human tendency to gain well-being from feeling superior to others ("downward comparison"; Wills, 1981). Yet any additional financial gain does not result in additional happiness, or the effect is so minimal that it can be neglected (Boyce, Daly, Hounkpatin, & Wood, 2017).

Whoever complains about the fact that positive events do not increase happiness in the long run might be complaining about first-world problems, as Ed and Carol Diener proved (1996): The vast majority of people on this earth describe themselves as rather happy and content. Last but not least, a further relativisation should be noted. The just-described findings on hedonic adjustment are based on average values. These actually represent a variety of trajectories, which are disguised when only mean scores are reported. After all, a quarter of married people report an increased level of happiness many years after marriage. Others again are even worse off than before their marriage (Lucas, Clark, Georgellis, & Diener, 2003). It thus depends on how we deal with events – whereby social comparisons on the one hand and mindfulness and gratitude on the other seem to play an important role.

> Scenario: What world would you rather live in? In a world where you earn €50,000 a year and the others half as much, or in a world where you earn €100,000 a year and the others twice as much?

To a large degree, our satisfaction depends on how we see ourselves in comparison with others. In the scenario described earlier, most people choose the first option. It is not the absolute level of income that is relevant but the relative level that determines what financial possibilities I have compared to others. But social comparisons can be dangerous.

Western industrialised countries are highly competitive. Whereas in the past, we competed with neighbours, friends and direct colleagues, the spread of social media and online performance quantification have exponentially increased the possibilities for comparison. They predominantly concern material goods and status symbols: Who has the better grades, more likes, better looks, the more expensive car, more publications, the more desirable holiday? People who ask these questions train their attention to the identification of deficits. Dissatisfaction is therefore inevitable – and it also drives the hedonic treadmill:

With much anticipation, Paul expected his professional promotion. Now it has arrived, and they even increased his salary. Paul's colleague was also promoted, he learns. His pay rise was even higher than Paul's. This drastically reduces Paul's joy. After a few more years, Paul is also on the verge of a juicy pay rise, which he is looking forward to. However, it is highly probable that Paul will soon hear about someone who earns more than he does. . .

There is an obvious alternative: Paul could draw his attention to those in similar positions who earn less than he does. In contrast to the *upward comparison* described earlier, this would be a *downward comparison*, a comparison with people who are worse off. This type of comparison is generally accompanied by an increase in well-being (Sirgy, 2012). But what kind of worldview does this "happiness strategy" imply? Should we commit to a motto like "It's all right as long as there are enough people who are worse off than me"? There are more-decent alternatives.

For this purpose, it is helpful to know about typical distortions of perception. One of them is the negativity bias: People are more sensitive to negative signals than to positive ones (Rozin & Royzman, 2001). This phenomenon is easily explained from an evolutionary perspective. During the millennia-long development of our nervous system, it was vital to observe stimuli that might be harmful to us. The environment was full of dangers, including physical injuries, the consumption of poisonous plants, attacks by wild animals and hostile people. Overlooking such hints meant illness or death. This was not the case for positive signs. The consequences of ignoring the beauty of a blossoming tree, for instance, were much less serious. But our environment has changed. As long as we abide by a few rules, our lives are rarely in danger. However, our nervous system has not yet become accustomed to this relative safety; it continues to seek cues for danger. The main beneficiaries are insurance agencies.

Such concentration on potential dangers is rather detrimental to our well-being. It leads to more fear and anxiety than might be appropriate. It also causes us to be more impressed by negative events than by positive ones. Imagine a typical day that is quite pleasant and good. One negative event is enough to overturn our mood. Despite a high number of normal, pleasant or even beautiful events, a single unpleasant event can make us go to bed dissatisfied in the evening. Mindfulness and gratitude come to bear here, the importance of which has been proven in many studies.

Mindfulness is the deliberate and nonjudgemental attention to current events and experiences (Kabat-Zinn, 1990). It is about directing attention to everything that happens – not just to potential hazards. The attitude of nonjudgement demands an internal step back. This interrupts the automatism of evaluation, which all too often results in the attribution of danger or loss. As a consequence of practised mindfulness, we learn that our feelings and thoughts are changeable, that we are not determined by them. Studies show that this leads to improved self-control. We can assess situations more realistically and have a greater awareness of our own needs and values (Nakamura, 2012). Under such conditions, our well-being is less dependent on social comparisons.

Another way to balance negativity bias and to increase well-being on a long-term basis is to practise gratitude. While the idea may seem to imply a religious stance, it is not per se tied to any particular ideological background. Gratitude is understood as the appreciation of what one experiences as valuable and important (Sansone & Sansone, 2010). Many studies have shown that gratitude is related to well-being. Individuals who appreciate their living conditions, events, people, things and so on report a high sense of well-being. It is even possible to increase well-being by practising gratitude, as several studies demonstrated (Emmons, 2008). In Section 10.3, you will find the instructions for a typical gratitude exercise.

For some people, joy and satisfaction are natural: Their default value is a good mood. In fact, there is a genetic predisposition that determines our well-being. On the basis of behavioural genetic research – especially twin studies – and molecular genetic studies, researchers came to the conclusion that 32–41 percent of the variability in subjective well-being is due to genetic differences among people (Nes & Røysamb, 2017). Positive emotionality seems to be less attributable to genetic factors than negative emotionality (Zheng, Plomin, & von Stumm, 2016), which suggests that attention should be drawn to positive attitudes such as mindfulness and gratitude. The influence of living conditions is estimated to be relatively low, at around 10 percent, which leaves a lot of room for intentional action. Those of us who were not born with a predisposition to happiness will thus find it a bit harder to be happy. But better don't make happiness your ultimate goal. Instead, practise gratitude because you see reasons for it, not because you expect it to make you happy. Exercise mindfulness for the sake of being in the present, with all peaks and troughs . . . which brings us straight to another kind of well-being, namely eudaimonic well-being.

10.1.2 More than pleasant

> And as in the Olympic Games it is not the most beautiful and the strongest that are crowned but those who compete (for it is some of these that are victorious), so those who act win, and rightly win, the noble and good things in life.
>
> (Aristotle, 1999, p. 13)

There are many different ways of pursuing hedonic well-being. The route is nearly irrelevant; what counts is the result, the good feeling. The concept of eudaimonic well-being is more demanding. It is primarily concerned with the way of living. The word "eudaimonia" comes from Greek antiquity. Aristotle elaborated on the concept in his Nicomachean Ethics. He emphasised that eudaimonia is not a state but a way of acting. Only those who act will win "the noble and good things in life" (see the foregoing quote).

But how should we act? Aristotle does not make a general statement here. To him, good action is closely related to personal characteristics and the type of motivation we act on. The ideal, he suggests, is for each and every one to actively commit to the realisation of their talents and virtues. The goals we pursue will therefore vary, but they should all adhere to one principle: not to create injustice. Justice, for Aristotle, is "the most complete virtue." Accordingly, eudaimonia is "never only my personal happiness. I cannot strive for and realise it at the expense of my fellow human beings, and I cannot even strive for and realise it in isolation, without reference to my fellow human beings" (Jacobi, 1979, p. 320 f.; transl. TS).

We therefore need to consider the consequences of our actions and the reason for our actions (our motivation). According to Aristotle, actions are "good" when they are performed for their own sake. In psychology, we call this intrinsic motivation. The opposite is extrinsic motivation: the performance of an activity in order to earn a reward or avoid punishment. Again, this criterion of eudaimonia is difficult to generalise, because it refers to internal processes. Thus, one person can live out their thirst for knowledge for intrinsic reasons, because they regard knowledge itself as desirable. Another person may strive for knowledge because they expect to improve their reputation from it. In the latter case, Aristotle would not speak of eudaimonic action.

Last but not least, acting well presupposes that we voluntarily commit to our action. Aristotle saw humans as reasonable beings, capable of insight and discernment. This supposed autonomy implies responsibility. On this basis – but not through force or mindless adaptation – eudaimonia is possible (Schnell, 2013).

What distinguishes Aristotle from other ancient thinkers is the importance he attaches to the satisfaction of basic material needs. Pragmatically and realistically, he declares the necessity of sufficient means: "For our nature is not self-sufficient for the purpose of contemplation, but our body must also be healthy and must have food and other attention" (Aristotle, 1999, p. 176 f.). He thus agrees with the findings of modern happiness research as presented in Section 10.1.1. For a eudaimonic life, basic material needs have to be fulfilled. A further increase in financial means, however, is no guarantee of an increase in quality of life. Instead, under certain circumstances even the opposite may happen, as Aristotle subtly points out:

> Still, we must not think that the man who is to be happy will need many things or great things, merely because he cannot be supremely happy without external goods; for self-sufficiency and action do not involve excess, and we can do noble acts without ruling earth and sea; for even with moderate advantages one can act virtuously (this is manifest enough; for private people are thought to do worthy acts no less than despots – indeed even more); and it is enough that we should have so much as that.
>
> (Aristotle, 1999, p. 177)

Despite all the talk about good and virtuous action, Aristotle also sees the importance of enjoyment. For him, pleasure and happiness are not an end in themselves but positive side effects of eudaimonia. They are closely linked to the action that produces them – and that at the same time is completed by joy. In other words, happiness is not considered detached from the character of an action. It is the natural consequence of a life lived in accordance with personal talents and virtues, voluntarily, responsibly and under appropriate living conditions.

Several studies show that Aristotle's theory is transferable to contemporary life. Meaningfulness can be understood as an expression and indicator of eudaimonic well-being, whereas subjective well-being, positive mood and life satisfaction are regarded as indicators of hedonic well-being. Michael Steger and colleagues (2008) asked their study participants how often they exercised certain hedonic and eudaimonic activities per week. Examples of hedonic actions were sex only for pleasure, buying jewellery or electronic devices, getting drunk, taking drugs or eating more than you want because it tastes so good. Eudaimonic activities included volunteering, giving money to a needy person, writing down one's future goals, thanking someone or entrusting someone with personal thoughts (Steger, Kashdan, & Oishi, 2008). The participants were also asked about their hedonic and eudaimonic well-being: their mood, life satisfaction and meaningfulness. The results confirmed Aristotle's assumptions: Hedonic activities neither contributed to a good mood nor to life satisfaction or meaningfulness. Eudaimonic activities, on the other hand, were accompanied by meaningfulness and by positive mood and satisfaction with life.

Stephen Schueller and Martin Seligman (2010) asked respondents to what degree they pursued pleasure, task engagement or meaningfulness in their lives. Here too, the lowest hedonic well-being was found among those who were striving for pleasure; both the striving for meaning and the striving for task engagement were accompanied by significantly more happiness, positive mood and life satisfaction. Ethan McMahan and Maggie DeHart Renken (2011) also found no connection between a pleasure-oriented lifestyle and positive mood, life satisfaction or meaningfulness, whereas a meaning-oriented, eudaimonic lifestyle was associated with higher meaningfulness and with more life satisfaction and positive mood.

In a longitudinal study carried out by Bernadette Vötter and me, we examined subjective well-being and meaning in life among highly gifted people. The data again supported the earlier-reported association: Participants who reported high meaningfulness at the first measurement showed higher subjective well-being at the second measurement, about four years later. This was not the case the other way round: Subjective well-being did not predict later meaningfulness (Vötter & Schnell, 2019).

10.2 Meaning without happiness

Happy, then, are those who succeed in living according to their personal talents self-determinedly, responsibly, in the knowledge of being connected to fellow human beings and under good external conditions. Yet again and again, we find ourselves in restrictive situations. Or we are faced with the choice between a pleasant option and an alternative that seems right but promises to be demanding. Especially in the short term, meaningful options often appear less pleasant. They are the more difficult choice; they may be challenging. But this is one of the reasons why they usually have positive long-term consequences: Those who challenge themselves gain more experiences and get to know themselves as more active and self-effective than those who tend to choose the momentarily more pleasant option.

But meaning can also be experienced when situations are void of happiness. Such experiences demonstrate that meaningfulness is independent of pleasure and pain and that it is possible even in moments of suffering. Memorably, Viktor Frankl here referred to the "defiant power of the mind" (2011, p. 147). He experienced this power of defiance when he suffered under unspeakable conditions in a concentration camp but refused to give up his dignity. Although the atrocious situation severely restricted his options, Frankl experienced a remaining spiritual freedom. The Nazi subordinates had no access to his innermost being. Frankl managed to rise above degradation and humiliation, to turn suffering into an achievement, as he later said.

Thus, it is possible to defy external conditions with our attitude. As long as we are fully conscious, we retain the power of interpretation over what happens. And depending on how this appraisal turns out, the resulting experience and action will be shaped. Frankl has thus succeeded in transforming what at first sight appears to be a hopeless situation into a challenge with a future perspective; a perspective which, as he said, saved his life.

Another example of a victory of the "defiant power of the spirit" is documented in the diaries of Etty Hillesum (2002). Etty Hillesum was a young Jewish woman who lived in Amsterdam during Nazism. In 1941 and 1942, she wrote in her diary, which was published decades later. On these pages, she shares her inner world of experience. While the outer world is marked by anti-Semitic laws that isolate and oppress Jewish people, deny them professional activity and restrict their residence, Etty Hillesum experiences her life as rich, beautiful and meaningful:

> I am not alone in my tiredness or sickness or fears, but at one with millions of others from many centuries, and it is all part of life, and yet life is beautiful and meaningful too. It is meaningful even in its meaninglessness, provided one makes room in one's life for everything, and accepts life as one indivisible whole, for then one becomes whole in oneself.
>
> (Etty Hillesum, 2002, p. 466)

She radically explores herself through an ongoing dialogue with a god whom she finds in her heart. She loves and suffers on a large scale. Love is fundamental to her, both for individuals and for all humanity, including those who oppress her and who will eventually kill her. And she considers the suffering that is part of her life to be just as fundamental (see also Schnell, 2018).

But Etty Hillesum does not stop there. From her inner experience of peace and meaning, she gains the strength to be there for others, to practise generativity. With great effort, she stands up for those who are already subjected to stronger limitations. When more and more of her family and friends are deported to a transit camp, she joins them voluntarily. In the camp, under difficult conditions and with poor health, she works in a hospital. She also repeatedly uses a special permit to return to Amsterdam, putting her life in danger by exchanging information and maintaining contact with underground groups (see Greif, 2004).

> I work and continue to live with the same conviction, and I find life meaningful – yes, meaningful – although I hardly dare say so in company these days.
>
> (Etty Hillesum, 2002, p. 461)

Etty Hillesum sets an example for the claim that meaningfulness is possible even under the worst conditions. Meaning arises from coherent and convinced action, from a sense of integrity that we maintain on our path, from experiences of belonging and the significance of our action for others. Such experiences are far from maximising pleasure and reducing pain; they are anything but pleasant. Nevertheless, they can evoke a deep satisfaction, in the sense of peace with oneself and even, as in the case of this special and courageous woman Etty Hillesum, in the sense of peace with the world.

10.3 Know thyself!

SELF-EXPLORATION: GRATITUDE

VERSION 1 – ON YOUR OWN

Take about five minutes every evening to write down three things for which you are grateful that day, or which you experienced as particularly valuable. Use a digital or analogue diary for your notes and continue the exercise for one week.

VERSION II – WITH COMPANIONS OR FAMILY

Over dinner, for example, share your experiences of the past day with everyone present, telling them about three things that you are grateful for that day or that you experienced as particularly valuable. Continue the exercise for one week.

(Of course, nothing should prevent you from continuing the exercise over a longer period of time. Our son also reminds us time and again to talk about the "three things," which he has obviously enjoyed – as we have, too).

SELF-EXPLORATION: MYTHS OF HAPPINESS

The American psychologist Sonja Lyubomirsky (2014) warns us of two types of beliefs that can prevent our experience of happiness. The first concerns the assumption that we can be happy only when a certain event occurs (e.g. partnership/marriage, higher income, child, moving to another house). The second is the belief that when an event occurs, happiness is definitely no longer possible (e.g. separation, illness, loss of employment). Try to find out whether you are – more or less consciously – attached to such "myths of happiness":

Once I . . .

———

———

———

. . ., then I will be happy!

I can't be happy if . . .

———

———

———

10.4 Literature

Aristotle. (1999). *Nicomachean ethics* (W. D. Ross, trans.). Kitchener: Batoche Books.

Boyce, C. J., Daly, M., Hounkpatin, H. O., & Wood, A. M. (2017). Money may buy happiness, but often so little that it doesn't matter. *Psychological Science*, *28*(4), 544–546.

Brickman, P., Coates, D., & Janoff-Bulman, R. (1978). Lottery winners and accident victims: Is happiness relative? *Journal of Personality and Social Psychology, 36*(8), 917–927.

Diener, E., & Diener, C. (1996). Most people are happy. *Psychological Science, 7*(3), 181–185.

Diener, E., Lucas, R. E., & Scollon, C. N. (2006). Beyond the hedonic treadmill: Revising the adaptation theory of well-being. *American Psychologist, 61*(4), 305.

Easterlin, R. A. (1974). Does economic growth improve the human lot? Some empirical evidence. *Nations and Households in Economic Growth, 89*, 89–125.

Easterlin, R. A., McVey, L. A., Switek, M., Sawangfa, O., & Zweig, J. S. (2010). The happiness – income paradox revisited. *Proceedings of the National Academy of Sciences, 107*(52), 22463–22468.

Emmons, R. A. (2008). *Thanks! How practicing gratitude can make you happier*. Boston, MA: Houghton Mifflin Company.

Frankl, V. (2011). *Man's search for meaning*. London: Rider.

Greif, G. (2004). *Ein abgeschnittenes Leben–Das Tagebuch von Etty Hillesum 1941–1943*. Retrieved from www.suesske.de/greif_hillesum.htm

Hillesum, E. (2002). *Etty: The letters and diaries of Etty Hillesum 1941–1943*. Grand Rapids: Wm. B. Eerdmans Publishing Company.

Jacobi, K. (1979). Aristoteles' Einführung des Begriffs 'eudaimonia' im I. Buch der 'Nikomachischen Ethik'. In *Philosophisches Jahrbuch 86* (pp. 300–325). Freiburg: Verlag Karl Alber.

Kabat-Zinn, J. (1990). *Full catastrophe living: The program of the stress reduction clinic at the university of Massachusetts medical center*. New York: Delta.

Kahneman, D., & Deaton, A. (2010). High income improves evaluation of life but not emotional well-being. *Proceedings of the National Academies of Science, 107*(38), 16489–16493.

Kahneman, D., Diener, E., & Schwarz, N. (Hrsg.). (1999). *Well-being: The foundations of hedonic psychology*. New York: Russell Sage Foundation.

Lucas, R. E., Clark, A. E., Georgellis, Y., & Diener, E. (2003). Reexamining adaptation and the set point model of happiness: Reactions to changes in marital status. *Journal of Personality and Social Psychology, 84*(3), 527–539.

Lyubomirsky, S. (2014). *The myths of happiness: What should make you happy, but doesn't, what shouldn't make you happy, but does*. New York: Penguin.

Mauss, I. B., Tamir, M., Anderson, C. L., & Savino, N. S. (2011). Can seeking happiness make people happy? Paradoxical effects of valuing happiness. *Emotion, 11*(4), 807–815.

McMahan, E. A., & DeHart Renken, M. (2011). Eudaimonic conceptions of well-being, meaning in life, and self-reported well-being: Initial test of a meditational model. *Personality and Individual Differences, 51*, 589–594.

Nakamura, Y. (2012). Achtsamkeit. In C. Steinebach, D. Jungo, & R. Zihlmann (Eds.), *Positive psychologie in der praxis* (pp. 60–66). Weinheim and Basel: Beltz.

Nes, R. B., & Røysamb, E. (2017). Happiness in behaviour genetics: An update on heritability and changeability. *Journal of Happiness Studies, 18*(5), 1533–1552.

Rozin, P., & Royzman, E. B. (2001). Negativity bias, negativity dominance, and contagion. *Personality and Social Psychology Review, 5*(4), 296–320.

Sansone, R. A., & Sansone, L. A. (2010). Gratitude and well-being: The benefits of appreciation. *Psychiatry, 7*(11), 18–22.

Schnell, T. (2013). Mehr als angenehm – über Partizipation und Sinnerleben. In T. Köhler & C. Mertens (Eds.), *Jahrbuch für Politische Beratung 2012/2013* (pp. 39–49). Wien: Böhlau.

Schnell, T. (2018). Einlassen, Zulassen, Loslassen. Ein philosophisch-psychologischer Zugang zu einem aktiven Leidensbegriff. *Zeitschrift für Palliativmedizin, 19*, 249–255.

Schueller, S. M., & Seligman, M. E. P. (2010). Pursuit of pleasure, engagement, and meaning: Relationships to subjective and objective measures of well-being. *The Journal of Positive Psychology, 5*(4), 253–263.

Sirgy, M. J. (2012). Effects of social comparisons on subjective QOL: The psychology of quality of life. *Social Indicators Research Series, 50*, 223–233.

Steger, M. F., Kashdan, T. B., & Oishi, S. (2008). Being good by doing good: Daily eudaimonic activity and well-being. *Journal of Research in Personality, 42*, 22–42.

Vötter, B., & Schnell, T. (2019). Cross-lagged analyses between life meaning, self-compassion, and subjective well-being among gifted adults. *Mindfulness, 10*(7), 1294–1303.

Wills, T. A. (1981). Downward comparison principles in social psychology. *Psychological Bulletin, 90*(2), 245–271.

Zheng, Y., Plomin, R., & von Stumm, S. (2016). Heritability of intraindividual mean and variability of positive and negative affect: Genetic analysis of daily affect ratings over a month. *Psychological Science, 27*(12), 1611–1619.

Chapter 11

Meaning, health and illness

11.1 Can meaning in life improve your health?

Research findings suggest that the more meaning a person experiences, the healthier they are – both mentally and physically. Effect sizes range from small to moderate with regard to physical health and from moderate to large regarding mental health. Meaningfulness thus does not *guarantee* health. We should say instead that people who see meaning in their lives have a higher likelihood to be healthy. We can further claim that when people with high meaningfulness do become ill, they deal with it differently than people with a low sense of meaning. They suffer less from it, and often, the symptoms are much less pronounced.

As far as mental health is concerned, it has been shown that meaningful people are more hopeful and optimistic than people who see little meaning in their lives (Damásio, Koller, & Schnell, 2013). They experience themselves as more competent, more self-determined and better integrated socially (Kashdan & Breen, 2007). It is easier for them to accept their weaknesses and mistakes, in the sense of self-compassion (Vötter & Schnell, 2019). Their self-efficacy, resilience and self-regulation skills are also more pronounced. They are better able to activate, motivate and calm themselves, to direct their attention and to cope with failures (Hanfstingl, 2013; Sørensen et al., 2019). In addition, meaningfulness is accompanied by fewer psychological problems. It correlates negatively with neuroticism, depression, anxiety and the severity of posttraumatic stress disorders (Owens, Steger, Whitesell, & Herrera, 2009; Pedersen et al., 2018; Pinquart, 2002; Schnell, 2009). The magnitude of these effects is considerable, ranging from medium to large.

Nathan Lewis and colleagues (2017) investigated the relationship between meaning in life and cognitive functioning in Americans between the ages of 32 and 84. Their data showed that people with a high level of meaningfulness fared better in performance tests. They had better scores on memory, problem-solving, decision-making and attention. Kim and colleagues (2019) confirmed this finding in a longitudinal study: In more than 11,000 Americans aged 50 and older, meaning in life predicted cognitive performance six years later. It proved to be an important protective factor against cognitive ageing.

Also with regard to physical health, meaning in life has been established as a crucial factor. A meta-analysis (Czekierda, Banik, Park, & Luszczynska, 2017) found moderate correlations between meaningfulness and objective health measures (such as availability of natural killer cells, heart rate, etc.) and medium correlations with subjective health measures (such as self-assessed health, symptom severity or perceived functional limitations). The effects were replicated not only in cross-sectional but also in experimental and longitudinal studies. This suggests that we can indeed assume that meaning contributes to health.

Here are some more-specific results: In Japan, a large prospective cohort study (over 43,000 people) was conducted, which in this case meant that members of a national health insurance scheme were interviewed over several years. One of the questions asked at the beginning was whether the participants felt that their lives were meaningful and worth living – whether they had *ikigai* in their lives. They could answer "yes," "no" or "uncertain." Those who initially affirmed a sense of meaning in life showed significantly better physical health, less pain and less impairment of physical functioning seven years later (Sone et al., 2008). A nationwide American study confirmed the connection between meaningfulness and self-assessed health and physical functioning (Krause, 2009). A smaller German study with older participants also found a positive relationship between meaningfulness and physical functioning (Wiesmann & Hannich, 2011). An American prospective longitudinal study showed that the risk of developing Alzheimer's disease was significantly lower for people with a high level of meaning in life (Boyle, Buchman, Barnes, & Bennett, 2010). A more recent study with a similar design (Kim, Kawachi, Chen, & Kubzansky, 2017) showed that meaningfulness also predicted the mobility of older adults four years later. This was measured by walking speed and, as in all studies reported here, by controlling for other health-related conditions, such as marital status, education, income, health status, experienced stress, BMI, smoking, alcohol, exercise, sleep duration and medical history.

Several studies even discovered that risk of mortality is significantly lower for people with high meaning in life (Alimujiang et al., 2019; Boyle, Barnes, Buchman, & Bennett, 2009; Hill & Turiano, 2014;

Krause, 2009; Sone et al., 2008). This result was established in all age groups – that is, in adolescents as well as in middle and late age – and while controlling for other factors known to influence one's risk of mortality. An American study found that high meaningfulness reduced general risk of mortality by 23 percent and reduced the risk of heart attack, stroke or need for bypass surgery or stent implantation by 19 percent (Mount Sinai Medical Center, 2015). Another American study, which examined nearly 7,000 adults aged 50 years and older for over four years, found a two-and-a-half times greater risk of mortality among those who reported very low meaningfulness compared to those who reported very high meaningfulness. For cardiovascular and blood diseases, the cause-specific mortality was 166 percent higher for those with low meaningfulness than those with high meaningfulness (Alimujiang et al., 2019). The Japanese study described earlier (Sone et al., 2008) found a 50 percent higher risk of mortality within the seven years studied for those with no meaning in life (*ikigai*). The risk of cardiovascular death and fatal stroke was 60 percent higher in both cases when meaning was absent, the cause-specific death from pneumonia was 80 percent higher, and the probability of dying from suicide was twice as high compared to people who had stated that they saw meaning in their lives. A meta-analysis from 2016, which systematically searched for studies that addressed the relationship between meaning in life, cardiovascular disease and mortality, confirmed the validity of the meaning effect (Cohen, Bavishi, & Rozanski, 2016): Across all studies, the probability of cardiovascular disease was 17 percent lower when meaning was present. Overall mortality was reduced by the same amount.

How can we explain these effects? Why should people who see meaning in their lives be psychologically and physically healthier and even live longer? There is evidence that meaning has a positive influence on our health in two ways: meaning motivates, and meaning moderates.

11.1.1 Meaning in life as a motivator

Aaron Antonovsky, the father of salutogenesis, has vividly demonstrated and justified the motivating power of meaningfulness. In the 1970s, he initiated a change of perspective in the social sciences: Instead of investigating disorders and their aetiology, Antonovsky explored the origins of health (1979). He was particularly interested in how people succeed in maintaining their health even when they experience severe stressors. He arrived at this perspective when he examined how women from different ethnic groups dealt with menopause. One of these groups was born in Central Europe between 1914 and 1926. Antonovsky later wrote that he no longer really knew why, but he had asked them, among other things, whether they had been in a Nazi concentration camp. When he included the answer in his analyses, he found that 29 percent of the former internees had good mental health. This finding was a turning point for him: How was it possible to survive the Holocaust, to live as displaced people for years, to build up a new existence in Israel, where again wars were raging, and still be reasonably healthy? Through further studies, he came to the conclusion that it is a fundamental conviction that allows for a health-promoting way of coping with stress. He coined the term "sense of coherence" and described it as a fundamental trust in the comprehensibility, manageability and meaningfulness of one's own life.

Comprehensibility means that we can understand and, to a certain extent, predict the events we encounter in the course of our lives, whether they originate in our inner world or the environment. When comprehensibility is low, we perceive internal and external stimuli as unexpected and disordered; they appear to be unexplainable or random. Of course, our perception of comprehensibility also affects how prepared we feel to cope with our lives. Manageability is the second component of Antonovsky's sense of coherence. It is a person's trust to have sufficient internal or external resources available to cope with demands. If it is low, we feel overwhelmed by life.

The third and, according to Antonovsky, most important component of the sense of coherence is meaningfulness. If we perceive our lives as meaningful, we also evaluate demands as worthwhile challenges. This implies a sense of significance: My actions matter; the requirements, problems and goals are worth the effort because they make sense; they have a meaning. The motivational function of meaning thus comes into view. Meaning motivates us to constructively deal with efforts and stressors. Without meaning, we rather perceive them as a burden, as impositions that we are not willing to face.

The three components of the sense of coherence are instructive for understanding human health behaviour. Only when we perceive our lives as meaningful are we at all willing to invest in life – even if it might be stressful. Health behaviour is one such effort. This includes specific conduct such as regular exercise, a balanced diet, sufficient sleep and exercising restraint with regard to luxury foods and potentially harmful substances. In general, health behaviour stands for a willingness to take responsibility for one's own health (Wiesmann & Hannich, 2011; Wikler, 2002).

The perception of life as meaningful thus motivates us take responsibility for our health; we believe it is worth the effort and engagement (Antonovsky). The health-promoting function of meaningfulness can be illustrated by the hierarchic model of meaning (Figure 11.1). If meaningfulness is present, it motivates people to invest in health: one of the sources of meaning. This in turn suggests the pursuit of certain objectives, such as "increasing endurance," "eating healthily," "maintaining physical resilience" and so on. These goals result in corresponding actions (e.g. eating lots of fruit and vegetables, drinking little alcohol, not smoking), which in turn guide the evaluation and interpretation of perceived stimuli (e.g. the perceived attractiveness of healthy and unhealthy food).

Several empirical studies demonstrate the motivating function of meaningfulness. An American research group (Holahan, Holahan, & Suzuki, 2008) studied 130 cardiac outpatients undergoing treatment for coronary artery disease, myocardial infarction, angina, arrhythmias and other coronary problems. The researchers asked the patients for an

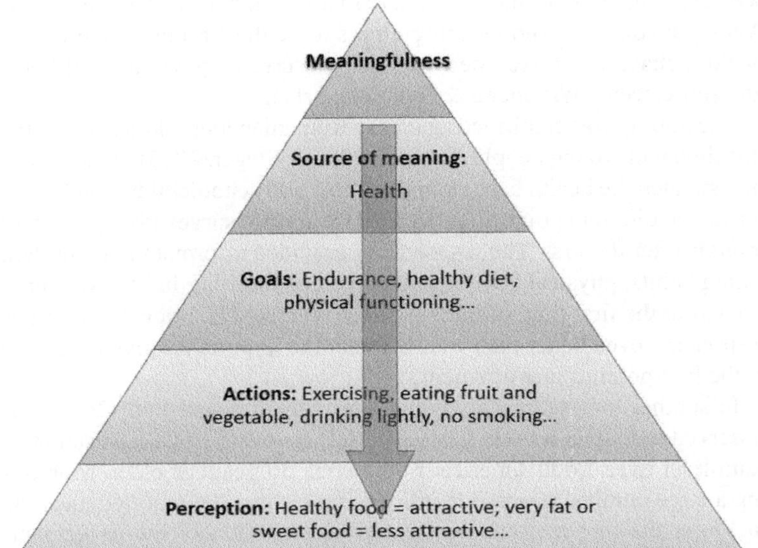

Figure 11.1 Meaningfulness motivates health-related behaviour in the hierarchic model of meaning

assessment of their own health and for information about their physical activity and purpose in life. It turned out that the more meaning the outpatients saw in their lives, the healthier they felt. The correlation was mediated by physical activity, indicating that meaningfulness motivated the patients to exercise regularly (they reported going for walks, doing routine housework, gardening and sports) and that these physical activities in turn contributed to their sense of health.

Another US study (Homan & Boyatzis, 2010) aimed to explore the reasons for older people to live healthy lives. They interviewed 160 senior Americans about their religiosity, meaningfulness and health behaviour. Meaningfulness turned out to be the most robust predictor of health behaviour. A high level of meaningfulness apparently motivated people to be physically active, take responsibility for their health and manage stress constructively. German researchers conducted a similar study to investigate older people's motives to live healthy lives. They consulted 170 adults who were 67 years, on average. To assess healthy living, they asked whether the respondents paid attention to their personal hygiene, went to the doctor regularly, ate a healthy diet, got sufficient exercise and relaxation, slept enough and demonstrated responsibility in dealing with alcohol, nicotine and drugs, in road traffic and in sexual intercourse. Again, the data showed meaningfulness to be the strongest predictor of health behaviour. It exceeded various measures of physical well-being and self-esteem (Wiesmann & Hannich, 2011).

The finding was confirmed again in a Romanian longitudinal study, but this time with young people (Brassai, Piko, & Steger, 2015). Researchers investigated the health behaviour of almost 500 schoolchildren in Romania at two different points in time, with the second survey taking place 13 months after the first. The respondents provided information about their eating habits, physical activity and perceived meaning in life. Meaningfulness at the first time of measurement predicted health behaviour one year later – even better than well-being or the importance given to health at the first point of measurement.

In another longitudinal study, by Kim, Strecher, and Ryff (2014), the observed time span was six years. The authors examined a representative sample of over 7,000 Americans who were 50 years or older. Monitoring a large number of possible influencing factors, the reported meaning in life at the first measurement could predict whether the participants would undergo cholesterol tests, colonoscopy, mammograms or prostate examinations six years later. The number of hospital stays was also significantly lower among those who had reported a high meaningfulness six years earlier.

The studies show that people are more likely to behave in a health-conscious way if they see meaning in their lives. Meaningfulness motivates people not to be negligent with their health but instead to take responsibility for their well-being. Life seems valuable enough to accept restrictions or efforts in return. The specific consequences of such behaviour are better physical and mental health, fewer functional limitations in old age and a longer life. In addition to the motivating function of meaning in life, a moderating function has been observed, which plays an important role in maintaining and regaining health.

11.1.2 Meaning in life as a moderator

A moderator is a regulator. It affects the relationship between two other variables, by reducing or strengthening it (Figure 11.2).

Various studies have shown that personal meaningfulness has an influence on the consequences of stressors (Boyle et al., 2012; Krause, 2007; Park, Edmondson, Fenster, & Blank, 2008). Stressors are all those events that can lead to psychological or physical suffering. These include everyday hassles as well as traumatic events like a separation, an accident or a serious illness. Such events can be destructive, interrupt life and cause great suffering. However, if a person is strengthened by the presence of meaning in life, then suffering is less serious in most cases. The existential foundation can prevent a loss of perspectives and goals. People can deal with the stressor more constructively, which also goes hand in hand with better coping. Meaning therefore acts like a "stress buffer." Let's look at some examples of the buffering effect of meaning in life.

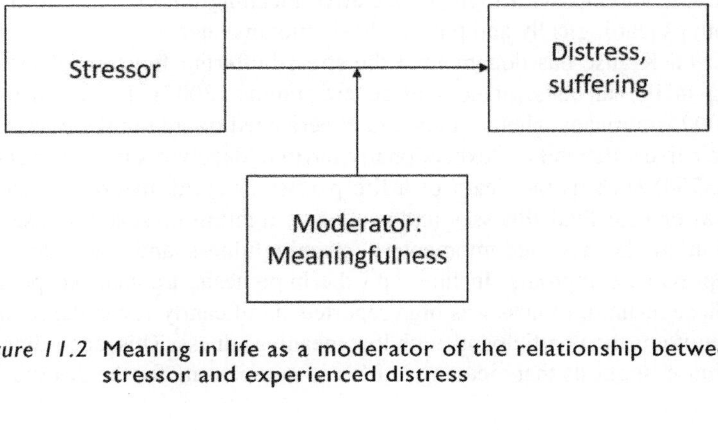

Figure 11.2 Meaning in life as a moderator of the relationship between stressor and experienced distress

An American longitudinal study (The Rush Memory and Aging Project; Bennett et al., 2005) examined the health course of the ageing population, with a special focus on Alzheimer's disease. More than 1,000 people participated annually in interviews and clinical and psychological tests, including questions on meaning in life. This benefited the participants, who received up-to-date information on their health status, and it benefited the researchers. A large number of patients also agreed to an autopsy after death, which meant an additional gain in knowledge for the researchers. Patricia Boyle and colleagues (2012) investigated 246 cases, including autopsies. They found higher levels of meaning to reduce the deleterious effects of Alzheimer's disease on cognitive function. When patients had reported high meaningfulness, their cognitive performance declined much more slowly than it did in people with low meaningfulness. The authors interpret the findings as indicating that meaning in life contributes to building up "neuronal reserve," which allows people to function better despite the presence of pathological changes like amyloid and tangles. Here the buffer function of meaning in life may arise from meaningfulness being accompanied by a goal and action orientation that trains resistance and thus increases the strength and efficiency of the nervous system (Boyle et al., 2012).

Another study from the US provided further evidence of the stress-buffering function of meaning in life in the – perhaps somewhat surprising – context of knee surgery (Smith & Zautra, 2000). The authors examined elderly patients who were given a knee joint replacement due to arthrosis. After such an operation, pain and functional limitations may still occur for several months afterwards. Six months after the surgery in Smith and Zautra's study, those patients who had reported low meaningfulness before the operation especially suffered from pain and limitations. Patients with high preoperative meaningfulness had improved both psychologically and physically six months later.

Neil Krause has documented the stress-buffering function of meaning in life in consequences of severe trauma (2007). He asked over 1,000 Americans whether they had experienced trauma in the course of their lives, defined as "exceptionally terrible, deeply disturbing events" (p. 794) such as the death of a life partner or child, natural disasters, fatal or near-fatal illnesses and accidents, fighting or sexual abuse. In addition, he assessed momentary meaningfulness and the extent of depressive symptoms. In line with the hypothesis, traumatised people whose meaningfulness was high reported significantly fewer depressive symptoms than participants with low meaningfulness. This, according to Krause, suggests that meaning in life can compensate for the destructive consequences of experienced traumas. This assumption is supported by a recent study of 1,119 Mississippi coastal residents affected by the Deepwater Horizon disaster (also known as the Gulf oil spill). For many of the residents, the drilling rig explosion and subsequent oil spill caused financial, social and/or health problems. More than one-third of the sample experienced posttraumatic stress disorder (PTSD). In this context, too, the perception of life as meaningful proved to be an important buffer: Those who reported meaningfulness were significantly less affected by posttraumatic stress symptoms (Aiena, Buchanan, Smith, & Schulenberg, 2016).

Many studies have investigated connections between meaning in life and mental suffering in cancer patients. Cancer is also regarded as a trauma, because it interrupts the course of life in a disturbing and dangerous way. Those who are affected are burdened with physical symptoms and the side effects of treatments, but in many cases, they also have depression, anxiety and a multitude of other negative feelings and moods. A team of researchers compared 62 studies on meaning in life and the mental suffering of cancer patients in a meta-analysis (Winger, Adams, & Mosher, 2016). Overall, the results confirmed that the mental suffering of cancer patients is less pronounced when they perceive their lives as meaningful. The buffer effect of meaningfulness was thus again confirmed.

Findings suggest that meaningfulness can directly reduce or compensate for negative experiences. Moreover, there is evidence that meaningfulness reduces the burden of rumination. When negative events occur, we usually ask questions like "Why me?" and "Why did this happen to me?" We search for a specific meaning of the incident. This search, however, is not productive and often represents an additional burden (Park, 2010; Park et al., 2008). Instead, it is more important to view life as meaningful per se, in spite of – or including – suffering. This overall sense of meaning provides a stable existential foundation, a foothold from which we can deal with events even without attributing specific meaning to them. This is different, however, if a person's meaning in life is based on positive illusions: unrealistically favourable attitudes that people have towards themselves or the world (Section 8.5). Such illusions include the belief in a just world, the above-average effect, unrealistic optimism and the illusion of control. These assumptions are jeopardised by negative events, and people whose meaning hinges on their veracity tend to search for meaning in specific events – mostly unsuccessfully.

Another potentially harmful belief is connected with a specific type of instrumental-reciprocal religiosity. Such a – rather widespread – faith is based on the principle of reciprocity: "do ut des" (Latin for "I give, so that you give") (Streib, 1997). Here the following assumption prevails: Whoever follows religious rules and commandments is rewarded for it – such as by a happy, healthy and prosperous life. When a negative event occurs, believers are motivated to seek the cause in their own misconduct and thus find meaning in the event.

However, the matter is complex and great care should be taken in practice. Searching for meaning in negative events cannot simply be dismissed as obstructive. Several studies show that the *search* for meaning in an illness, an accident or other critical events tends to have negative effects. At the same time, it is known that *finding* such meaning can be beneficial. Those who "succeed" in finding a meaning in cancer can actually deal with it better; in many cases, it even leads to an increase in quality of life. This phenomenon of posttraumatic growth is described in more detail in Section 11.4. It is therefore not a question of preventing the attribution of meaning. Rather, only the unsuccessful search for it has a destructive effect. The psychotherapist Elmar Reuter, who has been working in psycho-oncology for several decades, advises people to be patient when questions about the cause of their own illness arise:

> Things are not easy. It is not about getting immediate answers, it is about the process of regaining control, gradually regaining security. The process of asking questions should be seen as a struggle to move from initial helplessness to more inner security.
>
> (Reuter, 2010, p. 28; transl. TS)

In summary, we can say that an existing meaning in life acts as a buffer against the negative consequences of stressors. A stable existential foundation can prevent our life from becoming dominated by a disease, injury or other limitation. In addition to motivating health behaviour, meaningfulness also has a moderating function: It reduces or averts the negative consequences of stressors. But how can this happen? What are the paths that run from the abstract construct of meaning in life to our mental and physical health?

11.2 From mind to body

Various biological systems are responsible for our health. These include the immune system, the cardiovascular system (heart and blood vessels) and the neuroendocrine system (pituitary glands, parathyroid gland, adrenal medulla, etc.) They determine whether and how quickly we fall ill, how fast we recover and how well our body functions. There is clear evidence that a meaningful life is related to the effective functioning of these systems. The most important findings to date are presented here.

11.2.1 Meaning in life and biomarkers

In a sample of older women, Carol Ryff and colleagues found that with regard to several biomarkers, those with higher meaningfulness differed significantly from those with lower meaningfulness (Ryff, Singer, & Dienberg Love, 2004). Participants who saw meaning in their lives produced less cortisol, both after getting up and throughout the day. (High cortisol levels in the morning and throughout the day are considered indicators of chronic stress.) In addition, fewer pro-inflammatory cytokines (interleukin 6) were detected, which, when present, indicate chronic inflammatory processes. The risk for cardiovascular diseases was lower among women who reported meaning, which was expressed in a better waist–hip ratio and in higher HDL cholesterol values. (The high-density lipoprotein is considered "good" cholesterol because it is a protective factor against cardiovascular diseases.) Last but not least, a calmer and thus more effective sleep pattern could be demonstrated in participants with higher meaning.

A different study design was used to examine how socioeconomic status and health are related in older women and whether meaningfulness might play a moderating (regulating) role. As a health indicator, the American research team (Tsenkova, Love, Singer, & Ryff, 2007) used glycosylated haemoglobin (HbA1c). HbA1c – colloquially known as long-term blood sugar – is an important indicator of the course of type 1 and type 2 diabetes. Moreover, HbA1c has been shown to be informative for non-diabetics' health. According to epidemiological studies, a small increase in non-diabetic HbA1c is associated with a multiple increase in risk of cardiovascular disease and general mortality (Tsenkova et al., 2007). As the researchers had expected, household income was inversely related to HbA1c levels: The less money available, the more critical the health score. And again, the moderating function of meaning in life was confirmed. Women with a low household income but a high sense of purpose achieved similarly good scores as more financially solvent women. Apparently, meaningfulness compensated for the negative effects of low income. A lack of meaning, on the other hand, even led to an increase in the negative effects of low income.

A moderating (regulating) function of meaningfulness has also been demonstrated for the relationship between chronic diseases in old age and inflammation markers (interleukin 6 and C-reactive protein) (Friedman & Ryff, 2012). Many older people have multiple chronic disorders such as hypertension, arthritis, asthma, diabetes, autoimmune diseases and so on. These lead to further inflammatory processes, which are associated with additional functional limitations. In the national sample examined by Friedman and Ryff, multiply-affected participants who reported meaning in life had significantly lower levels of inflammatory processes than would have been expected, given the co-morbidity. This suggests that meaning in life does not necessarily prevent disorders but it mitigates their negative effects.

Another group of researchers (Zilioli, Slatcher, Ong, & Gruenewald, 2015) studied a subset of the previously described national sample. These participants had been willing – ten years after the first survey – to again undergo a detailed examination. Just under 1,000 people had their complete medical history taken. In addition, researchers collected blood, urine and saliva samples and assessed various cardiovascular parameters. For this specific study, the authors broadened the perspective from the observation of individual diseases and health parameters to the assessment of allostatic load. Allostatic load refers to the physiological consequences of cumulative physiological stress that the body endures when it is repeatedly or persistently adapting to the demands of the environment. The term "allostasis" refers to the changes that the cardiovascular, autonomic, neuroendocrine, immunological and metabolic systems undergo in stressful situations. Too long or too frequent cycles of allostasis make us biologically "fragile" – in other words, allostatically stressed. This stress, in turn, is associated with a higher risk of disease, cognitive decline and mortality (Seeman, McEwen, Rowe, & Singer, 2001; Seeman et al., 2004).

When analysing the data, Zilioli and his team also discovered the expected role of meaning: People who had reported high meaning in life at the first measurement showed a significantly lower allostatic load ten years later. In addition, these people were also more convinced that they could influence their health. This conviction, in turn, was associated with lower allostatic stress. It "mediated" the connection between meaningfulness and allostatic biomarkers. The finding highlights the importance of "manageability" according to Antonovsky (Section 11.1.1) – that is, the assumption that we can take care of things that are important to us: High meaningfulness seems to strengthen our trust that we can contribute to our health; given its motivating function, meaningfulness also influences our actual attempts to live healthily, thus increasing our sense of manageability with regard to health. This in turn appears to be an important link to regulate and maintain our physical health.

A good example of how people with high meaning in life regulate their allostatic load was documented in an experimental study by Fogelman and Canli (2015). They exposed 44 elderly Americans to the Trier Social Stress Test, in which participants have to complete two tasks in front of two cameras and a jury of two people in white coats. First, they have to deliver a free five-minute speech concerning their suitability for employment in a mock job interview; then the task is to count backwards in steps of 17 from a high number of thousands. The procedure reliably ensures that physical stress reactions occur. Fogelmann and Canli now found that study participants with high meaning in life had a normal stress reaction – but that they recovered faster than others. Such accelerated stress reduction decreases the allostatic load. Again, it indicates that having meaning in life helps to better deal with stressors.

11.2.2 Social genomics: meaning in life and gene expression

The relatively new research area of social genomics is based on findings that show that our genes do not have a constant state of activity but are switched on or off by certain environmental conditions. Importantly, it is not the conditions themselves that have predictable genetic consequences but rather how we perceive them. This is where our view of ourselves and the world comes into play, which differs in many ways between people with high meaningfulness and people with low meaningfulness (see also the hierarchic model of meaning in Section 4.1).

The social geneticist Steven Cole (2014, 2019) demonstrated in his studies how stress perception is reflected in the genes. There is ample evidence that subjective experiences of social stress upregulate systemic inflammatory processes, which have destructive effects on health. The result is known as conserved transcriptional response to adversity (CTRA). It is a typical profile of "switched-on" genes that becomes active as a result of stress. Specifically, the CTRA profile implies an increased expression of pro-inflammatory genes and a decreased expression of genes related to the innate antiviral response and antibody synthesis. In other words, inflammation is promoted and the immune response to viruses and the synthesis of antibodies is reduced.

Of course, such a genetic profile does not exist without reason. It prepares the body to deal with wounds and bacterial infections. Inflammatory processes are responsible for keeping pathogens in check, rejecting damaged tissue and carrying out repairs. For our ancestors, these processes were vital, but under current conditions, the CTRA gene profile appears to be activated to an excessive degree. Alarmingly, CTRA profiles are found more often in people with low socioeconomic status, in mourning people, caring relatives, people with PTSD and those who have been diagnosed with cancer (Cole, 2014). All these situations have in common that they can easily be perceived as uncontrollable stressors. They exert a strong influence on life, and it is difficult to escape them. Chronic stress results, which – mediated by CTRA gene expression – promotes the development of other disorders, such as cardiovascular diseases, Alzheimer's disease, type 2 diabetes and metastatic cancers. At the same time, the body's defences against viral infectious diseases are reduced (Cole, 2014).

Steven Cole, Californian researcher Barbara Fredrickson and colleagues (Fredrickson et al., 2013, 2015) have successfully demonstrated that meaning in life can inhibit CTRA gene expression. Given the findings that chronic stress – mediated by gene expression – impairs health, the research team assumed that high well-being should have positive effects on health, also mediated by gene expression. According to the current state of research, they distinguished between eudaimonic and hedonic well-being (Section 10.1). The results were partly quite surprising given that they did not confirm the assumption of positive psychology that positive feelings are beneficial to health. Hedonic well-being (positive mood and satisfaction with life) was *not* systematically related to CTRA. Eudaimonic well-being (purpose in life, personal growth, generativity), on the other hand, was associated with reduced CTRA gene expression (Fredrickson et al., 2013). In the analysis of individual subscales, purpose in life proved to be a relevant antagonist of CTRA gene expression, along with self-acceptance, environmental mastery, autonomy and positive relationships (Fredrickson et al., 2015).

In 2017, Nelson-Coffey and colleagues investigated a similar question in a controlled randomised study. They wanted to know if CTRA gene expression would be affected if over a period of four weeks, participants did something good for themselves (e.g., pampered themselves, practised a hobby), did something good for others (e.g., invited somebody for coffee, lightened somebody's workload) or did something that would benefit the world in general (e.g., picked up garbage, donated money). As was to be expected from previous studies, the hedonistic task – doing good for oneself – had no effect on gene expression. Also, becoming active for the world in general had no effect. But when others benefited directly from the good deed, improvements in the leukocyte expression of CTRA indicator genes were observed. It thus seems to be relevant for our health to actually experience the (positive) consequences of our deeds.

This finding confirms the crucial role of "significance" in meaning (see Section 2.3.2). It also reflects another insight that I gained from numerous case studies: Volunteers who spend time working for rather abstract and long-term goals such as social justice or climate change are often more exhausted than people who directly contribute to the well-being of others through their actions (and thus receive immediate feedback on the significance of their work). A society that relies on individuals and groups committing themselves to long-term goals should therefore support them in the best possible way, both ideally and materially (see also Schickedanz, 2018).

11.2.3 More meaning, less inflammatory processes

Summarising the various findings, meaning in life appears to cushion the effects of stress on biological systems by limiting inflammatory processes. Contemporary medicine has established connections between chronic inflammation and many diseases, such as autoimmune diseases of the central nervous system (such as multiple sclerosis) and neurodegenerative diseases such as Alzheimer's and Parkinson's (Kaplin & Anzaldi, 2015). Inflammation is caused by the activity of the immune system –and in principle, this is a good thing. As a weapon of the body's own defence system, inflammation fights infections and contributes to wound healing. However, our immune system not only becomes active when it encounters pathogens that invade the body but also reacts to psychosocial stress – the Trier Social Stress Test is a good example. Our brain (especially the hypothalamus and pituitary gland) signals to the adrenal gland that a stressor is present, whereupon the latter releases the stress hormone cortisol. This suppresses the immune system, but only for a short time. When we endure psychosocial stress for a longer period of time, such as from ongoing professional overload, separation anxiety, financial worries or loneliness, the immune system no longer reacts so sensitively to cortisol. Instead, it becomes even more active and thus produces persistent, often silent inflammations that cause or aggravate diseases.

Some of the studies presented earlier are directly related to inflammatory markers such as interleukin 6, C-reactive protein and the upregulation of pro-inflammatory genes. When we look at other biological markers that are related to meaning in life (Section 11.2.1), associations with inflammatory processes can also be detected here: Daily profiles of cortisol release are positively correlated with inflammatory processes (and are considered to be reactions to psychosocial stressors; DeSantis et al., 2012). The waist–hip ratio is considered an indicator of overweight and obesity associated with subclinical systemic inflammatory processes (Visser, Bouter, McQuillan, Wener, & Harris, 1999). HDL cholesterol – the high-density lipoprotein – has anti-inflammatory properties. By activating a transcriptional regulator (ATF3), HDL cholesterol is responsible for the downregulation of inflammatory gene expression; it thus protects against persistent inflammation (De Nardo et al., 2014). Sleep disorders and resulting sleep deprivation are associated with increased levels of pro-inflammatory cytokines and C-reactive protein (Simpson & Dinges, 2007). The blood glucose level HbA1c is related to subclinical inflammation too (Temelkova-Kurktschiev et al., 2002). One review article (Rohleder, 2014) concludes that people with low meaning in life are particularly likely to respond to stress with inflammatory stress reactions.

The data suggest the following explanation: According to Lazarus and Folkman's (1984) groundbreaking stress theory, events can be appraised as threats, losses or challenges. When we perceive a stressor as an uncontrollable threat or a loss that has already occurred, genes are activated that put the body into a state of defence and cause inflammatory processes. At the same time, there is an increased release of the stress hormone cortisol. Also, sleep disorders occur more frequently, which triggers additional inflammatory processes. Low motivation and/or a lack of internal resources can limit the willingness to exercise and eat healthily. Resulting overweight leads to further inflammatory reactions, and with a reduction in HDL cholesterol, an important anti-inflammatory factor is eliminated.

If, on the other hand, stressors are regarded as worthwhile and manageable challenges – to which the moderating and motivating functions of meaningfulness contribute significantly – then the dangerous inflammatory processes are more likely to be absent. Without their threatening character, stressors do not elicit a defensive reaction of the body, such as CTRA gene expression. Finally, meaningfulness prevents a loss of perspective. Instead of directing all attention to the stressors experienced as threatening, they are put into perspective: "I am not determined by being a cancer patient/unemployed person/abuse survivor/widow." The availability of various sources of meaning – including selfactualisation; wellbeing and relatedness; order and selftranscendence – can compensate for limitations. This way, we can realise that there is a lot of life worth living besides the challenging stressors.

11.3 "I can't go on!" Crises of meaning prevent recovery

Meaningfulness affects health by motivating healthy behaviour and by moderating the influence of stressors. The observed effects are usually of medium size. This indicates that there must be other important influences, such as self-acceptance, environmental mastery and positive relationships. The situation is different for crises of meaning. Here we find drastic effects, indicating that when there is a crisis of meaning, life energy dwindles – and thus, health suffers.

As described in Chapter 8, a crisis of meaning is a painful state of affairs. During a crisis of meaning, feelings of happiness, joy, curiosity and satisfaction are almost impossible. Trust in one's own strengths diminishes; internal and external demands can hardly be dealt with. With the loss of such resources, the occurrence of depression, anxiety and suicidal tendencies becomes more likely (Damásio et al., 2013; Schnell, 2009; Schnell, Gerstner, & Krampe, 2018; Sørensen et al., 2019; Wood & Joseph, 2010). A crisis of meaning often occurs as a result of a severe stressor, and it can prevent constructive coping. It therefore has a mediating function.

11.3.1 Mediating desperation

A mediator is a go-between – in everyday life and in statistics. Mediators explain why two variables, for example a stressor and drug use, are related. The principle is illustrated in Figure 11.3: The mediator, here a crisis of meaning, is a consequence of the stressor and evokes the next

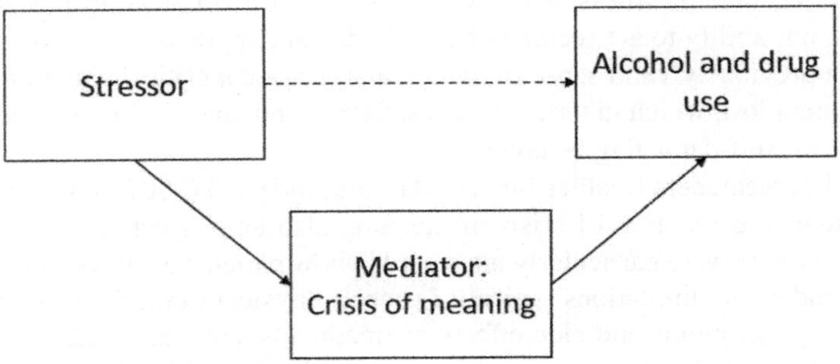

Figure 11.3 Crisis of meaning as a mediator between stressor and alcohol and drug use

characteristic, in this case the use of alcohol and drugs. The mediator crisis of meaning thus explains why there is a connection between the stressor and the use of alcohol and drugs.

The mediation shown in Figure 11.3 illustrates the result of a study by Lisa Harlow, Michael Newcomb, and Peter Bentler (1986). Their aim was to explore why, and under which conditions, young people consume alcohol and drugs. Their assumption was that both alcohol and drugs are used to cope with stress, especially when the stressors are experienced as uncontrollable. This might be the case when children or adolescents are exposed to their parents' separation; when their family is undergoing financial difficulties, accidents, serious illness or death; or when a relocation with a change of school is unavoidable. In such cases, Harlow and colleagues postulated that some young people experience a loss of control that could result in a crisis of meaning. This in turn could lead to increased alcohol and drug use. In fact, two mediators were assumed here: loss of control and crisis of meaning. In a cross-sectional study with almost 400 students, the hypothesis was clearly confirmed: When participants experienced stressors resulting in a loss of control and then a crisis of meaning, they reported more frequent use of alcohol and drugs. In a subsequent longitudinal study, crisis of meaning also explained alcohol and drug consumption four years later.

The study shows that it is not the stressor per se that leads to self-damaging behaviour or other forms of mental suffering. Problems occur when the stressor cannot be understood and mastered as a worthwhile challenge but instead is perceived as a severe threat or a loss that has already occurred (see also Section 11.2.3). Appraisals of stressors as threats or losses suggest a loss of control: When believing that our competences and resources are insufficient to successfully avert a threat, we experience helplessness. When we perceive a stressor as an irrevocable loss, our ability to act seems to be limited. Both appraisals can jeopardise a previously valid sense of meaning and cause a critical situation of meaning lost, which in turn prompts suffering and, under certain circumstances, self-damaging behaviour.

The researchers Heather Jim and Barbara Andersen (2007) have found a mediating function of crisis of meaning also among cancer patients. The authors were particularly interested in how patients dealt with physical and social limitations typical of cancer. Physical limitations include disease symptoms and side effects of treatments, such as nausea, pain, fatigue, cognitive impairment and sexual dysfunction. Also, the interruption of daily activities due to such complaints counts as a physical limitation. Moreover, social restrictions occur. People who are often tired or experience pain or nausea easily fall out of the social fabric. The network of social relationships shrinks, and the number of interpersonal contacts decreases. In some cases, entire role identities are lost, such as when it is no longer possible to pursue one's professional activity or when physical ailments preclude voluntary work or certain hobbies. All these are social limitations.

Hence, cancer is a traumatic, disturbing and on many levels limiting event. It is therefore not surprising that cancer patients often develop depression, anxiety and negative moods such as anger, rage, nervousness and tension. Nevertheless, such mental suffering is not a necessary consequence of cancer. Some patients are much better off than others. Jim and Andersen wanted to know what this depends on. They assumed that the cause of suffering might be found in physical and social limitations. But they also posited that it was not the restrictions themselves that were causing the suffering. Rather, it should be a question of how the limitations are built into one's life. Are they perceived as a challenge that can be overcome or as a threat or loss? If the latter is the case, the researchers postulated, then the personal meaning system is shaken. A crisis of meaning arises, which in turn leads to mental suffering.

The data confirmed this assumption, both in a cross-sectional survey and in a longitudinal survey. For many of the cancer patients, physical and social limitations led to a crisis of meaning, which in turn was responsible for mental suffering. We can thus conclude that a breakdown in personal meaning causes a lot of additional suffering, beyond the inevitable consequences of illness and other severe stressors. Those who work in healthcare professions are therefore well advised to develop a sensitivity for this dimension of human experience, which lies beyond the biopsychosocial model. Even with appropriate medication, self-confidence and a tight social network, a loss of meaning can prevent healing and lead to suffering.

11.3.2 Existential despair at the end of life

This problem is particularly striking in the context of incurable diseases. The psychiatrist William Breitbart has in his work with terminally ill people, especially cancer and HIV patients, come across a phenomenon that he describes as "despair at the end of life." It is a syndrome of hopelessness, suicidal thoughts and desire for hastened death (Breitbart et al., 2000, 2015). Such "despair at the end of life" occurs repeatedly in patients who are confronted with the fact that their disease is incurable and the end of their life is foreseeable. While some take the news calmly, settle their legacies and prepare to die in peace, others show signs of despair, expressing their desire to die soon and possibly asking for euthanasia. Breitbart describes his experiences as follows:

> Close to 20%–25% of the patients whom I was seeing were people in great despair who wanted to die, and who wanted their death hastened. Although not all of them were asking their doctors to assist them specifically by giving a prescription or euthanizing them, they wanted to die fast. They could not deal with the suffering, and saw no meaning or value in living.
>
> (Breitbart & Heller, 2003, p. 979 f.)

Breitbart initially assumed that these were depressive symptoms. He focused his attention on correctly diagnosing and treating depression in the final stages of life. In the process, he notes, he came across some common misconceptions. One is the assumption that it is "normal" for people who have only four to eight weeks to live to be depressed. In fact, he and his colleagues found a depression rate of only 17 percent in a sample of people who had on average one month to live. A second misconception is that depression cannot be effectively treated in the last weeks of life. Breitbart contradicts this and explains that there are various drugs available that can lift the mood and vitality of the patients. Such measures are just as important as the alleviation of physical symptoms, emphasises Breitbart, since those affected perceive mental suffering as at least as painful.

However, the syndrome of despair at the end of life could not be attributed to depression. Apparently, it is a phenomenon that can occur in addition to depression or independently of it, and it makes the last phase of life immensely difficult. After further investigation, Breitbart and his team identified a critical lack of meaning as the cause of despair at the end of life: To those affected, their entire life seemed meaningless. Consequently, they saw no meaning in structuring the few remaining weeks or months or even in living them consciously.

It is a potentially bleak scenario that is unfolding here. If at the end of life, we look back and judge our life as inadequate or unacceptable, there is no time for corrections. And yet the "final chapter" still holds many possibilities, says Breitbart. Whether restricted in movement or because of pain – as long as a person is conscious, they can grow spiritually. This is why Breitbart is committed to palliative medicine and care that goes beyond the goals of support and guidance. He would like to see more help for dying people to accept their life and – as a consequence – their death.

> Many suggest such a goal of care is not achievable by all and perhaps inappropriate for many. I would suggest that tasks of life completion are achievable and essential at this phase of life. Acknowledging or facing death (i.e., the finiteness of life) is the impetus for transformation. Facing death forces us to turn around and face life – the life one has lived. . . . It allows for realization that the last chapter of one's life is the last opportunity to live to one's full potential, to leave behind an authentic legacy, to connect with the beyond, and to transcend life as we know it. . . . The paradox of the end-of-life dynamic is that through acceptance of the life one has lived comes acceptance of death. The lessons of the dying can inform the living of the value of life.
>
> (Breitbart, 2015)

The crisis of meaning here is the reaction to the announcement of imminent death. It is accompanied by a "devaluation" of life, which is perceived as meaningless and something that the patient wants to be "overcome" as quickly as possible. Hopelessness, suicidal thoughts and the desire for hastened death are in the foreground. This prevents a conscious confrontation with life and with death. William Breitbart acted on this knowledge by developing an intervention to strengthen meaning in terminally ill patients. The procedure is presented in Chapter 12.

11.3.3 Crises of meaning are not clinical depression

From the outside, depression and crisis of meaning are easily confused. A sad, depressed mood prevails in both. Nevertheless, they are different phenomena. In a study of 318 students in Ecuador aged 16–18 years (Schnell et al., 2018), we found that 82 percent of those who met the criteria for clinical depression also experienced a crisis of meaning. However, when we looked at all those who reported a crisis of meaning, we found increased depression rates in only 35 percent. We can conclude that a crisis of meaning is a common component of depression – but that many crises of meaning occur without clinical depression.

In another study, we investigated whether crises of meaning were correlated with specific symptoms of clinical depression. Surprisingly, there were no systematic associations. Instead, we found a link between crises of meaning and increased symptoms related to anxiety: People dealing with a crisis of meaning reported feelings of tension and worry (Schnell, in preparation). However, tension and worry do not yet constitute a mental disorder, even if they are pronounced. Mental disorders are considered "expressions of dysfunctional psychological, biological or developmental processes" (Falkai & Wittchen, 2015, p. 26; transl. TS). But what is "dysfunctional"? In the German dictionary (Duden, 2019), dysfunctional means "detrimental to an effect." Synonyms are "impractical" and "unfunctional." It remains open which effect, which function, is aimed at. Psychology and psychiatry in this respect are oriented towards what is "normal," what the majority of society thinks, experiences, does. In many cases, however, people in a crisis of meaning experience precisely this: What is considered normal, what everyone does, suddenly becomes questionable. They are thus in agreement with a remarkable sentence attributed to Mark Twain: Whenever you find yourself on the side of the majority, it is time to reform (or pause and reflect).

11.3.4 Crisis of meaning and suicidality

Falling out of familiar, "normal" references and functions can be stressful. A crisis of meaning disillusions; it calls into question what has previously served as basis of existence; it deprives everyday life of meaning. This is accompanied by a feeling of isolation and solitude (see Chapter 8). Thoughts of suicide are a common consequence. In our study of Ecuadorian adolescents (Schnell et al., 2018), we also examined the connection between crisis of meaning and suicidal tendencies. Suicidality is understood to be a way of thinking, experiencing and acting that strives for or accepts one's death. In this context, hopelessness and lack of perspective prevail (see e.g. Wolfersdorf, 2012). Certain factors can further promote a desire to die by suicide, such as low self-esteem, lack of social integration and the burden of critical life events. We have controlled these characteristics in our study and found that crises of meaning were as closely linked to suicidal tendencies as depression was. For male adolescents, they were an even-more-important predictor of suicidal tendencies than for young women. The results show that in suicide prevention, it might be vital to go beyond the diagnosis of depression.

11.4 Posttraumatic growth

Life asks a lot of us. Death, accidents, illness and violence are traumatic events that can hurt us emotionally, destroy our existential foundation, lead to crises of meaning and thus take away our will to live. And yet there are also quite different developments that follow life crises. Many people succeed in coping with stressful life events and thereby grow psychologically. The term "posttraumatic growth" emphasises that those affected not only recover from trauma but also use it as an opportunity for further personal development. The pioneers of research on posttraumatic growth, Richard Tedeschi and Lawrence Calhoun, illustrate the phenomenon by using an earthquake metaphor: Trauma shakes fundamental assumptions about ourselves and the world. If we succeed in adapting our own psychological reality to the new situation, posttraumatic growth can happen. In the process, a new worldview is created that is more mature, robust and in tune with reality than the previous one, thus bringing new strength (Calhoun & Tedeschi, 2014). The following quotation illustrates this from the perspective of a person who has survived cancer:

> I have had the opportunity to gain so many positive experiences: with myself; my thinking; my inner strength to deal with crises. I have also had many positive experiences with my fellow human beings, with my family. You only notice this when you are in need; how many people stand by me. I notice that I approach my studies and education in a much more mature way. Maybe I needed the disease. I go so far as to say that I am grateful for the illness. Perhaps it doesn't have to be this illness, but the process, the crisis-like experience and what then happened to me and around me has made me more mature, more human in a deeper sense.
>
> (Thomas K., in Reuter, 2010, p. 16; transl. TS)

Posttraumatic growth can affect different areas of life. Research has identified five changes that are frequently mentioned, but they do not always occur simultaneously (Calhoun & Tedeschi, 2014):

1. A more intense appreciation of one's own life: Those affected state that they have a new view of what is essential in life. They are aware of the finiteness of their life, which makes life more valuable. They also perceive the "little things in life" more consciously and appreciatively, such as the sunrise, the embrace of a child or the beauty of a flower.
2. An intensification of personal relationships, closer relationships with people who have proven to be "true friends" and a distancing from incriminating or superficial contacts. Likewise, many people report that they have developed greater compassion for other people.

3 Becoming aware of one's own strength: Coping with the trauma conveys an awareness of one's strength, but also vulnerability is increased. Evidently, the two are closely related. The knowledge of constant vulnerability represents an acknowledgement of reality, which is experienced as an inner preparation for further blows of fate. The fact that a terrible event has already been overcome once strengthens confidence in the ability to cope with hardships in the future.
4 Discovering new possibilities: Priorities change, and the interruption from the outside allows those affected to escape from structures that previously seemed unalterable. A frequent consequence is that people turn away from professional lives that took up (too much) time and energy and turn towards occupations that seem more meaningful to them.
5 An intensified spiritual awareness: Last but not least, many affected people find a new and deeper access to spirituality or religiosity.

As might be expected, posttraumatic growth is associated with meaning in life (Cann, Calhoun, Tedeschi, & Solomon, 2010; Paterno, 2012; Triplett, Tedeschi, Cann, Calhoun, & Reeve, 2012). People who say their life has changed for the positive after a trauma report more meaningfulness than people without posttraumatic growth. Tedeschi and Calhoun have recently taken this into account by adding existential change to the fifth domain of posttraumatic growth, which is now termed "spiritual-existential change" (Tedeschi et al., 2017). It covers a greater clarity about life's meaning; better ability to face questions about life and death; more connectedness with existence and a greater sense of harmony with the world (Tedeschi et al., 2017). In one of our studies, people who reported posttraumatic growth attached particular importance to communion, attentiveness, social commitment and health as sources of meaning (Paterno, 2012).

It is not yet fully understood why posttraumatic growth occurs in some people and not in others. The results are contradictory in terms of age, gender and severity of trauma. However, there is consensus in the literature that fundamental assumptions must have been shaken for posttraumatic growth to ensue. The typical consequence of such a shock is intrusive rumination, a severe form of brooding that can hardly be controlled deliberately. If this rumination leads to a conscious, active confrontation with the trauma, then it is another condition for posttraumatic growth. What is necessary for this is the willingness to allow the suffering, to accept it – and thus to finally release it (cf. Schnell, 2018).

It is also helpful if other people treat with compassion those who were affected, stand by them and are prepared to react empathically to revelations of traumatic experiences, which are often difficult to bear even for those who are close (Cann et al., 2010; Calhoun & Tedeschi, 2014).

11.5 Know thyself!

ESSENTIAL QUESTIONS: DEATH AND DYING

- How often do you think of your own death and of your dying?
- Do you find dying frightening?
- Are you afraid of death?
- Do you think that seriously ill people should be confronted with their death and dying by medical, therapeutic and/or nursing staff?
- Can *you* talk to seriously ill people about death and dying?
- Talk to someone about your attitude towards death and dying!

FOR CONTEMPLATION

For traumatised people, the hint of the possibility of posttraumatic growth is often of little help; it might even be experienced as a slap in the face. Dealing with the findings on posttraumatic growth requires great caution. The experiences of American journalist Barbara Ehrenreich, who was diagnosed with breast cancer, are revealing:

> The cheerfulness of breast cancer culture goes beyond mere absence of anger to what looks, all too often, like a positive embrace of the disease. . . . Writing in 2007, *New York Times* health columnist Jane Brody faithfully reflected the near universal bright-siding of the disease. She gave a nod to the downside of breast cancer and cancer generally: "It can cause considerable physical and emotional pain and lasting disfigurement. It may even end in death." But for the most part her column was a veritable ode to the uplifting effects of cancer, and especially breast cancer. . . . In the most extreme characterization, breast cancer is not a problem at all, not even an annoyance – it is a "gift," deserving of the most heartfelt gratitude.
>
> (Ehrenreich, 2010, p. 27ff)

> And in our implacably optimistic breast cancer culture, the disease offers more than the intangible benefits of spiritual upward mobility.

> You can defy the inevitable disfigurements and come out, on the survivor side, actually prettier, sexier, more femme.
>
> (Ehrenreich, 2010, p. 30)

> Clearly, the failure to think positively can weigh on a cancer patient like a second disease. . . . Breast cancer, I can now report, did not make me prettier or stronger, more feminine or spiritual. What it gave me, if you want to call this a "gift," was a very personal, agonizing encounter with an ideological force in American culture that I had not been aware of before – one that encourages us to deny reality, submit cheerfully to misfortune, and blame only ourselves for our fate.
>
> (Ehrenreich, 2010, p. 43 f.)

11.6 Literature

Aiena, B. J., Buchanan, E. M., Smith, C. V., & Schulenberg, S. E. (2016). Meaning, resilience, and traumatic stress after the deepwater horizon oil spill: A study of Mississippi coastal residents seeking mental health services. *Journal of Clinical Psychology*, *72*(12), 1264–1278.

Alimujiang, A., Wiensch, A., Boss, J., Fleischer, N. L., Mondul, A. M., McLean, K., . . . Pearce, C. L. (2019). Association between life purpose and mortality among US adults older than 50 years. *JAMA Network Open*, *2*(5), e194270.

Antonovsky, A. (1979). *Health, stress and coping*. San Francisco: Jossey-Bass.

Bennett, D. A., Schneider, J. A., Buchman, A. S., Mendes de Leon, C., Bienias, J. L., & Wilson, R. S. (2005). The rush memory and aging project: Study design and baseline characteristics of the study cohort. *Neuroepidemiology*, *25*(4), 163–175.

Boyle, P. A., Barnes, L. L., Buchman, A. S., & Bennett, D. A. (2009). Purpose in life is associated with mortality among community-dwelling older people. *Psychosomatic Medicine*, *71*(5), 574.

Boyle, P. A., Buchman, A. S., Barnes, L. L., & Bennett, D. A. (2010). Effect of a purpose in life on risk of incident Alzheimer disease and mild cognitive impairment in community-dwelling older people. *Archives of General Psychiatry*, *67*(3), 304–310.

Boyle, P. A., Buchman, A. S., Wilson, R. S., Yu, L., Schneider, J. A., & Bennett, D. A. (2012). Effect of purpose in life on the relation between Alzheimer disease pathologic changes on cognitive function in advanced age. *Archives of General Psychiatry*, *69*(5), 499–504.

Brassai, L., Piko, B. F., & Steger, M. F. (2015). A reason to stay healthy: The role of meaning in life in relation to physical activity and healthy eating among adolescents. *Journal of Health Psychology*, *20*(5), 473–482.

Breitbart, W. (2015, May 25). Potential power of meaning-centered group psychotherapy in patients with advanced cancer. *The Asco Post*, *6*(9).

Breitbart, W., & Heller, K. S. (2003). Reframing hope: Meaning-centered care for patients near the end of life. *Journal of Palliative Medicine*, *6*(6), 979–988.

Breitbart, W., Rosenfeld, B., Pessin, H., Applebaum, A., Kulikowski, J., & Lichtenthal, W. G. (2015). Meaning-centered group psychotherapy: An effective intervention for improving psychological well-being in patients with advanced cancer. *Journal of Clinical Oncology*, *33*(7), 749–754.

Breitbart, W., Rosenfeld, B., Pessin, H., Kaim, M., Funesti-Esch, J., Galietta, M., & Brescia, R. (2000). Depression, hopelessness, and desire for hastened death in terminally ill patients with cancer. *JAMA*, *284*(22), 2907–2911.

Calhoun, L. G., & Tedeschi, R. G. (Eds.). (2014). *Handbook of posttraumatic growth: Research and practice*. New York: Routledge.

Cann, A., Calhoun, L. G., Tedeschi, R. G., & Solomon, D. T. (2010). Posttraumatic growth and depreciation as independent experiences and predictors of well-being. *Journal of Loss and Trauma*, *15*(3), 151–166.

Cohen, R., Bavishi, C., & Rozanski, A. (2016). Purpose in life and its relationship to all-cause mortality and cardiovascular events: A meta-analysis. *Psychosomatic Medicine*, *78*(2), 122–133.

Cole, S. W. (2014). Human social genomics. *PLoS Genetics*, *10*(8), e1004601.

Cole, S. W. (2019). The conserved transcriptional response to adversity. *Current Opinion in Behavioral Sciences*, *28*, 31–37.

Czekierda, K., Banik, A., Park, C. L., & Luszczynska, A. (2017). Meaning in life and physical health: Systematic review and meta-analysis. *Health Psychology Review*, *11*(4), 387–418.

Damásio, B. F., Koller, S. H., & Schnell, T. (2013). Sources of meaning and meaning in life questionnaire (SoMe): Psychometric properties and sociodemographic findings in a large Brazilian Sample. *Acta de Investigación Psicológica*, *3*(3), 1205–1227.

De Nardo, D., Labzin, L. I., Kono, H., Seki, R., Schmidt, S. V., Beyer, M., & Latz, E. (2014). High-density lipoprotein mediates anti-inflammatory reprogramming of macrophages via the transcriptional regulator ATF3. *Nature Immunology*, *15*(2), 152–160.

DeSantis, A. S., DiezRoux, A. V., Hajat, A., Aiello, A. E., Golden, S. H., Jenny, N. S., & Shea, S. (2012). Associations of salivary cortisol levels with inflammatory markers: The multi-ethnic study of atherosclerosis. *Psychoneuroendocrinology*, *37*(7), 1009–1018.

Duden. (2019). *Dysfunktional*. Retrieved from www.duden.de/rechtschreibung/dysfunktional

Ehrenreich, B. (2010). *Smile or die: How positive thinking fooled America and the world*. London: Granta Books.

Falkai, P., & Wittchen, H.-U. (2015). *Das Diagnostische und Statistische Manual Psychischer Störungen (DSM-5)*. Göttingen: Hogrefe.

Fogelman, N., & Canli, T. (2015). 'Purpose in life' as a psychosocial resource in healthy aging: An examination of cortisol baseline levels and response to the trier social stress test. *NPJ Aging and Mechanisms of Disease*, *1*, 15006.

Fredrickson, B. L., Grewen, K. M., Algoe, S. B., Firestine, A. M., Arevalo, J. M., Ma, J., & Cole, S. W. (2015). Psychological well-being and the human conserved transcriptional response to adversity. *PLoS One*, *10*(3), e0121839.

Fredrickson, B. L., Grewen, K. M., Coffey, K. A., Algoe, S. B., Firestine, A. M., Arevalo, J. M., & Cole, S. W. (2013). A functional genomic perspective on human well-being. *Proceedings of the National Academy of Sciences*, *110*(33), 13684–13689.

Friedman, E. M., & Ryff, C. D. (2012). Living well with medical comorbidities: A biopsychosocial perspective. *The Journals of Gerontology Series B: Psychological Sciences and Social Sciences*, *67*(5), 535–544.

Hanfstingl, B. (2013). Ego- and spiritual transcendence: Relevancies for psychological resilience and the role of age. *Evidence-Based Complementary and Alternative Medicine*, 9 pages.

Harlow, L. L., Newcomb, M. D., & Bentler, P. M. (1986). Depression, self-derogation, substance use, and suicide ideation: Lack of purpose in life as a mediational factor. *Journal of Clinical Psychology*, *42*(1), 5–21.

Hill, P. L., & Turiano, N. A. (2014). Purpose in life as a predictor of mortality across adulthood. *Psychological Science*, *25*(7), 1482–1486.

Holahan, C. K., Holahan, C. J., & Suzuki, R. (2008). Purposiveness, physical activity, and perceived health in cardiac patients. *Disability and Rehabilitation*, *30*(23), 1772–1778.

Homan, K. J., & Boyatzis, C. J. (2010). Religiosity, sense of meaning, and health behavior in older adults. *The International Journal for the Psychology of Religion*, *20*(3), 173–186.

Jim, H. S., & Andersen, B. L. (2007). Meaning in life mediates the relationship between social and physical functioning and distress in cancer survivors. *British Journal of Health Psychology*, *12*(3), 363–381.

Kaplin, A., & Anzaldi, L. (2015, May). New movement in neuroscience: A purpose-driven life. *Cerebrum: The Dana Forum on Brain Science*. PMID:26380036. Dana Foundation.

Kashdan, T. B., & Breen, W. E. (2007). Materialism and diminished well-being: Experiential avoidance as a mediating mechanism. *Journal of Social and Clinical Psychology*, *26*(5), 521–539.

Kim, E. S., Kawachi, I., Chen, Y., & Kubzansky, L. D. (2017). Association between purpose in life and objective measures of physical function in older adults. *JAMA Psychiatry*, *74*(10), 1039–1045.

Kim, E. S., Strecher, V. J., & Ryff, C. D. (2014). Purpose in life and use of preventive health care services. *Proceedings of the National Academy of Sciences*, *111*(46), 16331–16336.

Kim, G., Shin, S. H., Scicolone, M. A., & Parmelee, P. (2019). Purpose in life protects against cognitive decline among older adults. *The American Journal of Geriatric Psychiatry*, *27*(6), 593–601.

Krause, N. (2007). Evaluating the stress-buffering function of meaning in life among older people. *Journal of Aging and Health, 19*(5), 792–812.

Krause, N. (2009). Meaning in life and mortality. *The Journals of Gerontology Series B: Psychological Sciences and Social Sciences, 64*(4), 517–527.

Lazarus, R. S., & Folkman, S. (1984). Coping and adaptation. In W. D. Gentry (Ed.), *The handbook of behavioral medicine* (pp. 282–325). New York: Guilford.

Lewis, N. A., Turiano, N. A., Payne, B. R., & Hill, P. L. (2017). Purpose in life and cognitive functioning in adulthood. *Aging, Neuropsychology, and Cognition, 24*(6), 662–671.

Mount Sinai Medical Center. (2015, March 6). Have a sense of purpose in life? It may protect your heart. *Science Daily*. Retrieved from www.sciencedaily.com/releases/2015/03/150306132538.htm

Nelson-Coffey, S. K., Fritz, M. M., Lyubomirsky, S., & Cole, S. W. (2017). Kindness in the blood: A randomized controlled trial of the gene regulatory impact of prosocial behavior. *Psychoneuroendocrinology, 81*, 8–13.

Owens, G. P., Steger, M. F., Whitesell, A. A., & Herrera, C. J. (2009). Posttraumatic stress disorder, guilt, depression, and meaning in life among military veterans. *Journal of Traumatic Stress, 22*(6), 654–657.

Park, C. L. (2010). Making sense of the meaning literature: An integrative review of meaning making and its effects on adjustment to stressful life events. *Psychological Bulletin, 136*(2), 257.

Park, C. L., Edmondson, D., Fenster, J. R., & Blank, T. O. (2008). Meaning making and psychological adjustment following cancer: The mediating roles of growth, life meaning, and restored just-world beliefs. *Journal of Consulting and Clinical Psychology, 76*(5), 863.

Paterno, D. (2012). *Posttraumatisches Wachstum und Sinnerleben–Sinnressourcen für die Traumatherapie* (Unpublished Master thesis), University of Innsbruck, Innsbruck.

Pedersen, H. F., Birkeland, M. H., Jensen, J. S., Schnell, T., Hvidt, N. C., Sørensen, T., & la Cour, P. (2018). What brings meaning to life in a highly secular society? A study on sources of meaning among Danes. *Scandinavian Journal of Psychology, 59*(6), 678–690.

Pinquart, M. (2002). Creating and maintaining purpose in life in old age: A meta-analysis. *Ageing International, 27*(2), 90–114.

Reuter, E. (2010). *Leben trotz Krebs – eine Farbe mehr*. Stuttgart: Schattauer.

Rohleder, N. (2014). Stimulation of systemic low-grade inflammation by psychosocial stress. *Psychosomatic Medicine, 76*(3), 181–189.

Ryff, C. D., Singer, B. H., & Dienberg Love, G. (2004). Positive health: Connecting well-being with biology. *Philosophical Transactions-Royal Society of London Series B Biological Sciences*, 1383–1394.

Schickedanz, L. (2018). *Die mentale Infrastruktur offener Räume: eine Fallstudie in Innsbruck, Österreich* (Unpublished Master thesis), University of Innsbruck, Innsbruck.

Schnell, T. (2009). The sources of meaning and meaning in life questionnaire (SoMe): Relations to demographics and well-being. *Journal of Positive Psychology*, *4*(6), 483–499.

Schnell, T. (2018). Einlassen, Zulassen, Loslassen. Ein philosophisch-psychologischer Zugang zu einem aktiven Leidensbegriff. *Zeitschrift für Palliativmedizin*, *19*, 249–255.

Schnell, T., Gerstner, R., & Krampe, H. (2018). Crisis of meaning predicts suicidality in youth independently of depression. *Crisis–The Journal of Crisis Intervention and Suicide Prevention*, *39*, 294–303.

Seeman, T. E., Crimmins, E., Huang, M. H., Singer, B., Bucur, A., Gruenewald, T., . . . Reuben, D. B. (2004). Cumulative biological risk and socio-economic differences in mortality: MacArthur studies of successful aging. *Social Science & Medicine*, *58*(10), 1985–1997.s

Seeman, T. E., McEwen, B. S., Rowe, J. W., & Singer, B. H. (2001). Allostatic load as a marker of cumulative biological risk: MacArthur studies of successful aging. *Proceedings of the National Academy of Sciences*, *98*(8), 4770–4775.

Simpson, N., & Dinges, D. F. (2007). Sleep and inflammation. *Nutrition Reviews*, *65*(12, part 2), 244–252.

Smith, B. W., & Zautra, A. J. (2000). Purpose in life and coping with knee-replacement surgery. *OTJR: Occupation, Participation and Health*, *20*(1), 96–99.

Sone, T., Nakaya, N., Ohmori, K., Shimazu, T., Higashiguchi, M., Kakizaki, M., & Tsuji, I. (2008). Sense of life worth living (ikigai) and mortality in Japan: Ohsaki study. *Psychosomatic Medicine*, *70*, 709–715.

Sørensen, T., la Cour, P., Danbolt, L. J., Stifoss-Hanssen, H., Lien, L., DeMarinis, V., . . . Schnell, T. (2019). The sources of meaning and meaning in life questionnaire in the Norwegian context: Relations to mental health, quality of life, and self-efficacy. *The International Journal for the Psychology of Religion*, *29*(1), 32–45.

Streib, H. (1997). Religion als stilfrage. *Archive for the Psychology of Religion*, *22*, 48–69.

Tedeschi, R. G., Cann, A., Taku, K., Senol-Durak, E., & Calhoun, L. G. (2017). The posttraumatic growth inventory: A revision integrating existential and spiritual change. *Journal of Traumatic Stress*, *30*(1), 11–18.

Temelkova-Kurktschiev, T., Siegert, G., Bergmann, S., Henkel, E., Koehler, C., Jaro, W., & Hanefeld, M. (2002). Subclinical inflammation is strongly related to insulin resistance but not to impaired insulin secretion in a high risk population for diabetes. *Metabolism*, *51*(6), 743–749.

Triplett, K. N., Tedeschi, R. G., Cann, A., Calhoun, L. G., & Reeve, C. L. (2012). Posttraumatic growth, meaning in life, and life satisfaction in response to trauma. *Psychological Trauma: Theory, Research, Practice, and Policy*, *4*(4), 400.

Tsenkova, V. K., Love, G. D., Singer, B. H., & Ryff, C. D. (2007). Socioeconomic status and psychological well-being predict cross-time change in glycosylated hemoglobin in older women without diabetes. *Psychosomatic Medicine*, *69*(8), 777–784.

Visser, M., Bouter, L. M., McQuillan, G. M., Wener, M. H., & Harris, T. B. (1999). Elevated C-reactive protein levels in overweight and obese adults. *JAMA*, *282*(22), 2131–2135.

Vötter, B., & Schnell, T. (2019). Cross-lagged analyses between life meaning, self-compassion, and subjective well-being among gifted adults. *Mindfulness*, *10*(7), 1294–1303.

Wiesmann, U., & Hannich, H. J. (2011). Salutogenic perspectives on health maintenance: The role of resistance resources and meaningfulness. *GeroPsych: The Journal of Gerontopsychology and Geriatric Psychiatry*, *24*(3), 127.

Wikler, D. (2002). Personal and social responsibility for health. *Ethics & International Affairs*, *16*(2), 47–55.

Winger, J. G., Adams, R. N., & Mosher, C. E. (2016). Relations of meaning in life and sense of coherence to distress in cancer patients: A meta-analysis. *Psycho-Oncology*, *25*(1), 2–10.

Wolfersdorf, M. (2012). Suizid und Suizidalität auspsychiatrisch-psychotherapeutischer Sicht. *Psychotherapie im Dialog*, *13*, 2–7.

Wood, A. M., & Joseph, S. (2010). The absence of positive psychological (eudemonic) well-being as a risk factor for depression: A ten year cohort study. *Journal of Affective Disorders*, *122*(3), 213–217.

Zilioli, S., Slatcher, R. B., Ong, A. D., & Gruenewald, T. L. (2015). Purpose in life predicts allostatic load ten years later. *Journal of Psychosomatic Research*, *79*(5), 451–457.

Chapter 12

Meaning-centred interventions

Although the importance of meaning in life in the context of health and illness has been established many times, meaning-related communication or interventions are not regular elements of health treatments. Major approaches to psychotherapy, such as psychoanalysis and psychodynamic therapies and cognitive-behavioural and systemic therapies do not focus on existential concerns, thus leaving a majority of licensed psychotherapists without knowledge and expertise in this regard (Utsch, 2018). But existential communication is not limited to the psychological field. Also in medical care, patients expect physicians to be present as human beings, showing social responsibility (Halperin, 2010). A Norwegian research team (Agledahl et al., 2011) conducted a revealing qualitative study of 101 video-recorded patient–doctor encounters. They found doctors to be courteous, polite, friendly and approachable. However, the physicians actively redirected the focus from existential concerns to medical facts, thus overriding personal aspects and, in particular, existential issues. The authors call for an acknowledgement of what they term a “moral offence” experienced by patients when their existential concerns are ignored. They also note that improving social and communication skills will not suffice to solve this problem, but rather, a deeper awareness of existential concerns is necessary.

This has also been proposed for other healthcare workers. After conducting focus groups with healthcare professionals involved in treatment of people at risk of suicide, Søberg and colleagues (2018) saw no clear connection between the professionals’ understanding of existential issues and the practical implementation thereof. They conclude that competencies regarding existential matters ought to be strengthened, such as through mandatory courses in healthcare education. With regard to caring professions, Camilla Udo (2014) writes that

> caring is a process with no fixed answers, there is a need for continuous reflective discussions, in addition to education and training, to

> inspire a common philosophy and development of skills which will enable nurses to provide high-quality care and address the uniquely personal and intimate existential issues.
>
> (p. 352)

This is a high level of ambition and a source of anxiety for many care workers. Although experienced as rewarding and fulfilling, many report the challenge they perceive when realising that they cannot relieve patients' spiritual or existential anguish (Tornøe, Danbolt, Kvigne, & Sørlie, 2015a). This can even result in moral distress, grief and burnout among care workers (Tornøe, Danbolt, Kvigne, & Sørlie, 2014). Education in dealing with existential problems in the healthcare system is therefore highly necessary. An exemplary initiative is Norway's mobile spiritual and existential care teaching team, whose members, expert hospice nurses with several years' experience as clinical supervisors in end-of-life care, teach care workers to identify spiritual and existential suffering, initiate appropriate conversations and convey consolation through "active presencing" and silence (Tornøe, Danbolt, Kvigne, & Sørlie, 2015b).

Beyond educational initiatives, numerous existential interventions have been developed. Among those that focus on meaning in life, several have been subjected to rigorous validation studies and proven their worth. A large part of these has been designed for cancer patients or for palliative contexts, but some newer developments can be used in the treatment of depression and dementia or also in rehabilitation and in nursing homes. In the following, life-review procedures are described first, followed by individual and group therapeutic interventions.

12.1 Gaining meaning from a meta-perspective – life reviews

Life reviews are used mostly in palliative settings. They can counteract mental suffering, despair and loss of meaning in terminally ill and dying people. However, there is no reason why they should not be used for healthy and younger people, since a review of life can be experienced as a clarifying and integrating process at every point of life.

12.1.1 Functions of life stories

By looking back at our lives from a meta-perspective, we become aware of our identity – not only at the end, but at different times in our lives. The term "identity" is instructive: It comes from the Latin word *idem*, which means "same." Identity thus stands for being the same, across different situations and phases of life, in inner self-perception and in outer expression. But we change, develop and experiment over the course of our lives, and this can complicate the perception of "sameness," or identity. A retrospective view of life can be of much help in this regard; it allows for putting different appearances and events in a meaningful order. This works best in the form of a story, as narrative psychology has proven (Bruner, 1990; McAdams, 1993, 2001).

A story is characterised by a beginning, a middle and an end. The same applies to a life story. It explains us to ourselves and creates meaning and identity by relating the now to the past and the future: Where do I come from? What difficult, exciting or beautiful things have I experienced in life? What have I achieved and mastered? What have I failed at? What goals and ideas of the future do I have? Through the narrative form a connection is established – coherence is created, a central feature of meaningfulness (Section 2.3.2).

In fact, such a story is not a chronological retelling of life but an innovation that arises at the moment of telling it. It is not about reproducing one's own life in detail and correctly. Rather, life stories are based on a narrative truth that should appear coherent, consistent and convincing in itself (McLean et al., 2007; Schnell, 2004/2009). If this succeeds, our life takes on a meaningful form before our eyes. "To tell *how* things came into existence is to explain them and at the same time indirectly to answer another question: *Why* did they come into existence?" (Eliade, 1959, p. 97).

The verbalisation of our life story brings to mind basic assumptions about ourselves and the world. As long as they are unconscious, they are powerful; they direct and control our experience. Expressing them can help to uncover dysfunctional beliefs that prevent us from taking a constructive and accepting view of our own life. In such cases, raising awareness is of great advantage, since only in this way is it possible to check and possibly relativise these assumptions. By adopting alternative perspectives and explanatory patterns, a constructive reinterpretation (reframing) can succeed.

While all life-review procedures refer to the cohesive and thus meaning-making power of the life story, the uncovering of dysfunctional structures is aspired only by some. In the following, two short-term and two longer-term forms of life-review interventions are presented in more detail.

12.1.2 Short-term life reviews

The following interventions can be carried out over one or two sessions. There is no need for a long-term commitment, which is helpful in some palliative settings and in outpatient or other short-term treatments.

12.1.2.1 Dignity therapy

Dignity therapy (DT) (Chochinov et al., 2005) is an individualised short-term therapy developed with the aim of counteracting a loss of dignity at the end of life. Palliative patients often complain of such a loss of dignity. On an empirical basis, Chochinov and colleagues developed a model of dignity that includes the following three dimensions:

1 *Illness-related concerns*: preserving the highest possible degree of independence and limiting the burden of symptoms.
2 *Social dignity*: safeguarding privacy, social support and respectful care.
3 *Personal dignity-preserving repertoire*: dignity-preserving perspectives (continuity of self, maintenance of roles, generativity/legacy, self-esteem, hope, autonomy/control, acceptance and fighting spirit) and actions (living in the moment, maintaining normality, seeking spiritual support).

Respecting all three dimensions helps to maintain or strengthen the dignity of terminally ill and dying people. DT focuses on the dimension of the personal dignity repertoire. It is a life review in which a conversation is guided by a set of nine questions. The conversation is intended to create an awareness of the meaningfulness of one's own life and thereby reduce mental suffering (Chochinov et al., 2005). The questions aim to identify issues that are particularly close to the dying person's heart and characteristics or events that the patient wishes to remember.

The following are some sample questions (Chochinov, 2002, p. 2258):

- "When did you feel most alive?"
- "Are there particular things that you feel still need to be said to your loved ones or things that you would want to take the time to say once again?"
- "Are there words or perhaps even instructions that you would like to offer your family in order to provide them with comfort or solace?"

Conversation on these issues should last up to two one-hour sessions. It is recorded and transcribed by using an audio device. The therapist then creates a revised version that puts what has been said into a chronological structure. In addition, content that could injure others is eliminated after consultation with the patient, and an appropriate final passage is selected. The document is read out in full to the patient in a concluding session and then handed over. Depending on the patient's wishes, it can be shared with relatives or bequeathed to certain people as a legacy (Chochinov et al., 2005). In total, the intervention takes about five to six hours, excluding the time for interview transcription (Chochinov, 2012).

A randomised clinical trial compared DT with a life review without a final document/legacy and a control group (Vuksanovic, Green, Dyck, & Morrissey, 2017). Individuals who had participated in DT later reported increased generativity (caring for future generations, leaving traces) and ego integrity (accepting the life lived and the person you have become; no fear of death). Pure life review was not accompanied by such an increase. Accordingly, the authors conclude that the process of developing a legacy that goes beyond one's own death has specific advantages: It seems to strengthen a generative attitude and help people to perceive and accept their past life as meaningful. In a study at two German palliative care centres, the majority of patients (N = 18 of 19) and relatives (N = 24 of 26) confirmed the feasibility and acceptance of the method (Mai et al., 2018).

A systematic review of studies on the effectiveness of DT was presented by a research team in 2015 (Fitchett, Emanuel, Handzo, Boyken, & Wilkie, 2015). From a total of 25 publications, 17 articles, referring to 12 studies, reported high satisfaction of patients who had participated in the therapy. Patients stated that they and their relatives had benefited from the procedure. However, the findings were rather weak with regard to specific changes. There was no convincing evidence of an increase in meaningfulness, dignity or hope or of a reduction in psychological and physical symptoms.

Two later overview studies from 2017 could not report much improved findings. Marina Martínez and her team (2017) related that DT improved anxiety and depression in two cases. Moreover, in addition to the patients, relatives and healthcare staff have also been found to experience DT as positive and supportive in coping with the last phase of life. Brenda Bentley and colleagues (2017) confirmed that DT is well accepted in most instances. However, they emphasised that in many cases, the intervention is not effective, therapeutically appropriate or practical.

A Swedish-Australian research team (Lindqvist, Threlkeld, Street, & Tishelman, 2015) compiled a number of points of criticism that had become apparent during their implementation of DT. One of the questions that arose was who actually benefits from DT. Because the life review is conducted with a view to a potential legacy for family members, patients may find themselves in conflict over what to say and what they would be better off not saying. The cultural appropriateness of the guiding questions was also questioned. For some patients, the procedure had been too burdensome, because it provoked conflict but offered neither space nor support for resolving it. In addition, the procedure for editing the final document proved to be risky. The role of therapists, here, is inevitably an active one, which can lead to patients feeling that they are losing control over their own life story. The researchers concluded that while this specific procedure is problematic, they would continue to use life-review procedures, because they have great potential to strengthen the sense of meaning at the end of life.

The Bentley and colleagues review (2017) confirmed several of the criticisms mentioned by Lindqvist and colleagues. The authors noted, for instance, that the use of DT may be contraindicated in people with high levels of distress. If these result from social or economic problems or from physical symptoms and pain, addressing these issues would be more urgent than reflecting on concerns of dignity and meaning.

The practical implementation was criticised by several researchers too. All studies reported that the time required to implement DT was significantly longer than the five to six hours specified by Chochinov (see Bentley, Connor, Shaw, & Breen, 2017). Furthermore, Bentley and colleagues referred to several studies in which relatives reported negative experiences with DT. These entailed ensuing family conflicts, worries and problems that were perceived as making an already-difficult time even more difficult (see also Scarton et al., 2018).

Only recently did Chochinov and colleagues present *dignity talk*, a method designed to facilitate conversation between patients and family members (Guo, Chochinov, McClement, Thompson, & Hack, 2018). Dignity talk is reported to have emerged from the revision of DT's guiding questions.

Finally, it is worthwhile to again raise Bentley and colleagues' (2017) question of who benefits from DT and who should implement it. Staff in the palliative care sector have consistently assessed the implementation of DT positively. This is understandable given that in an area where generally little can be done, the intervention can generate a sense of doing something useful and meaningful. However, due to the lack of evidence of success in increasing the experience of dignity and meaning and in reducing depression and anxiety, it is necessary to reflect on whether it is not the staff who primarily benefit from DT and how potentially negative effects on patients relate to this. It is also necessary to consider the professionalism of the users. DT is carried out by psycho-oncologists, psychiatrists, students of various disciplines, nursing staff, social workers, pastoral workers, volunteers, psychologists, geriatric nursing staff and researchers. Guidelines defining necessary qualifications, skills and experience would certainly be advantageous (Bentley et al., 2017).

12.1.2.2 Short-term life review

Short-term life review is another life-review intervention that has already been validated. It is very similar to DT, but avoids some of the disadvantages mentioned earlier. A Japanese research group around the psychologist Michiyo Ando developed the intervention, which can be carried out in two sessions (Ando, Morita, Okamoto, & Ninosaka, 2008). The target group are cancer patients at the end of their lives who experience a loss of meaning, relationship problems or religious conflicts, often in addition to depression and anxiety (Ando et al., 2008). A question-guided life review is seen as a suitable intervention, because it gradually recalls earlier experiences, allows for a reassessment and thus makes it possible to resolve and integrate conflicts. This should increase meaningfulness and reduce psychological problems.

Seven guiding questions, some of which overlap with the questions of DT, steer the conversation. Patients are asked to name both good and bad memories that come to their mind. The following are some sample questions (Ando et al., 2008, p. 886f):

> "In your life, what was the event that or the person who affected you the most?"
> "What is the most important role in your life?"
> "What advice would you wish to pass on to the important people in your life or to a younger generation?"

The conversation is recorded and transcribed. Significant sentences and keywords are then transferred to an album. Both positive and negative statements are recorded. The album is brought to life by matching pictures and photos from books and magazines. In the second session, the therapist and patient look at the album together, and the patient is given the opportunity to re-evaluate, reframe and appreciate their life in this retrospective.

Unlike in DT, the album is not intended as a legacy for relatives. There is no pressure to convey a certain positive image of oneself. (The positive effect in terms of generativity and ego integrity that Vuksanovic and colleagues (2017) found for the legacy in DT is therefore not guaranteed here. However, it is certainly conceivable that clients of the short-term life review will also pass on their album if it seems reasonable to them). Ando's suggestion that both positive and negative memories are relevant and worth communicating seems to have additional clarifying potential. Facilitating re-evaluation in the second session and creating the possibility, at least to some extent, to deal with conflicts, are further advantages over DT.

Clinical studies provide clear indication of the procedure's effectiveness. A pilot study has shown improvements in meaningfulness, anxiety, depression, mental suffering and subjective well-being (Ando et al., 2008). In a subsequent randomised controlled trial, improvements were found in meaningfulness, hope and emotional distress. After the intervention, patients stated that they perceived their lives as positively completed, were prepared for death and did not experience themselves as a burden to their relatives. Improvements were shown in comparison to the initial measurement and in comparison to the control group (Ando, Morita, Akechi, Okamoto, & Japanese Task Force for Spiritual Care, 2010).

In this procedure too, the therapist's editorial influence on the final version of the written document is strong. This critique is somewhat weakened, however, by the fact that the document is introduced as a discussion template for a subsequent reconstruction and appreciation of the life story and not as a legacy. The therapist's editorial interference is thus unlikely to cause major problems. Finally, designing an album with supplementary photos is a complex and time-consuming task. Let's hope that both therapists and patients enjoy the creativity involved in this exercise.

12.1.3 Longer-term life reviews

The following interventions take place in multiple sessions over several weeks. Life reviews are at the core of all methods, but they are supplemented by further elaboration or reflection. While life-review therapy is conducted in one-on-one sessions, the other two (cognitive reminiscence therapy [CRT] and remembering yesterday, caring today [RYCT]) are group procedures.

12.1.3.1 Life-review therapy

Life-review therapy by Serrano and colleagues (2012) is based on autobiographical retrieval, focusing on childhood, adolescence, adulthood and summary. In each of four weekly individual sessions, one particular life period is discussed, guided by 14 questions that are designed to evoke specific positive memories. The following are some sample questions (Serrano et al., 2012, p. 227): "What did your mother or father do one day when you were a child that astonished you?" "Tell me about a day when you were an adolescent and you did something out of the ordinary."

"Tell me a time that you remember experiencing the most pride at work." Controlled randomised studies for this therapy (Serrano et al., 2012) and variations thereof (Korte, Bohlmeijer, Cappeliez, Smit, & Westerhof, 2012; Lamers, Bohlmeijer, Korte, & Westerhof, 2015) are available.

12.1.3.2 Cognitive reminiscence therapy (CRT)

In *cognitive reminiscence therapy* (CRT), by Watt and Cappeliez (2000), individuals are guided to two types of adaptive use of autobiographical memory: *Integrative reminiscence* is intended to enable reconciliation with negative events in the past, the perception of continuity across experiences and the perception of the meaningfulness of one's life (Wong, 1995). *Instrumental reminiscence* involves recollecting past coping and problem-solving experiences in order to improve self-efficacy and perceived control and to resort to past problem-solving experiences (Wong, 1995). In six weekly sessions of 90 minutes each, small groups (two to four people) meet to evoke memories on specific topics. These include family history, special achievements, important turning points, love and hate, stress experiences, life meaning and purpose. The integrative perspective encourages participants to process or accept past negative events and to recognise the past self in the present. The instrumental perspective focuses attention on successful problem-solving and goal attainment in the past and transfers these experiences to current problems. Controlled randomised studies are available (Hallford & Mellor, 2016a, 2016b).

12.1.3.3 Remembering yesterday, caring today (RYCT)

Remembering yesterday, caring today (RYCT) is a manualised intervention developed by the European Reminiscence Network (Schweitzer & Bruce, 2008) to support informal carers of dementia patients. In weekly groups, leaders and volunteers meet with people who have dementia, to explore patients' past and present through creative means. Drama, music and visual arts are used. Several controlled, randomised studies are available (Charlesworth et al., 2016; Orrell et al., 2017; Thorgrimsen, Schweitzer, & Orrell, 2002; Woods et al., 2016). Beautiful examples and suggestions can be found at www.storiedlives.institute/remembering-yesterday-caring-today [as of 01.02.2020].

12.1.4 Overview of the effectiveness of life reviews

In recent years, several reviews and meta-analyses on the effectiveness of life reviews have been published. In doing so, the authors also took various psychological disorders into consideration. Wang and colleagues (2017) reported improved quality of life, increased meaningfulness and reduced subjective suffering in advanced or terminal cancer. For patients with various types of life-threatening diseases, improvements in depression and an increase in quality of life and self-esteem were confirmed (Chen, Xiao, Yang, & Lan, 2017). Lan, Xiao, and Chen (2017) summarised studies that had conducted life reviews with people aged 60 and over (without cognitive impairment or dementia and not under psychotherapeutic treatment). The overview established evidence of significantly reduced depression and hopelessness and increased well-being. In older people who had depression, life-review procedures contributed to a reduction in symptoms; this was effective both in nursing homes residents and in community settings (Holvast, Massoudi, Voshaar, & Verhaak, 2017).

Two randomised clinical trials investigated the effectiveness of life reviews in young depressed adults (Hallford & Mellor, 2016a, 2016b). The authors observed reduced depressive symptoms and reduced anxiety. Moreover, meaning in life, self-esteem, self-efficacy and optimism were increased. Lamers and colleagues (2015) conducted a clinical study with adults aged 40 years and older who had moderate depressive symptoms. In contrast to other studies, the life review here was carried out as online-supported self-help. Again, depressive symptoms decreased and emotional and psychological well-being improved.

12.2 Meaning-oriented psychotherapy

Apart from life reviews, several other methods can be used to strengthen meaning in life. Numerous reviews (Guerrero-Torrelles, Monforte-Royo, Rodríguez-Prat, Porta-Sales, & Balaguer, 2017; Keall, Clayton, & Butow, 2015; LeMay & Wilson, 2008; Teo, Krishnan, & Lee, 2019) and meta-analyses (Park et al., 2019; Vos, Craig, & Cooper, 2015) have examined the effectiveness of different meaning-oriented therapies. In the following, some interventions that have already proven empirically effective are presented in more detail.

12.2.1 The SoMe-Card Method

The SoMe-Card Method (la Cour & Schnell, 2019, 2020) presented in Section 3.3 is an instrument to identify and explore personal sources of meaning. It can be used for diagnostic purposes but also represents an intervention. Through a guided exploration of a comprehensive inventory of sources of meaning, clients are supported in discovering their personal ultimate concerns and what place these occupy in their lives.

The intervention can be applied in a variety of areas, such as counselling, therapy, coaching, education and palliative care.

The card method can be completed within an hour. The client receives a set of 26 cards on which statements about the 26 sources of meaning are printed. These are sorted until a maximum of five cards have been selected as particularly relevant. The multiple sorting process is designed to support slow, step-by-step processing. In most cases, after a first reading, clients feel overwhelmed by the multitude of statements and the emotions that are awakened by them (flooding). In the second step, the statements are already known, and clients can concentrate on developing their position in this respect (structuring). In the third step, clients have a good overview and can concentrate on the relative importance of the cards (prioritising).

Next, a semi-structured conversation on the selected sources of meaning follows. It focuses on the respective card's interpretation, meaning, importance, threat and potential for change. Optionally, the backsides of the cards can be used to introduce a meta-level by naming the corresponding sources and dimensions of meaning and to clarify the balance of personal sources of meaning: According to our study results, meaningfulness is at its highest when at least three of the five dimensions of meaning (vertical selftranscendence; horizontal selftranscendence; selfactualisation; order; and well-being and relatedness) are realised in a person's life (see Section 6.2.2; Schnell, 2011).

During the conversation, the administrator takes notes of the chosen statements and essential considerations uttered by the client, especially with regard to possible changes and actions. Finally, the notes are handed over to the client in a standardised format.

As a short-term intervention, the SoMe-Card Method can be integrated into a wide variety of settings and forms of therapy. Ideally, there should be an opportunity to further discuss the insights gained through the conversation at a later date, particularly with regard to practical applications (Böhmer, 2017; Böhmer, la Cour, & Schnell, under review). We recommend that only professionals with sufficient competence in counselling, coaching or therapy use the method. Its implementation should take place in a protected and professional environment.

So far, three feasibility studies and a randomised controlled trial have been carried out on the effectiveness of the procedure. In a feasibility study involving 47 adults (primarily healthcare workers; Schnell & la Cour, 2018), 11 percent rated the procedure as moderately worthwhile (a 2 or a 3 out of 0–5 points); 17 percent rated it as very worthwhile (4 points); and 72 percent rated it as extremely worthwhile (5 out of

5 points). The method was found to be helpful ("My most important priorities in life were summarised in a few words on the cards. This creates clarity." "A good exercise that puts into words something that is not usually talked about."). Concentrating on a maximum of five cards was experienced as an important challenge ("It was hard to choose, but I was forced to – and that was good!"). Many participants reported positive impulses for the future ("I now know which first step I have to take to make change possible." "I have gained the courage to change my situation.").

We conducted a randomised controlled study (Böhmer et al., under review) with 42 chronic pain patients. Twenty-one of these received the intervention, while the others were put on a waiting list (and participated later on). Following the intervention, participants reported less anxiety, depression and crisis of meaning and higher pain acceptance. Increased pain acceptance and reduced anxiety were still present after two months; in addition, pain medication had decreased. In the control group, no improvements were observed.

Of the 21 chronic pain patients who participated in the intervention, 10 percent rated the procedure as moderately worthwhile, 28 percent as very worthwhile; and 62 percent as extremely worthwhile. Patients experienced the interview as "intense, exhausting, enriching" and as

> very interesting and also very easy to understand. The application of the cards and what they are used for seems well conceived. . . . I have never felt uncomfortable. This is not always the case when it comes to 'me.' Time has passed incredibly fast. The conversation was good and very informative.

Throughout, the participants experienced the method as a key to a complex, often ineffable dimension of human existence.

An abridged version of the card method was designed for use in palliative contexts. It aims to keep the cognitive burden on conversation partners as low as possible (Struer-Tranberg, 2019). A qualitative study with eight palliative patients confirmed its feasibility (Struer-Tranberg, 2019). Eighty-eight percent stated that the procedure enabled them to verbalise what was important to them. Seventy-five percent were inspired to act accordingly. Sixty-three percent found the procedure worthwhile. Nobody stated the opposite. Four participants reported that they learned more about themselves and their sources of meaning through the interview, and three of the other four reported that they had already achieved a high level of self-knowledge. Further feedback confirmed the usefulness of the procedure (important awareness, new view of the self, restructuring, conversation free of distortions and prejudice by those conducting it, natural and effortless).

The SoMe-Card Method enables the identification and exploration of personal sources of meaning; integrating gained insights is the responsibility of the users in further sessions. Critical situations might arise if administrators lack expertise to deal with existential questions raised by the intervention. In Denmark, therefore, training courses on the use of the card method are offered, and licences are granted (www.somecam.org).

12.2.2 Meaning-making intervention (MMi)

As a nursing scientist, Virginia Lee has often experienced how stressful a cancer diagnosis can be for those affected – both emotionally and physically. Frequently, also existential distress occurs when patients are confronted with the prospect of early death. Therefore, Lee developed an intervention for the time shortly after the cancer diagnosis, to support patients who are in danger of losing orientation and who accordingly experience a loss of meaning (Lee, 2004).

The intervention, called meaning-making intervention (MMi), can take place at the patient's home or in hospital. It consists of one to four sessions, lasting 30 to 90 minutes. (Flexibility should be maintained with regard to the patients' psychological and physical needs and capacities). MMi is a manualised procedure that has three primary objectives (Henry et al., 2010):

1 Reviewing the meaning and impact of the cancer diagnosis for the present.
2 Exploring past significant life events and identifying successful coping strategies as related to the present experience.
3 Discussing current priorities and new goals that can create meaning in the current situation, taking into account the limitations caused by cancer.

The three objectives relate to the recognition of the present, a reflection on the past and an orientation towards the future. Patients are asked to narrate these three perspectives by using a lifeline, drawn as a simple horizontal line on a sheet of paper. The therapist asks patients to imagine that the left pole signifies their birth and the right pole the end of their physical life. The patients' task is then to mark their present position by a circle on the line. They are invited to tell their stories from the diagnosis of cancer to the current situation. Questions relating to symptoms, feelings, thoughts and so on can stimulate a deepening involvement.

To place the cancer disease in a biographical context of life events already mastered, patients are then asked to mark earlier turning points in their lives on the lifeline. The therapist encourages them to work out the strengths and coping strategies that were helpful in these situations.

The third task is to develop a fulfilling vision of the future. Life goals and sources of meaning are rearranged. Given the current situation, short-term and longer-term goals and related activities are identified and drawn on the right side of the lifeline (Henry et al., 2010; Lee, Cohen, Edgar, Laizner, & Gagnon, 2006a, 2006b).

The effectiveness of MMi has been evaluated with promising results. In a randomised controlled trial, patients reported higher meaningfulness one and three months after the MMi than before, whereas no such effect was found in the control group (Henry et al., 2010). In previous studies, increases in self-esteem, optimism and self-efficacy had been established (Lee et al., 2006a, 2006b). Patients consistently reported high acceptance of the procedure, considered it helpful and stated that they would recommend it to others who had a cancer diagnosis (Henry et al., 2010).

Henry and colleagues reported an actual duration of the conversations of 75 to 120 minutes, which is not in accordance with the manual. However, anyone who has ever worked with the narrative method knows about the difficulty in limiting a conversation once the "narrative flow" has started. Given the existential importance of the MMi topics, it is realistic to plan at least one and a half hours per conversation, from the outset.

12.2.3 Outlook – a preparation and life completion intervention

Outlook is an intervention for use in palliative care. The American authors criticise the fact that in terminal care, the control of symptoms and pain is given high priority, whereas the psychosocial and spiritual dimensions of experience are not sufficiently taken into account (Steinhauser et al., 2008). This can be for many reasons, including a lack of time, inadequate training of medical and nursing staff and the staff's fear of confronting their own vulnerability (Keall, Butow, Steinhauser, & Clayton, 2011). For some patients, ignoring these dimensions means that they are overburdened with the preparation of their approaching death, which can be accompanied by despair and the desire for hastened death (Breitbart et al., 2015).

Outlook is a manualised procedure that allows for a guided processing of existential topics. It consists of three individual sessions of about one hour each, which are carried out in one-week intervals. The first session includes a life review; the second session deals with the topic of forgiveness; and the third session addresses the question of legacy. Each session is guided by a number of thematically relevant questions. The following are some sample questions for a life review (Keall, Butow, Steinhauser, & Clayton, 2013):

"What are cherished times?"
"Of what are you most proud?"
"If someone were to make a movie of your life, what would be important to include?"

The second topic, forgiveness, is related to past actions (or non-actions), with questions such as the following:

- "If you were to do things again, what might you do differently?"
- "Are there things or times that you regret?"
- "Is there anyone to whom you would like to offer forgiveness?"

The third session, which deals with what to leave behind, is guided by questions such as the following:

- "What would you like to share with future generations?"
- "What are the most valuable lessons that you learned?"
- "If you could choose one thing to pass on as your legacy, what would that be?"

The effectiveness of the intervention has been tested in three studies. In a first randomised controlled trial, there was a trend towards improvements in functional status, anxiety, depression and preparation for death, measured one week and two weeks after the intervention. No comparable changes were observed in two control groups. However, because of the small sample size, no significant changes were observed (Steinhauser et al., 2008). A later qualitative evaluation of the procedure, which was conducted in an Australian context, concluded that eight of the ten participants considered the intervention helpful and that nine out of ten would recommend it to others. Seven of the ten indicated that they were supported by the procedure in reflecting on their lives (Keall et al., 2011). In this Australian study, the three sessions were recorded with an audio device. At the end, the recording was offered to the participants. Interestingly, only four of the ten people accepted the offer, and only one person, a man, reported that he enjoyed listening to the recording with his family. A randomised controlled trial in 2017 (Steinhauser et al., 2017) compared outlook with relaxing meditation and the usual course of treatment. In the first follow-up survey after five weeks, patients who had participated in outlook appeared to be slightly better prepared for death than those who had been treated as usual, but this effect did not last. Otherwise, outlook did not bring about any positive changes in meaningfulness, depression and anxiety, and the method did not prove to be more effective than relaxing meditation.

As has also been noted with regard to life-review procedures, it is not clear for whom this intervention is suitable. Steinhauser and colleagues (2008) stated that 61 percent of the patients in question refused to participate. An explicit preoccupation with death, as also envisaged in outlook, is an unreasonable burden for many people, which they do not want to face (Perry, 2015). What is even more serious, however, is that the only sufficiently large clinical trial to date has not provided any indication of the procedure's effectiveness.

12.2.4 Managing cancer and living meaningfully (CALM)

A Canadian research group led by Gary Rodin, Sarah Hales and Christopher Lo sees a particular difficulty in the fact that many cancer patients have to cope with a "double consciousness": the knowledge of physical decay and imminent death on the one hand and the task of living until then and making this remaining life meaningful on the other (Lo et al., 2013). The researchers thus developed managing cancer and living meaningfully (CALM), a manualised procedure that aims to reduce mental suffering in people with metastatic cancer. At the same time, psychological well-being and growth should be promoted.

CALM consists of three to eight individual sessions of 60 minutes each, over a period of up to half a year. The primary caregiver is invited to participate in one or more sessions if the patient agrees. Compared to other procedures, CALM is a comprehensive programme in that it combines existential and practical concerns that come to the fore as the disease progresses. The following four areas are addressed:

1 Symptom management and communication with healthcare providers.

2 Changes in the self and relationships with close others.
3 Spiritual well-being and meaningful values and commitments.
4 Preparation for the future and dealing with mortality.

The most important element of CALM is the relationship between therapist and patient. It is characterised by openness, empathy and authenticity. Fluctuations in the patient's physical and mental state are flexibly addressed. In the course of the joint discussions, patients are supported to regulate their feelings to an appropriate degree, to deal with conflicts of dependence and attachment and to become aware that hopelessness or discouragement are not inevitable but changeable mental constructs (Hales, Lo, & Rodin, 2015).

Together, patient and therapist strive to understand the disease, explore ways to control symptoms and make informed decisions about possible treatments. The continuity of the therapeutic relationship allows for the maintenance of the self, which is increasingly stripped of its roles and identity by the limitations imposed by the disease. Difficult questions regarding existing relationships, family ties and children are discussed.

Patients are further invited to tell their life story in order to maintain or recreate a sense of meaning. Joint reframing and co-construction help to achieve a sense of coherence and completion of life. Current priorities and future goals for the foreseeable future are worked out; implicit or explicit assumptions about the meaning of the disease are discussed. Last but not least, the focus is on acknowledging the fear of dying and death while maintaining a balance between living and dying. Patients are given the opportunity to discuss specific points concerning the dying process, the end of life, burial arrangements and inheritance matters (Hales et al., 2015).

The authors stress that CALM is suitable for patients who have sufficient interest and capacity for self-reflection. Also, a certain degree of physical and cognitive functioning is needed to actively participate in the sessions. The authors also emphasise that the intervention is not suitable for patients who only wish to "think positively"; the programme requires a willingness to deal with experiences of loss and approaching death (Hales et al., 2015).

Clinical studies have shown CALM to reduce depressive symptoms (Lo et al., 2013, 2019; Rodin et al., 2018). However, the intervention did not show robust effects on dealing with one's own mortality, spiritual well-being and other aspects of quality of life. Although the focus of the procedure is on a meaningful life, the experience of meaningfulness was not assessed.

CALM is a comprehensive concept that combines practical medical counselling with the treatment of psychological and existential problems. Nevertheless, with three to eight sessions over several months, the procedure is not excessively time-consuming and can be flexibly adapted to the situation and needs of the patients. It is critical to note, though, that despite the comprehensive approach, the procedure apparently has no measurable effects beyond a reduction in depression. This could also be achieved with less-time-consuming instruments.

12.2.5 Meaning-centred psychotherapy

For almost 20 years, researchers around William Breitbart at the Memorial Sloan Kettering Cancer Center in New York have been working on meaning-centred psychotherapy and subjected it to multiple evaluations (Greenstein & Breitbart, 2000; Breitbart et al., 2010, 2012, 2015). The procedure is based on the principles of Frankl's logotherapy and adapts some of the methods suggested there. Its aim is to support people who have advanced cancer in maintaining their meaning in life and thus limit mental suffering and despair.

The interventions were designed both as group and individual therapies. Meaning-centred group therapy takes place in eight weekly sessions of 90 minutes each. Three methods are combined to uncover potential sources of meaning (Greenstein & Breitbart, 2000):

1 Didactic presentations of the philosophical foundations on which the method is based.
2 Experiential exercises and homework.
3 Discussions related to meaning and advanced cancer.

Participants are encouraged to read Frankl's texts before the first session begins; in particular, the book *Man's Search for Meaning* (Frankl, 1985) is recommended.

The intervention combines a didactic approach and an experiential approach. Furthermore, the group setting encourages each group member to assume responsibility for the others, by supporting them in discovering personally relevant sources of meaning. An altruistic aspect thus comes into play, which adds to the meaning-making impact (Greenstein & Breitbart, 2000).

A first randomised controlled study (Breitbart et al., 2010) showed that meaningfulness and spiritual well-being increased significantly after subjects participated in meaning-centred group therapy. After two months, the effects were still present; they had increased even further. In the control group, engaging in supportive group therapy as usual, no changes were observed. Contrary to expectations, meaning-centred psychotherapy did not result in reduced depressive symptoms. A decrease in the desire for hastened death and anxiety became apparent only in the follow-up after two months. In 2015, a randomised controlled trial (Breitbart et al., 2015) showed meaning-centred group therapy to be associated with significantly greater changes than the control group, a supportive group therapy, was. Improvements appeared in quality of life, spiritual well-being, depression, hopelessness, desire for hastened death and physical symptoms. For reasons not mentioned, meaning in life was not assessed in this study.

As the authors themselves critically note, a group intervention for patients with advanced cancer is associated with some problems. Fluctuations in health and well-being can lead to individual sessions being missed. In general, the intervention cannot be adapted to the course of the disease, but it is carried out according to a predetermined schedule. Breitbart and colleagues therefore adapted meaning-centred psychotherapy to an individual therapy setting. In a randomised controlled study in 2012 (Breitbart et al., 2012), improvements in meaningfulness, spiritual well-being, general quality of life and physical symptoms were observed immediately after the intervention. They exceeded the improvements found in the control group (therapeutic massage). Surprisingly, however, two months later, no differences between the two groups were to be found. Another randomised controlled trial on the effectiveness of individual meaning-centred therapy among patients with advanced cancer in 2018 (Breitbart et al., 2018) provided support for its efficacy as a treatment for psychological and existential distress. In this regard, the meaning-oriented intervention exceeded the results of usual care (small to moderate effects) and supportive group psychotherapy (modest effects).

Moreover, Breitbart and colleagues further adapted the method to use it with cancer survivors. Besides changing the theme “a good and meaningful death” to “continuing with life despite limitations,” a short mindfulness exercise was integrated into the adapted programme. In a randomised controlled study (van der Spek et al., 2017), immediately after treatment, meaning-centred group therapy resulted in significantly higher improvements in comparison to treatment as usual with regard to personal meaning, goal-orientedness, positive relations, purpose in life and fighting spirit; however, these effects were not stable. Six months after the treatment, though, participants in the meaning-centred group showed lower distress and depression scores. When compared to a non-meaning-centred group therapy, the intervention resulted in higher personal growth three months later and higher environmental mastery six months later.

12.2.6 Logotherapy

Logotherapy is the earliest meaning-centred psychotherapy. It was developed by Viktor Frankl in the 1930s. Generally referred to as logotherapy and existential analysis, this Third Viennese School of Psychotherapy (after Freud and Adler) assumes that human beings are motivated primarily by a search for meaning. According to Frankl, frustrating feelings of meaninglessness and worthlessness arise if this will to meaning cannot be brought to bear on everyday life.

The term *logotherapy* includes the Greek word *logos*, which can be translated as "reason" or "meaning." Frankl emphasised the spirit-oriented dimension of being human, which is often ignored in psychotherapy. By using the term "existential analysis," Frankl established a relationship to existential philosophy, which had a strong influence on his work. He adopted several concepts from the philosophy of Max Scheler, who posited that human beings, unlike animals, have the possibility to self-distance. From this follows freedom of self-determination – a special status held by human beings. This can result in existential uprooting, but it also offers the opportunity to live in accordance with our own values (Scheler, 1928).

Logotherapy and existential analysis take place in therapeutic and counselling settings (e.g. Längle & Bürgi, 2011; Riedel, Deckart, & Noyon, 2015; Schlieper-Damrich & Kipfelsberger, 2008) and in meaning-centred educational activity (Schechner & Zürner, 2013). Individual settings typically employ Socratic dialogue in order to support clients in gaining insight into their own situation. The aim is to recognise and realise the "meaning of the moment." Additionally, various other methods are applied, such as education, paradoxical intention, imagination, de-reflection, humour, enneagram and attitude modulation (Biller & de Lourdes Stiegeler, 2008). Riemeyer (2007) stresses that logotherapy is "completely open to other helpful methods and therapies" (p. 151). He emphasises that Frankl has called for individualisation from person to person and improvisation from hour to hour.

Empirical studies on the effectiveness of logotherapy and existential analysis that satisfy generally accepted scientific criteria hardly exist. In a meta-analysis of clinical studies on existential therapies, with an explicit search for logotherapeutic procedures, Vos et al. (2015) found only two – rather old – randomised controlled trials that investigated logotherapeutic interventions. Both were conducted about 40 years ago and had a sample size of N = 37 (Starck, 1981) and N = 20 (Zuehlke & Watkins, 1977). Currently, there is a slight increase in empirical studies on the effectiveness of logotherapy. These originate mainly from Iranian research institutes, but they have not yet appeared in psychological journals that meet the standards of scientific quality.

In view of the widespread use of logotherapy, the lack of clinical studies – especially in Western countries – should be viewed critically. Casuistics and anecdotal case descriptions have their place in the "creative development phase" of novel interventions, as Krampen and colleagues (Krampen, Schui, & Wiesenhütter, 2008, p. 50) emphasise. Subsequently, however, empirically valid findings need to be made available. A focus on the preservation of Frankl's doctrine (see Logotherapie und Existenzanalyse, 2019), as represented by many logotherapeutic institutes and training centres (personal communication), contradicts a scientific stance and prevents critical examination and further development.

With regard to Frankl's "doctrine," a number of substantial points can be questioned or criticised. For example, it has been shown (Chapter 9) that the assumption of a universal, primary will to meaning is not empirically tenable (Schnell, 2010). A significant proportion of the population lives without meaning in life but does not suffer as a result. Depending on the person and phase of life, the question of meaning can be of greater or lesser relevance (see also Cooper, 2016). As early as 1980, Irvin Yalom put forward the thesis that the primacy of meaning is not universal but rather a Western myth, a cultural artefact.

Moreover, the metaphysics underlying logotherapy can be viewed critically, since Frankl postulated the existence of "objective meaning." Several authors pointed out the undisclosed contradictions in Frankl's theory, arising from this ontological assumption (Landau, 2017; Pytell, 2006; Reitinger, 2015; Yalom, 2010); some even speak of a "religious" basis of the logotherapeutic approach (May, 1961; Yalom, 2010). A presupposition of objective meaning contradicts the subjectivity of meaning, which existential thinkers such as Kierkegaard, Heidegger, Binswanger, Sartre, May and Yalom have emphasised (see also the definition of meaning in Chapter 2). Frankl's assertion of objective meaning and his directive style of communication, as criticised for example by Cooper (2016), May (1961) and Yalom (2010), are also in opposition with much of contemporary psychotherapy.

In addition to the interventions described in this chapter, there are a number of other approaches that aim to strengthen meaning in life or

Figure 12.1 Life-review exercise: my life as a book

overcome crises of meaning. These are so-called supportive-expressive therapies and experiential existential therapies. The aforementioned meta-analysis by Vos and colleagues (2015) concluded that these types of therapies yielded no or only minor effects; therefore, they will not be presented here. Interested readers are referred to Classen and colleagues (2008), Kissane and colleagues (2007) and Barren (2005).

12.3 Know thyself!

SELF-EXPLORATION: MY LIFE AS A BOOK

The following exercise can serve as a helpful entry to a life review, supplemented by a future perspective (cf. Schnell, 2004/2009):

Think of your life as a book. Divide it into several chapters, and assign titles to them. You are free to choose the number of chapters (ideally, there should be no fewer than three and no more than seven). It is useful to draw an arrow as a timeline or lifeline for this purpose (Figure 12.1).

12.4 Literature

Agledahl, K. M., Gulbrandsen, P., Førde, R., & Wifstad, Å. (2011). Courteous but not curious: How doctors' politeness masks their existential neglect. A qualitative study of video-recorded patient consultations. *Journal of Medical Ethics, 37*(11), 650–654.

Ando, M., Morita, T., Akechi, T., Okamoto, T., & Japanese Task Force for Spiritual Care. (2010). Efficacy of short-term life-review interviews on the spiritual well-being of terminally ill cancer patients. *Journal of Pain and Symptom Management, 39*(6), 993–1002.

Ando, M., Morita, T., Okamoto, T., & Ninosaka, Y. (2008). One-week short-term life review interview can improve spiritual well-being of terminally ill cancer patients. *Psycho-Oncology, 17*(9), 885–890.

Barren, J. R. (2005). Use of existential-phenomenological counseling for police officers. *Policing: An International Journal of Police Strategies & Management, 28*, 255–268.

Bentley, B., O'Connor, M., Shaw, J., & Breen, L. (2017). A narrative review of dignity therapy research. *Australian Psychologist, 52*(5), 354–362.

Biller, K., & de Lourdes Stiegeler, M. (2008). *Wörterbuch der Logotherapie und Existenzanalyse von Viktor Emil Frankl*. Wien: Böhlau.

Böhmer, M. (2017). *Sinnerfüllung bei chronischen Schmerzpatienten: Durchführung einer sinnorientierten Intervention anhand der Sources of Meaning Card Method* (Unpublished Master thesis), University of Innsbruck, Innsbruck.

Böhmer, M., la Cour, P., & Schnell, T. (under review). *Randomized controlled trial of the sources of meaning card method: A new meaning-oriented approach predicts depression, anxiety, pain acceptance, and crisis of meaning in chronic pain patients*.

Breitbart, W., Pessin, H., Rosenfeld, B., Applebaum, A. J., Lichtenthal, W. G., Li, Y., . . . Fenn, N. (2018). Individual meaning-centered psychotherapy for the treatment of psychological and existential distress: A randomized controlled trial in patients with advanced cancer. *Cancer*, *124*(15), 3231–3239.

Breitbart, W., Poppito, S., Rosenfeld, B., Vickers, A. J., Li, Y., Abbey, J., & Cassileth, B. R. (2012). Pilot randomized controlled trial of individual meaning-centered psychotherapy for patients with advanced cancer. *Journal of Clinical Oncology*, *30*(12), 1304–1309.

Breitbart, W., Rosenfeld, B., Gibson, C., Pessin, H., Poppito, S., Nelson, C., & Olden, M. (2010). Meaning-centered group psychotherapy for patients with advanced cancer: A pilot randomized controlled trial. *Psycho-Oncology*, *19*(1), 21–28.

Breitbart, W., Rosenfeld, B., Pessin, H., Applebaum, A., Kulikowski, J., & Lichtenthal, W. G. (2015). Meaning-centered group psychotherapy: An effective intervention for improving psychological well-being in patients with advanced cancer. *Journal of Clinical Oncology*, *33*(7), 749–754.

Bruner, J. (1990). *Acts of meaning*. Cambridge, MA: Harvard University Press.

Charlesworth, G., Burnell, K., Crellin, N., Hoare, Z., Hoe, J., Knapp, M., Russell, I., . . . Orrell, M. (2016). Peer support and reminiscence therapy for people with dementia and their family carers: A factorial pragmatic randomised trial. *Journal of Neurology, Neurosurgery & Psychiatry*, *87*(11), 1218–1229.

Chen, Y., Xiao, H., Yang, Y., & Lan, X. (2017). The effects of life review on psycho-spiritual well-being among patients with life-threatening illness: A systematic review and meta-analysis. *Journal of Advanced Nursing*, *73*(7), 1539–1554.

Chochinov, H. M. (2002). Dignity-conserving care – a new model for palliative care: Helping the patient feel valued. *Journal of the American Medical Association*, *287*(17), 2253–2260.

Chochinov, H. M. (2012). *Dignity therapy. Final words for final days*. New York: Oxford University Press.

Chochinov, H. M., Hack, T., Hassard, T., Kristjanson, L. J., McClement, S., & Harlos, M. (2005). Dignity therapy: A novel psychotherapeutic intervention for patients near the end of life. *Journal of Clinical Oncology*, *23*(24), 5520–5525.

Classen, C. C., Kraemer, H. C., Blasey, C., Giese-Davis, J., Koopman, C., Palesh, O. G., & Spiegel, D. (2008). Supportive-expressive group therapy for primary breast cancer patients: A randomized prospective multicenter trial. *Psycho-Oncology, 17*, 438–447.

Cooper, M. (2016). *Existential therapies*. London: Sage.

Eliade, M. (1959). *The sacred and the profane: The nature of religion*. New York: Harcourt Brace.

Fitchett, G., Emanuel, L., Handzo, G., Boyken, L., & Wilkie, D. J. (2015). Care of the human spirit and the role of dignity therapy: A systematic review of dignity therapy research. *BMC Palliative Care, 14*(1), 8.

Frankl, V. E. (1985). *Man's search for meaning*. New York: Simon & Schuster.

Greenstein, M., & Breitbart, W. (2000). Cancer and the experience of meaning: A group psychotherapy program for people with cancer. *American Journal of Psychotherapy, 54*(4), 486–500.

Guerrero-Torrelles, M., Monforte-Royo, C., Rodríguez-Prat, A., Porta-Sales, J., & Balaguer, A. (2017). Understanding meaning in life interventions in patients with advanced disease: A systematic review and realist synthesis. *Palliative Medicine, 31*(9), 798–813.

Guo, Q., Chochinov, H. M., McClement, S., Thompson, G., & Hack, T. (2018). Development and evaluation of the dignity talk question framework for palliative patients and their families: A mixed-methods study. *Palliative Medicine, 32*(1), 195–205.

Hales, S., Lo, C., & Rodin, G. (2015). Managing cancer and living meaningfully (CALM) therapy. In J. C. Holland, W. S. Breitbart, P. N. Butow, P. B. Jacobsen, M. J. Loscalzo, & R. McCorkle (Eds.), *Psycho-oncology* (3rd ed., pp. 487–491). New York: Oxford University Press.

Hallford, D. J., & Mellor, D. (2016a). Autobiographical memory-based intervention for depressive symptoms in young adults: A randomized controlled trial of cognitive-reminiscence therapy. *Psychotherapy and Psychosomatics, 85*(4), 246–249.

Hallford, D. J., & Mellor, D. (2016b). Brief reminiscence activities improve state well-being and self-concept in young adults: A randomised controlled experiment. *Memory, 24*(10), 1311–1320.

Halperin, E. C. (2010). Preserving the humanities in medical education. *Medical Teacher, 32*(1), 76–79.

Henry, M., Cohen, S. R., Lee, V., Sauthier, P., Provencher, D., Drouin, P., & Mayo, N. (2010). The meaning-making intervention (MMi) appears to increase meaning in life in advanced ovarian cancer: A randomized controlled pilot study. *Psycho-Oncology, 19*(12), 1340–1347.

Holvast, F., Massoudi, B., Voshaar, R. C. O., & Verhaak, P. F. (2017). Non-pharmacological treatment for depressed older patients in primary care: A systematic review and meta-analysis. *PLoS One, 12*(9), e0184666.

Keall, R. M., Butow, P. N., Steinhauser, K. E., & Clayton, J. M. (2011). Discussing life story, forgiveness, heritage, and legacy with patients with life-limiting illnesses. *International Journal of Palliative Nursing, 17*(9), 454–460.

Keall, R. M., Butow, P. N., Steinhauser, K. E., & Clayton, J. M. (2013). Nurse-facilitated preparation and life completion interventions are acceptable and feasible in the Australian palliative care setting: Results from a phase 2 trial. *Cancer Nursing, 36*(3), E39–E46.

Keall, R. M., Clayton, J. M., & Butow, P. N. (2015). Therapeutic life review in palliative care: A systematic review of quantitative evaluations. *Journal of Pain and Symptom Management, 49*(4), 747–761.

Kissane, D. W., Grabsch, B., Clarke, D. M., Smith, G. C., Love, A. W., Bloch, S., & Li, Y. (2007). Supportive-expressive group therapy for women with metastatic breast cancer: Survival and psychosocial outcome from a randomized controlled trial. *Psycho-Oncology, 16*, 227–286.

Korte, J., Bohlmeijer, E. T., Cappeliez, P., Smit, F., & Westerhof, G. J. (2012). Life review therapy for older adults with moderate depressive symptomatology: A pragmatic randomized controlled trial. *Psychological Medicine, 42*, 1163–1173.

Krampen, G., Schui, G., & Wiesenhütter, J. (2008). Evidenzbasierte Psychotherapie und Therapie-Ressourcen. *Zeitschrift für Klinische Psychologie und Psychotherapie, 37*(1), 43–51.

la Cour, P., & Schnell, T. (2019). *The Sources of Meaning Card Method.* Innsbruck: Studia.

la Cour, P., & Schnell, T. (2020). Presentation of the sources of meaning card method: The SoMeCaM. *Journal of Humanistic Psychology, 60*(1), 20–42.

Lamers, S. M., Bohlmeijer, E. T., Korte, J., & Westerhof, G. J. (2015). The efficacy of life-review as online-guided self-help for adults: A randomized trial. *The Journal of Gerontology: Psychological Sciences and Social Sciences, 70*, 24–34.

Lan, X., Xiao, H., & Chen, Y. (2017). Effects of life review interventions on psychosocial outcomes among older adults: A systematic review and meta-analysis. *Geriatrics & Gerontology International, 17*(10), 1344–1357.

Landau, I. (2017). *Finding meaning in an imperfect world.* New York: Oxford University Press.

Längle, A., & Bürgi, D. (2011). *Sinnvoll leben: eine praktische Anleitung der Logotherapie*. Salzburg: Residenz.

Lee, V. (2004). *A meaning-making intervention for cancer patients – procedure manual* (Unpublished manuscript). McGill University, Montreal, Canada.

Lee, V., Cohen, S. R., Edgar, L., Laizner, A. M., & Gagnon, A. J. (2006a). Meaning-making and psychological adjustment to cancer: Development of an intervention and pilot results. *Oncology Nursing Forum, 33*(2), 291–302.

Lee, V., Cohen, S. R., Edgar, L., Laizner, A., & Gagnon, A. J. (2006b). Meaning-making intervention during breast or colorectal cancer treatment improves self-esteem, optimism, and self-efficacy. *Social Science & Medicine, 62*, 3133–3145.

LeMay, K., & Wilson, K. G. (2008). Treatment of existential distress in life threatening illness: A review of manualized interventions. *Clinical Psychology Review, 28*(3), 472–493.

Lindqvist, O., Threlkeld, G., Street, A. F., & Tishelman, C. (2015). Reflections on using biographical approaches in end-of-life care dignity therapy as example. *Qualitative Health Research, 25*(1), 40–50.

Lo, C., Hales, S., Chiu, A., Panday, T., Malfitano, C., Jung, J., . . . Rodin, G. (2019). Managing cancer and living meaningfully (CALM): Randomised feasibility trial in patients with advanced cancer. *BMJ Supportive & Palliative Care*, *9*(2), 209–218.

Lo, C., Hales, S., Jung, J., Chiu, A., Panday, T., Rydall, A., & Rodin, G. (2013). Managing cancer and living meaningfully (CALM): Phase 2 trial of a brief individual psychotherapy for patients with advanced cancer. *Palliative Medicine*, *28*(3), 234–242.

Logotherapie und Existenzanalyse. (2019, September 23). *Wikipedia*. Retrieved from https://de.wikipedia.org/wiki/Logotherapie_und_Existenzanalyse

McLean, K. C., Pasupathi, M., & Pals, J. L. (2007). Selves creating stories creating selves: A process model of self-development. *Personality and Social Psychology Review, 11*(3), 262–278.

Mai, S. S., Goebel, S., Jentschke, E., van Oorschot, B., Renner, K. H., & Weber, M. (2018). Feasibility, acceptability and adaption of dignity therapy: A mixed methods study achieving 360 feedback. *BMC Palliative Care*, *17*(1), 73.

Martínez, M., Arantzamendi, M., Belar, A., Carrasco, J. M., Carvajal, A., Rullán, M., & Centeno, C. (2017). "Dignity therapy," a promising intervention in palliative care: A comprehensive systematic literature review. *Palliative Medicine*, *31*(6), 492–509.

May, R. (1961). *Existential psychology*. New York: Random House.

McAdams, D. P. (1993). *The stories we live by: Personal myths and the making of the self*. New York: Guilford.

McAdams, D. P. (2001). The psychology of life stories. *Review of General Psychology*, *5*(2), 100.

Orrell, M., Hoe, J., Charlesworth, G., Russell, I., Challis, D., Moniz-Cook, E., . . . Rehill, A. (2017, February). *Support at home: Interventions to enhance life in dementia (SHIELD) – evidence, development and evaluation of complex interventions*. Retrieved from www.ncbi.nlm.nih.gov/books/NBK424174/

Park, C. L., Pustejovsky, J. E., Trevino, K., Sherman, A. C., Esposito, C., Berendsen, M., & Salsman, J. M. (2019). Effects of psychosocial interventions on meaning and purpose in adults with cancer: A systematic review and meta-analysis. *Cancer*, *125*(14), 2383–2393.

Perry, S. (2015). Practice issues in social work and psychosocial oncology in Israel. In G. Christ, C. Messner, & L. Behar (Eds.), *Handbook of oncology social work: Psychosocial care for people with cancer* (pp. 365–370). Oxford: Oxford University Press.

Pytell, T. (2006). Transcending the angel beast: Viktor Frankl and humanistic psychology. *Psychoanalytic Psychology*, *23*(3), 490–503.

Reitinger, C. (2015). Viktor Frankl's logotherapy from a philosophical point of view. *Existential Analysis*, *26*(2), 344–357.

Riedel, C., Deckart, R., & Noyon, A. (2015). *Existenzanalyse und Logotherapie: Ein Handbuch für Studium und Praxis*. Darmstadt: Wissenschaftliche Buchgesellschaft.

Riemeyer, J. (2007). *Die Logotherapie Viktor Frankls und ihre Weiterentwicklungen*. Bern: Huber.

Rodin, G., Lo, C., Rydall, A., Shnall, J., Malfitano, C., Chiu, A., . . . Li, M. (2018). Managing cancer and living meaningfully (CALM): A randomized controlled trial of a psychological intervention for patients with advanced cancer. *Journal of Clinical Oncology*, *36*(23), 2422.

Scarton, L. J., Boyken, L., Lucero, R. J., Fitchett, G., Handzo, G., Emanuel, L., & Wilkie, D. J. (2018). Effects of dignity therapy on family members: A systematic review. *Journal of Hospice & Palliative Nursing*, *20*(6), 542–547.

Schechner, J., & Zürner, H. (2013). *Krisen bewältigen: Viktor E. Frankls 10 Thesen in der Praxis*. Wien: Braumüller Lesethek.

Scheler, M. (1928). *Die Stellung des Menschen im Kosmos*. Darmstadt: Otto Reichl Verlag.

Schlieper-Damrich, R., & Kipfelsberger, P. (2008). *Wertecoaching: Beruflich brisante Situationen sinnvoll meistern*. Bonn: managerSeminare.

Schnell, T. (2004/2009). *Implizite Religiosität–Zur Psychologie des Lebenssinns* (2nd ed.). Lengerich: Pabst.

Schnell, T. (2010). Existential indifference: Another quality of meaning in life. *Journal of Humanistic Psychology*, *50*(3), 351–373.

Schnell, T. (2011). Individual differences in meaning-making: Considering the variety of sources of meaning, their density and diversity. *Personality and Individual Differences*, *51*(5), 667–673.

Schnell, T., & la Cour, P. (2018). Von der Tiefe im Leben sprechen. Erkenntnisse der empirischen Sinnforschung und exploration von Lebensbedeutungen mit der LeBe-Kartenmethode. *Wege zum Menschen*, *70*(1), 33–47.

Schweitzer, P., & Bruce, E. (2008). *Remembering yesterday, caring today: Reminiscence in dementia care: A guide to good practice*. London and Philadelphia: Jessica Kingsley Publishers.

Serrano, J. P., Latorre, J. M., Ros, L., Navarro, B., Aguilar, M. J., Nieto, M., & Gatz, M. (2012). Life review therapy using autobiographical retrieval practice for older adults with clinical depression. *Psicothema*, *24*(2), 224–229.

Søberg, A. I. B., Kjørven Haug, S. H., Danbolt, L. J., Lien, L., & Sørensen, T. (2018). Existential themes in the treatment of people at suicide risk: Understandings and practices of specialist healthcare professionals. *Mental Health, Religion & Culture*, *21*(6), 588–600.

Starck, P. L. (1981). Rehabilitative nursing and logotherapy: A study of spinal cord injured clients. *International Forum for Logotherapy*, *4*, 101–109.

Steinhauser, K. E., Alexander, S. C., Byock, I. R., George, L. K., Olsen, M. K., & Tulsky, J. A. (2008). Do preparation and life completion discussions improve functioning and quality of life in seriously ill patients? Pilot randomized control trial. *Journal of Palliative Medicine*, *11*(9), 1234–1240.

Steinhauser, K. E., Alexander, S. C., Olsen, M. K., Stechuchak, K. M., Zervakis, J., Ammarell, N., . . . Tulsky, J. A. (2017). Addressing patient emotional and existential needs during serious illness: Results of the outlook randomized controlled trial. *Journal of Pain and Symptom Management*, *54*(6), 898–908.

Struer-Tranberg, T. M. (2019). *Development and feasibility testing of a therapeutic interview to explore sources of meaning in palliative care patients* (Unpublished Master thesis), Syddansk Universitet, Odense.

Teo, I., Krishnan, A., & Lee, G. L. (2019). Psychosocial interventions for advanced cancer patients: A systematic review. *Psycho-Oncology, 28*(7), 1394–1407.

Thorgrimsen, L., Schweitzer, P., & Orrell, M. (2002). Evaluating reminiscence for people with dementia: A pilot study. *The Arts in Psychotherapy, 29*(2), 93–97.

Tornøe, K. A., Danbolt, L. J., Kvigne, K., & Sørlie, V. (2014). The power of consoling presence-hospice nurses' lived experience with spiritual and existential care for the dying. *BMC Nursing, 13*(1), Article 25.

Tornøe, K. A., Danbolt, L. J., Kvigne, K., & Sørlie, V. (2015a). The challenge of consolation: Nurses' experiences with spiritual and existential care for the dying-a phenomenological hermeneutical study. *BMC Nursing, 14*(1), Article 62.

Tornøe, K., Danbolt, L. J., Kvigne, K., & Sørlie, V. (2015b). A mobile hospice nurse teaching team's experience: Training care workers in spiritual and existential care for the dying-a qualitative study. *BMC Palliative Care, 14*(1), 43.

Udo, C. (2014). The concept and relevance of existential issues in nursing. *European Journal of Oncology Nursing, 18*(4), 347–354.

Utsch, M. (2018). Existenzielle Krisen und Sinnfragen in der Psychotherapie. In M. Utsch, R. M. Bonelli, & S. Pfeifer (Eds.), *Psychotherapie und Spiritualität* (pp. 15–27). Heidelberg and Berlin: Springer.

van der Spek, N., Vos, J., van Uden-Kraan, C. F., Breitbart, W., Cuijpers, P., Holtmaat, K., . . . Verdonck-de Leeuw, I. M. (2017). Efficacy of meaning-centered group psychotherapy for cancer survivors: A randomized controlled trial. *Psychological Medicine, 47*(11), 1990–2001.

Vos, J., Craig, M., & Cooper, M. (2015). Existential therapies: A meta-analysis of their effects on psychological outcomes. *Journal of Consulting and Clinical Psychology, 83*(1), 115–128.

Vuksanovic, D., Green, H. J., Dyck, M., & Morrissey, S. A. (2017). Dignity therapy and life review for palliative care patients: A randomized controlled trial. *Journal of Pain and Symptom Management, 53*(2), 162–170.

Wang, C. W., Chow, A. Y., & Chan, C. L. (2017). The effects of life review interventions on spiritual well-being, psychological distress, and quality of life in patients with terminal or advanced cancer: A systematic review and meta-analysis of randomized controlled trials. *Palliative Medicine, 31*(10), 883–894.

Watt, L. M., & Cappeliez, P. (2000). Integrative and instrumental reminiscence therapies for depression in older adults. Intervention strategies and treatment effectiveness. *Aging and Mental Health, 4*, 166–177.

Wong, P. T. P. (1995). The processes of adaptive reminiscence. In B. K. Haight & J. D. Webster (Eds.), *The art and science of reminiscing: Theory, research, methods, and applications* (pp. 23–35). Philadelphia: Taylor & Francis.

Woods, R. T., Orrell, M., Bruce, E., Edwards, R. T., Hoare, Z., Hounsome, B., . . . Russell, I. (2016). Remcare: Pragmatic multi-centre randomized trial of reminiscence groups for people with dementia and their family carers; Effectiveness and economic anlaysis. *PLoS One*, *11*(4), e0152843.

Yalom, I. (2010). *Existentielle Psychotherapie*. Bergisch Gladbach: Edition Humanistische Psychologie.

Zuehlke, T. E., & Watkins, J. T. (1977). Psychotherapy with terminally ill patients. *Psychotherapy: Theory, Research & Practice*, *14*, 403–410.

Chapter 13

Meaning in work

Professional work is a goal-oriented activity that directly or indirectly serves to secure existence. Gainful employment was not well regarded at the beginning of European culture. The ancient Greeks and Romans believed that it was above all trouble and a burden; it even spoiled character. Work was regarded as particularly morally reprehensible if it was not motivated by the product or the service itself but by the acquisition of money (Aßländer, 2005). This view has changed drastically to this day. We are now generally happy to have a job. It often serves not only our livelihood but also the realisation of personal interests and abilities and thus shapes a large part of our identity. In addition, the formerly frowned-upon money has come to the fore. The meaningful potential of work seems to suffer as a result.

13.1 The search for meaning in work

> A strange delusion possesses the working classes of the nations where capitalist civilization holds its sway. This delusion drags in its train the individual and social woes which for two centuries have tortured sad humanity. This delusion is the love of work, the furious passion for work, pushed even to the exhaustion of the vital force of the individual and his progeny.
>
> (Lafargue, 1883/2012, S. 7)

This polemical analysis by Paul Lafargue, son-in-law of Karl Marx, seems highly topical in view of today's working conditions. There is a "love of work" that is manifested in flexibility, availability and commitment to the point of self-exploitation. But it is a forced love, without emotional attachment, as the Gallup Engagement Index notes anew each year. For instance, the percentage of employees in Germany who feel emotionally connected with their employer has only ever been between 11 and 16 percent in the past ten years (Gallup, 2018).

At the same time – and this appears to be paradoxical – a majority of employees say that they are satisfied with their work (Manpower-Group Germany, 2019). This contradiction becomes more understandable if we consider the background against which this satisfaction is expressed: Few can choose between different jobs. In recent surveys, job security is always at the top of the list when it comes to the most important job characteristics (e.g. IMAS, 2018; Randstad, 2019). Without real choices, however, people are more likely to agree – that is, be satisfied – with the given circumstances. The spectre of unemployment looms large. In the face of this alternative, almost any kind of work may be preferred to being unemployed and marginalised. For some of the respondents, the reported satisfaction with work is thus "resigned satisfaction". This important differentiation of work satisfaction goes back to Agnes Bruggemann (1974). She understood job satisfaction as the result of comparing personal aspirations with the possibilities of realising them in the actual work situation. Resigned satisfaction occurs when professionals do not find their personal expectations met and do not expect a change for the better but take comfort in the belief that things could be even worse. Unterrainer, Jeppesen, and Jønsson (2013) reported that in studies examining the differentiated model of job satisfaction, "the proportion of resigned satisfied employees was impressively high, ranging between 25 to 45%" (p. 408).

Employees' "love" for their work thus seems to assume the form of a marriage of convenience, if not a marriage for maintenance. Unless there is another way, we remain loyal to our employer – even if the employer does not return our love. While companies expect loyalty and commitment from their employees, they often show little loyalty. This is typically justified by inherent necessity and the logic of market economy. The maximisation of profits and growth increase are the guiding principles, which "necessarily" go hand in hand with wage dumping, outsourcing, high income discrepancies between management and employees and precarious working conditions (Schnell, Höge, & Pollet, 2013; Schnell, Höge, & Weber, 2019; Zinn, 2015).

The exhaustion of the workforce, which Lafargue already spoke of, is expressed today in a high level of perceived stress. In a representative study carried out by the German Federation of Trade Unions in 2012, 80 percent of all employees were of the impression that in recent years, they had to invest more effort to complete more work in less time.

Forty-four percent of employees felt empty and burnt out after work (DGB-Index Gute Arbeit, 2013). In 2014, only 46 percent of those surveyed expected that they would be able to make it to retirement under current working conditions (DGB-Index Gute Arbeit, 2014). In the most recent German Federation of Trade Unions survey, the intensity of work again was judged to be critical throughout Germany (DGB Index Gute Arbeit, 2018).

In the context of these developments, the meaningfulness of work is increasingly brought into question (Schnell, 2018). For many working people, this is the consequence of growing disillusionment or excessive demands. But also for new entrants to the world of work, questions of meaning are vital: Almost two-thirds of 23–35-year-old employees stated that meaningful work was important for them; 31 percent even said that too little meaning could be a reason for changing jobs (Xing, 2014). A survey conducted by the Nuremberg Institute for Market Decisions and St. Gallen Symposium (2019) asked more than 1,000 future top talents (international young scientists, entrepreneurs and politicians aged around 30) about the importance of the question of meaning for their choice of career. Sixty-three percent said they were searching for meaning-oriented employers; 42 percent had decided to accept a lower salary by choosing a more meaningful job; 40 percent had opted against applying to an otherwise interesting employer because of a conflict of values; and 26 percent had rejected a job offer because of a conflict of values.

In a 2019 survey, Xing asked more than 22,000 employed people whether they would be willing to switch to a new job with more meaning or social responsibility if it meant earning less money: 49 percent of Austrians, 50 percent of Germans and 62 percent of Swiss participants responded "yes." In a representative German study, Andrea Waltersbacher and colleagues (2018) examined the meaning that German employees experienced in their work and its connection with their state of health. When asked about the importance of job characteristics, safety at work was most popular, at 94 percent, followed directly by the desire for more meaningful (93 percent), interesting (92.7 percent) and independent (88.9 percent) work. Market success (51.8 percent) was the least popular criterion. An IMAS Report 2018 came to similar conclusions in Austria. Asked to assign grades to various job characteristics, most of the nearly 1,000 Austrians gave top marks to two characteristics: job security and task significance. This was followed by organisational climate and independence of the activity (IMAS Report, 2018).

The German study by Waltersbacher and colleagues also showed that discrepancies between expectations and actual conditions were accompanied by poorer health: People who considered criteria such as a good level of cooperation, high quality of products/services or appreciation of their work to be important but missed them at their workplace reported more frequent absences and work-related health complaints. These related to both physical problems and psychological problems.

A need for more meaning in work was also identified internationally. In an early study of board members, middle managers and directors, two-thirds said that they missed meaning in their working lives (Holbeche, 2004). In a survey of more than 100,000 professionals in North America, Europe and Asia-Pacific, participants were asked, among other things, "Would you take on a lesser role or lower wage if you felt that your work contributed something more important or meaningful to you or your organization?" (Kelly Services, 2009). Of them, 51 percent said they would be willing to do so. In 2012, Kelly Services further explored how employees found meaning in their work. Three-quarters of respondents mentioned the opportunity to develop and gain expertise. A further 41 percent each said they found meaning in the relationship with colleagues and the alignment of work with personal values. Thirty-one percent felt that it was important to be able to tie in with corporate strategy, and another 28 percent said that corporate citizenship was a key source of meaning (Kelly Services, 2012).

Many – though not the majority – of managers now see the need for companies to address social issues. For example, 38 percent of senior executives surveyed by Mercer reported that they consider it their duty to take responsibility for social issues (Mercer, 2019). The Deloitte Global Human Capital Trends report surveyed nearly 10,000 international executives (Deloitte, 2019). When asked about the most important measure of success in 2019, 34 percent of CEOs cited "impact on society, including income inequality, diversity, and the environment" (p. 2). This is significantly less than in 2015, for example, when 50 percent considered a company's social and societal activities "very important" (Deloitte, 2015). It thus seems that there is still a long way to go from importance to implementation, from "ought" to "is." The majority of the Deloitte respondents in 2015 did *not* believe that their companies were willing and able to adequately implement corporate social responsibility concerns. (There was a "competence gap" between the assessed importance – 78 out of 100 points – and the assessed ability – 47 out of 100 points). Currently, only 53 percent of managers believe that they actually contribute to making work meaningful (Deloitte, 2019).

And how do employees perceive the situation? International surveys from 2012 to 2014 showed a negative trend: In 2012, 46 percent described their work as meaningful; in 2013, the figure was down to 42 percent; and in 2014, it was only 38 percent (Kelly Services, 2014). The sharpest decline was recorded in European countries. Should this development give us cause for concern? "It's all right as long as I'm employed" might be the pragmatic opinion of job seekers and workers. And for many companies, "meaning" still seems to be a vague construct that has little to do with economic hard facts. However, 77 percent of committed employees (and 60 percent of the overall workforce) rated employers high in terms of opportunities to be involved in interesting, meaningful work. Kelly Services cautions that "Of course, every worker will have their own perspective on meaningful work, but if they seek it at your organization, make sure they find it" (Kelly Services, 2016, p. 30). Employees increasingly want more than "just any job." And the difference between any job and a meaningful job is huge – both in personal experience and in its impact for employers. Before discussing these differences in more detail, let's turn to the question of what meaningful work actually is.

13.2 What is meaningful work?

In principle, all work should be meaningful. Work is a goal-oriented mental and/or physical activity. If this activity contributes to the achievement of the given work goal, it can be regarded as meaningful (see Section 4.1.). If the therapist's treatment leads to patients feeling better, the treatment makes sense. If the office clerk's administrative activities contribute to a company's consistent bookkeeping and accounting, her work has meaning. If a car salesperson helps to ensure that customers find vehicles that suit them, their work makes sense. These examples work at least in theory. After all, many people do not experience their work tasks as meaningful. The inherent meaningfulness of work processes seems to be disturbed. As a consequence, both employees and employers suffer. As a growing number of studies show, the wish to experience professional activity as meaningful is not just a personal whim of the better-off or an incentive to get the most out of employees. A meaningful professional life is about the core of work – which is either experienced as meaningful or as an annoying, frustrating or exhausting obligation.

13.2.1 Meaningful work: definition

Following the criteria of general meaningfulness, we define meaning in work as a sense of coherence, direction, significance and belonging in the context of working life (Schnell et al., 2013; Schnell & Hoffmann, in press). The four criteria mentioned determine whether a person experiences an occupation as more or less meaningful. "Significance" means the extent to which one's activity is perceived to be beneficial to others: Does my action have an impact on people inside or outside the organisation? Is it important or irrelevant? "Orientation" means the general direction of the professional activity. It is about the values, mission and vision that determine the strategies and goals that are pursued. Current management and leadership theories pick up this criterion when they address "purpose-drivenness in organisations" (e.g., Craig & Snook, 2014). "Coherence" means fit and consistency in two ways: vertically and horizontally. The hierarchic model of meaning (Figure 13.1) can help to illustrate both. Vertical coherence is present when lower levels of meaning coincide with higher levels – that is, when (professional) action contributes to the achievement of the desired (work) goals and when the work goals pursued harmonise with personal sources of meaning. Horizontal coherence is present when the processes within a level fit together in a reasonable way: when professional activities complement each other meaningfully, when work objectives are free of contradiction and when personally relevant sources of meaning follow the same direction. "Belonging" means a sense of being part of a larger whole. It is about identifying with the company, the organisation or the institution, which goes hand in hand with an awareness of being needed and granted responsibility.

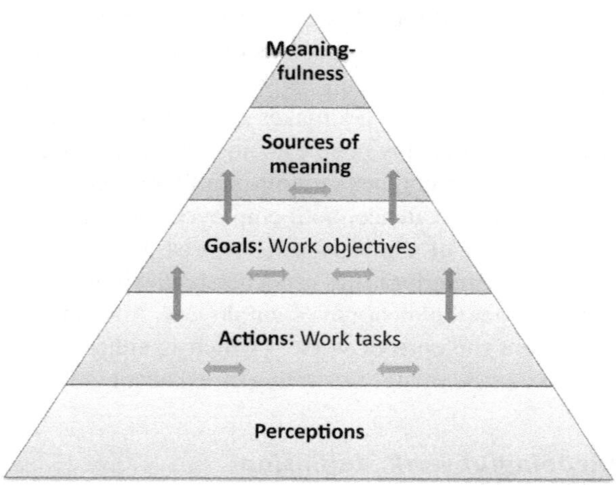

Figure 13.1 Vertical coherence and horizontal coherence at work

13.2.2 Predictors of meaningful work

We have examined the validity of this model of meaningful work in a study of German and Austrian employees (Schnell et al., 2013). For the criterion of significance, perceived task significance was assessed. As a measure of coherence, we asked to what extent the participants' actual professional activity coincided with their idea of an ideal, personally interesting activity. Belonging was measured by the perceived socio-moral atmosphere, which is characterised by an open approach to social problems and conflicts; reliable appreciation, care and support; and participative cooperation (Weber, Unterrainer, & Höge, 2008).

Orientation was assessed as the perceived organisational assumption of responsibility for society and the environment, in the sense of selftranscendent organisational orientation. In addition, we assessed demographics and personality traits. Figure 13.2 shows the extent to which the predictors contributed to the experience of meaningful work.

Perceived task significance proved to be the best predictor. The more that professionals believed that their work was useful to others, the more meaning they experienced. Perceived socio-moral atmosphere was strongly related to work meaningfulness too: When participants judged interaction at the workplace as open, appreciative and participative, they reported high work meaning. This also increased when employees believed that their employer was not interested in success at any price but instead took social and environmental concerns into account. A work–role fit with regard to personal interests appeared similarly important for work being perceived as meaningful.

The criteria we identified have thus in fact proved to be important conditions for the experience of meaning in work; overall, they can explain almost half of the variance in perceived work meaning. Figure 13.2 shows an additional finding of interest: Personality traits are not at all associated with experienced meaning in work – at least not beyond the four conditions described earlier. Of course, different people find meaning in different kind of jobs; this is not disputed here. Still, the four criteria of meaningful work seem to be beneficial to all kinds of personality types. So what would a meaningful workplace look like?

13.2.3 Task significance

As long as profit, growth and other economic parameters are paramount, the original significance of a given activity will easily fade into the background. However, significance is a value that does not even need to

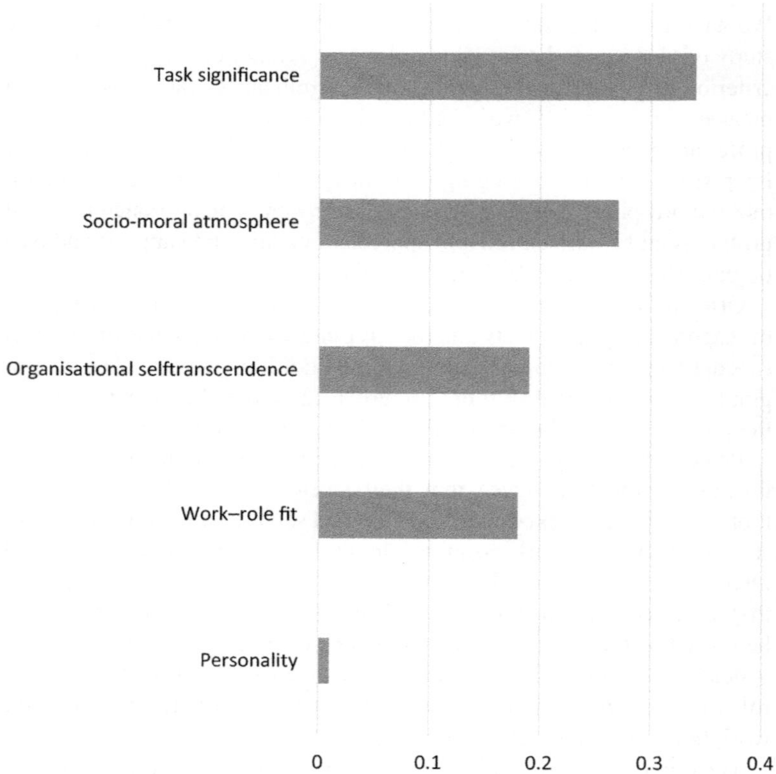

Figure 13.2 Predictors of meaningful work (beta weights)

be created, only disclosed, because the significance of an activity is its essence:

> In medicine this is health, in strategy victory, in architecture a house, in any other sphere something else, and in every action and pursuit the end; for it is for the sake of this that all men do whatever else they do.
>
> (Aristotle, 1999, p. 9)

The significance of an activity is what many job starters have in mind: the nurse who wants to provide good care for the sick; the construction worker who hopes to work on buildings that they can be proud of; the doctor who wishes to heal people of diseases and ailments. These original motivations often fade into the background when work is intensified under time pressure. When quantity comes before quality, the "real" meaning of work is forgotten.

It can be helpful for employees to keep reminding themselves of why they chose their profession, what activities and goals they "actually" wanted to pursue and strive for. For employers, depending on the area of work, there can be a variety of ways to highlight the significance that their service or product has for others. Think, for example, of contacts with customers or clients that go beyond the usual business relationships:

- Cleaning staff are invited to a reception by the office personnel, who benefit from daily cleanliness.
- Administrative organs provide visitors with insights into the secrets of their "work in the background" at an open to the public day.
- Sales staff select their favourite product and present it to customers.

American psychologist Adam Grant (2008) published a highly instructive example. He conducted an experimental study at a university fundraising organisation whose employees were tasked with soliciting donations for the university. Grant randomly divided the employees into three groups. The first group worked as usual. The second group read two stories from former employees who reported that working for the organisation had positively influenced their careers. The focus was thus placed on the self-serving aspects of the job. The third group also received two stories to read. They were grateful reports from two people who had received study grants from the donations that former callers had solicited. These stories hence emphasised the significance that the work had for others. The success rate in raising funds was measured before and one month after reading the stories. In the first group, which did not read any stories, nothing changed during this period. Neither did anything change in the second group. The third group, however, more than doubled the amount of weekly donation money that they raised.

13.2.4 Belonging: socio-moral atmosphere

The authoritarian leadership model, wherein decisions are made over the heads of the employees, is now considered obsolete. Nonetheless, it is still the standard model. A study among German managers concluded that the vast majority of managers reject such a top-down model. Instead, they would prefer employee participation and codetermination:

> Transparency of information, integration of different life plans, empathic involvement of employees and the promotion of comprehensive cooperation are high on the wish list. Managers agree that lonely decisions and ready-made concepts are no longer appropriate in view of the complex dynamics of globally interconnected markets.
>
> (INQA, 2014, p. 21; transl. TS)

At least in terms of ideas, this attests to a development that approaches the criteria of a socio-moral atmosphere at the workplace. The research group around my colleague Wolfgang Weber was able to demonstrate the many advantages of such an open, appreciative and participative organisational atmosphere: Employees showed greater empathy, reliability, helpfulness and solidarity both among themselves and in their dealings with their superiors and the company as a whole. They felt more closely tied to the company, which encouraged motivation, commitment and ultimately productivity (Weber & Unterrainer, 2015). Moreover, we found that a socio-moral atmosphere was connected with the experience of meaningful work (Höge & Weber, 2018; Schnell et al., 2013).

It will be a big step to change existing hierarchical structures in favour of democratic processes. But with Generation Y, employees have entered the job market who do not draw their motivation primarily from the level of salary and other material incentives: "Personal commitment is increasingly associated with appreciation, freedom of decision and personal responsibility. Autonomy is becoming more important than status symbols, and the perceived meaning of an activity determines the degree of commitment" (INQA, 2014, p. 9; transl. TS), is how the authors of the study Leadership Culture in Change summarise the statements of their 400 interview partners. To strengthen engagement and loyalty to the company, managers will hardly escape the necessity of changing their approach from a patriarchal-authoritarian one to an egalitarian, participative, appreciative and conflict-prepared one.

13.2.5 Selftranscendent organisations

Focusing primarily on profit has been another hallmark of the past decades, but it is being questioned, as the aforementioned INQA study shows: Less than a third of the managers surveyed favoured an efficiency-oriented management model geared to maximising profits (INQA, 2014). Instead, solidarity and social responsibility were endorsed, bringing to the fore perspectives that our study showed to be meaningful.

The concept of non-exclusive profit orientation seems difficult to implement within the prevailing ideology of the market economy. In some countries, however, an alternative approach has emerged, known as the fourth sector. These are enterprises that combine economic self-sufficiency with social benefits – as distinct from the public (government, public service), private (business, trade) and social (non-profit) sectors. The fourth sector includes initiatives such as corporate social responsibility, microfinance through small and micro-credits, entrepreneurial philanthropy (use of risk capital to support social, environmental or community projects), sustainable economic activity, social entrepreneurship and so on (Sabeti & Fourth Sector Network Concept Working Group, 2009).

Despite broad social recognition, the fourth sector cannot be said to be flourishing. Many institutional and structural obstacles still stand in the way of alternative organisational management, in terms of access to capital, legally valid forms of enterprise and tax laws. But even in the traditional private sector, there are developments towards more social responsibility. Terms such as "sustainability" and "corporate social responsibility" can be found in more and more mission statements. However, there are obviously major discrepancies with regard to active implementation. And according to the findings of a study of more than 1,800 managers, such discrepancies are dangerous: Employees indeed notice when mission statements exist only on paper and words are not followed by actions. Such perceptions of a lack of authenticity and integrity in management are typically accompanied by cynicism and a loss of meaning among employees (Holbeche & Springett, 2004). Consequences include declining commitment and loyalty to the employer.

If selftranscendent values are put into practice, however, then organisations can expect their employees' sense of meaning in work to rise. Management consultants Anja Förster and Peter Kreuz have witnessed how a company's practised "higher purpose" had an inspiring, energising and meaning-giving effect on employees:

> You can directly translate the term "higher purpose" into fundamental values like beauty, truth, setting out for new shores, freedom, justice, love, compassion, service to humanity. These are the moral imperatives that have always inspired people to achieve the extraordinary. If companies succeed in translating these values into their

> own set of goals, then the answer is found to why people should be involved in this company with all their creativity, initiative and passion.
>
> (Förster & Kreuz, 2009, p. 30; transl. TS)

The authors then specify that "it is also true that not everyone feels equally attracted to all values. Rather, it is about the fit of people and their values and companies that embody precisely these values" (Förster & Kreuz, 2009, p. 30; transl. TS). This point brings us to the fourth predictor of meaningful work, as confirmed in our study: work–role fit.

13.2.6 Work–role fit

A person should fit their job – in terms of education, skills, personality and interests. This may seem trivial and should really be a matter of course. Nevertheless, a good fit is still more of an exception. Thus, the majority of people we surveyed (Schnell et al., 2013) reported that their job "fits them more or less well" (62 percent). One-quarter of employees said that they and their job did not match well, and only 14 percent reported a high level of fit.

Consequences of poor job fit are manifold, including underchallenge and overchallenge. Overstrain and stress at work have been increasing for years. Pressure to perform and meet deadlines, workflow interruptions, lack of recognition and information overload are commonplace (Lohmann-Haislah, 2013; Techniker Krankenkasse, 2016). This results in musculoskeletal complaints (pain in neck, shoulders, back, arms, hands, legs, feet, hips and knees) and/or psycho-vegetative complaints (tiredness and exhaustion, sleep disorders, nervousness, irritability and depression). In a large German study conducted in 2012, 84 percent of the employees stated that they had frequently experienced at least one of these complaints in the past year. Almost 17 percent reported that they had often experienced physical and emotional exhaustion from work over the past 12 months (Lohmann-Haislah, 2013). In a survey carried out by a German health insurance company, termed Relax, Germany (Techniker Krankenkasse, 2016), almost half (49 percent) of full-time employees and 26 percent of part-time employees reported that they "often felt worn out and exhausted." According to Lohmann-Haislah, many complain about excessive demands from quantity of work but professional *under*-challenge. In numerous cases, work–role fit has not succeeded: "As far as qualifications are concerned, it has been shown that many employees feel they are not working in accordance with their skills. There still is extensive potential for improvement here" (Lohmann-Haislah, 2013, p. 122; transl. TS).

Although it may seem paradoxical in times of constant work intensification, the phenomenon of *boreout* is also attracting more and more attention – obviously justified. Thus, in Germany in 2011, just as many employees suffered from underchallenge as from overchallenge (DUW-Presseservice, 2011). In Austria, underchallenge was even more widespread than overchallenge: Whereas 7 percent described themselves as overchallenged, 23 percent said they suffered from underchallenge. These were mainly women who were working part time (Bauer, 2014). In one of our studies, we asked 492 Austrian professionals whether they felt underchallenged, overchallenged or properly challenged at work. Twenty-eight percent said they were underchallenged, 53 percent said they felt well fitted and 7 percent said they were overchallenged. A Randstad study from 2019 reported that a quarter of German respondents would like to change jobs for reasons of underchallenge or have already done so (Randstad, 2019). Underchallenge is accompanied by disinterest and boredom, which in the long run turn into frustrating emptiness that is hard to bear (Rothlin & Werder, 2014). The consequences are similar symptoms to those of burnout: physical exhaustion, emotional frustration, listlessness, social withdrawal and irritability. Depression or somatoform disorders may also follow (Brühlmann, 2015).

A report in an Austrian daily newspaper prompted a large wave of letters from readers, such as the following:

> On days when I have a lot to do, I go home feeling refreshed and rested. On days when I twiddle my thumbs for eight hours, I am completely exhausted in the evening from doing nothing. This may sound paradoxical, but it is a huge mental burden to always have the feeling that you are useless and cannot do anything significant.
>
> (User C.; Al-Kattib, 2013)

User A. wrote:

> I fall into despair because my life is passing me by and it turns completely meaningless. . . . My friends say I should quit, but when you feel so empty because the work is meaningless, you lose your self-confidence and don't know what kind of skills you actually have. And it takes strength and imaginativeness to apply for other jobs.
>
> (Al-Kattib, 2013; transl. TS)

The responses indicate that job matching should not be limited to filling positions with people who have the skills to do the job. Human needs for meaningful activity need to be taken seriously and appreciated, as analyses of the reasons for boreout show: Half of those affected report that they are not assigned challenging tasks and are not given responsibility. More than a third suffer from a lack of variety (DUW-Presseservice, 2011).

Why is it that so few people end up in jobs that suit them well? The author and entrepreneur Martin Gaedt has taken a closer look at career guidance in Germany. Job seekers have the choice between 329 recognised trades, 900 dual degree courses and 16,286 university courses. But in general, pupils are not even aware of one per mille of these options (Gaedt, 2014) – and apparently, the vocational guidance services provided by employment agencies have not been much help either (Stiftung Warentest, 2007). Dropout rates are correspondingly high; in Germany, they currently stand at 26 percent for recognised trades and as high as 30 percent for university studies. Too many people do not undergo any vocational training at all (14 percent in 2016; Federal Ministry of Education and Research, 2018). Those whose dropout entails a change of training or field of study can be credited with the courage to experiment. After all, school and training years are closely timed and geared towards efficiency and early entry into the labour market. They therefore lack precisely that: the opportunity to try things out, get to know oneself, gain experience and even take a detour without facing sanctions.

Internships and other interconnections between school education and the professional world are an important step in this direction. Another desideratum is to strengthen the self-knowledge of young people. I am regularly asked by parents or grandparents about recommendations for children who don't know what they want to do after school. Psychology offers various tests of vocational inclinations, which provide information about personality characteristics, interests and abilities. However, their implementation is usually left to the decision of the parents, who have to arrange for them at their own initiative and expense. In addition, skills and interests are not to be equated with activities that are considered meaningful for job starters. When there is a lack of insight into the meaningfulness of an apprenticeship or job, motivation is low. And both employees and employers suffer as a result, as the studies summarised below show.

13.3 Correlates of meaningful work

In a globalised, competitive economy, those organisations are at the forefront whose employees not only work to rule, but invest their energies and skills in the tasks ahead. Such work engagement (Bakker, Albrecht, & Leiter, 2011) shows in a positive affective-motivational state, characterised by vitality, dedication and absorption (Schaufeli, Salanova, González-Romá, & Bakker, 2002). People who are passionate about their profession, who are entirely absorbed in it and full of energy at work are said to have a high level of work engagement. Once this is present, we can safely assume that they experience work as meaningful. In our study at the University of Innsbruck, we found that meaningful work and work engagement are two sides of the same coin (Höge & Schnell, 2012). While work engagement represents the affective side – that is, feelings of vitality and enthusiasm – meaningful work represents the cognitive-evaluative side: From a meta-perspective, meaning and purpose of the job are evident; leadership is judged to be authentic and appreciative, and the goals pursued are in line with personal abilities, values and convictions.

There is thus a close connection between meaningful work and the extent to which an individual is involved in the workplace, is motivated, inspired and passionate about the job. Further positive relationships are found between meaningful work and job satisfaction, job performance, organisational commitment and duration of employment. Similarly, the higher the level of meaningfulness in work, the lower fluctuation, internal withdrawal, cynicism, exhaustion and distress (Claes & Ruiz-Quintanilla, 1994; Fairlie, 2011; Grant, 2007; Holbeche & Springett, 2004; Milliman, Czaplewski, & Ferguson, 2003; Rosso, Dekas, & Wrzesniewski, 2010).

In a 2019 meta-analysis, Allan, Batz-Barbarich and colleagues confirmed the following findings: Meaningful work showed strong correlations ($r = 0.70$ +) with work engagement, commitment and job satisfaction. Moderate to large effects ($r = 0.44$ to -0.49) emerged with regard to life satisfaction, meaning in life, general health and intention to quit. Small to moderate correlations ($r = -0.19$ to 0.33) were found with organisational citizenship behaviour, self-assessed work performance and negative affect. The data suggested that meaningful work predicts work engagement and satisfaction, which in turn predicts work performance, organisational citizenship behaviour and intention to quit.

These positive effects can also be interpreted in the opposite direction, of course. A lack of meaning in work corresponds to a painful state of emptiness. In the context of work, the absence of meaning is actually equivalent to the presence of a professional crisis of meaning: Those who experience their working life as meaningless and yet have to take up work every day, perform activities perceived as pointless and have to answer to superiors find this state frustrating, exhausting and burdensome. In addition to the personal suffering that arises here, employers also have to face considerable consequences. Such employees work without commitment, motivation and emotional ties. Their performance will inevitably decline, as will their loyalty to the company. Mobbing and damage to the company are possible consequences.

Burnout can also be a consequence of an increasing lack of meaning in work. The most prominent indicator of burnout syndrome is exhaustion, which over time leads to cynicism or indifference and is associated with occupational inefficiency and physical, emotional and mental problems (Maslach, Schaufeli, & Leiter, 2001). Typically, those who endure burnout have started their working lives with idealistic enthusiasm: Their work seemed meaningful to them and they invested a lot in it. "What started out as important, meaningful, and challenging work becomes unpleasant, unfulfilling and meaningless. Energy turns into exhaustion, involvement turns into cynicism, and efficacy turns into ineffectiveness" (Maslach et al., 2001, p. 416). The final state in burnout is characterised by feelings of alienation from oneself and others, up to the loss of a general meaning in life (Ekstedt & Fagerberg, 2005). Empirical evidence for the connection between a lack of meaning in work and burnout is provided, for example, by Fouché and colleagues (2017) for teachers; Rasmussen and colleagues (2016) for psycho-oncologists; and Allan, Owens and colleagues (2019) for counsellors.

But what causes the state of exhaustion that is so critical in the development of a burnout syndrome? A repeatedly confirmed explanation is excessive workload: too much work in too little time. If, in addition to work intensification, the personal scope for decision-making and control is restricted, then nothing remains but efficient, externally controlled functioning. This is particularly difficult for those who have started out full of motivation and ideas; who are less concerned with performance per unit of time than with high-quality, valuable work. In any case, they tend to perform more than is required. If, then, important resources such as scope for action, significance, belonging and coherence are lost, the danger of burnout is particularly serious. A high sense of meaning at work can therefore also be dangerous. The risks of meaningful work have been investigated in several recent studies.

13.4 You can't save the world every day! Risks of meaningful work

Meaningful work is a double-edged sword. Those who endure "sense-out" at the workplace are contrasted with those who are so pleased with their meaningful job as to exploit themselves. Good candidates for this kind of overcommitment are, for example, non-profit organisations – that is, organisations that pursue social, cultural or scientific goals rather than economic ones.

> NPOs [non-profit organisations] are particularly impressive in showing how important it is to convey the meaning of their work. In NPO, it is obviously fed by the mission. Motivation is high, both among employees and volunteers. "Sometimes too high," says Greenpeace CEO Alexander Egit. "We must then tell them 'You can't save the world every day.'" In extreme cases, excessive energy can lead to individual exhaustion and is also detrimental to the organisation, because efforts fizzle out if they are not used for strategically important goals.
>
> (Posch & Köttritsch, 2015; transl. TS)

The American research team Dempsey and Sanders (2010) analysed autobiographies of three social entrepreneurs: John Wood, who gave up a highly paid job at Microsoft to build libraries in developing countries (Room to Read); Greg Mortensen, who unsuccessfully tried to climb K2 in Pakistan and in doing so was moved by the magnanimity of the villagers; since then, he has dedicated himself to building schools in Pakistan, Afghanistan and Tajikistan; and Wendy Kopp, who while still an undergraduate developed her non-profit project Teach for America, which has since grown into a global network of independent NPOs. An analysis of the autobiographies revealed that social entrepreneurship is seen by the public as a convincing model of meaningful work, since the solution of urgent social problems is the main focus. The three selected protagonists, however, "paid" for the meaningfulness of their work with self-sacrifice. They accepted financial risks, underpayment, overtime and health problems. They exchanged a more or less regulated family life for a meaningful job:

> I have found the one thing I always wanted – a career with meaning and about which I feel passion. I wake up eager to jump out of bed and head to the office, excited for whatever it is that the day holds. That is a rare luxury in this world. . . . I saw my family less frequently than I would have preferred. . . . Our board of directors said that they were worried about my burning out. But the biggest downside kept rearing its ugly head: the long hours were absolute hell on my relationships. At times, I would begin dating a woman, and then,

> within a month, she would get extremely frustrated with how little time I had to devote to the burgeoning relationship. One frustrated woman opined that Room to Read was 'your wife, your mistress, your child, your family dog, and your career.' She then told me that nodding vigorously while grinning was not the proper response.
>
> (John Wood, cited after Dempsey & Matthews, 2010, p. 450)

Self-exploitation when doing meaningful work is not unknown in other occupational sectors either. In a series of successive studies, Hu and Hirsh (2017) demonstrated that people with a wide variety of professional backgrounds are willing to accept a lower salary for meaningful work. Two American researchers interviewed zookeepers about their meaning in work (Bunderson & Thompson, 2009) and concluded that there is an inherent tension in work that is experienced as meaningful: Such work implies responsibility, and a high sense of responsibility requires a certain degree of self-lessness. Zookeepers who saw their profession as a vocation and experienced it as meaningful identified strongly with their work. For them, their activity was a moral duty. Their zoos were better managed and met higher standards than those of colleagues who did not see their work as a calling. Yet zookeepers with a calling also accepted restrictions on their salary, leisure time and well-being in favour of their work.

Besides the advantages of meaningful work, it is therefore also important to be aware of possible dangers. Anyone who is prepared to accept personal disadvantages in favour of the quality of work is faced with potential exploitation. And indeed, such mechanisms – whether implicit or explicit – are already in operation. Bunderson and Thompson, for example, reported that in a sample of 982 zookeepers from the United States and Canada, those who saw their profession as a calling earned a lower income. Whoever identifies with the cause is all too easily prepared to accept material injustice. The authors Jing Hu and Jacob Hirsh, on the basis of their studies on the willingness of people to accept lower wages for meaningful work, came to a rather infamous conclusion: "An interesting implication of these studies is that companies may be able to save costs by hiring employees who find the work to be more personally meaningful" (Hu & Hirsh, 2017, p. 8).

In addition to attempts to deceive meaning-oriented employees with less money, managers should also avoid other stumbling blocks. Anyone who decides in favour of purpose-driven management must first of all face the task of representing this decision authentically and personally. As outlined earlier, employees have a particularly fine antenna for whether values and missions proclaimed in management are actually implemented or merely serve as a façade. The latter can cause cynicism and loss of meaning (Holbeche & Springett, 2004). It is also important to understand that professional meaning cannot be given or produced: It is a personal experience that can be facilitated and promoted through appropriate working conditions. Christian and colleagues (2011) accordingly advise managers to "'set the stage for engagement' by creating contextual conditions that facilitate employees' perceptions of meaningful work" (Christian, Garza, & Slaughter, 2011, p. 124). Bailey and colleagues (2017) argue that four approaches would seem appropriate in this regard, which are consistent with the aforementioned criteria of meaningful work:

- Job design that emphasises above all the prosocial aspects of work (significance).
- Human resources management that in addition to striving for the right fit focuses on the personal development of employees and their work–life balance (work–role fit, coherence).
- A leadership style that authentically embodies organisational values and thus inspires employees and serves as a role model for them. In this respect, the realisation of selftranscendent values is attributed a special potential (selftranscendent orientation).
- A corporate culture that emphasises cohesion and care for one another, thus strengthening the sense of belonging (belonging).

The authors close with a warning: Employees are well aware of the difference between authentic values and moral conduct on the one hand and attempts to control or manipulate on the other. When employees sense that the management is trying to manipulate experienced meaning in order to improve performance and productivity, this often leads to painful consequences – for individuals and for organisations.

The fact that meaningful action is associated with intrinsic motivation, voluntariness and the assumption of responsibility contributes to the ambivalence of meaningful employment. Autonomy and personal responsibility at the workplace, which many employers have meanwhile conceded, go hand in hand with a spatial and temporal boundarilessness of work. This results in a high potential for strain on employees and their private and family lives. In addition, there is often a gap between assigned tasks and the availability of time and material resources. In this way, employees may experience themselves as self-determined and fulfilled, but they can easily get caught in a vicious circle of stress and excessive demands (Rosa, 2014; Volpert & Weber, 2018).

13.5 The job as a source of meaning?

As important as the meaningfulness of work may be, it should not be overstretched. Not everyone expects their job to provide meaning to their life, and not every job has qualities that make it a suitable source of meaning. Regarding sources of meaning that can be found in the context of work, our data show that jobs primarily allow for selfactualisation. Sources of meaning like challenge, development, achievement, power, creativity and knowledge can be pursued in professional environments. But the more initiative, time and commitment that work requires, the less room there is for other sources of meaning. As explained in Section 6.2, a balance of sources of meaning is central to personal meaningfulness. Concentrating one-dimensionally on a job brings life into imbalance, as the – unfortunate – term *work–life balance* suggests. Of course, work is part of life. But it tends to take up our resources in such a way that other areas of life, especially the domain of well-being and relatedness, are neglected.

The temporal expansion of work (extra hours, increased retirement age) and its status as a central feature of identity can stand in the way of a balanced life. And they stigmatise those who, intentionally or unintentionally, do not play the game: homemakers, part-time workers and the unemployed. But a countertrend can be identified. While the traditional career path of steadily rising salaries has been experienced as motivating (and apparently meaningful enough) for decades, many professionals today question the inherent value of this pursuit.

There is even a seemingly paradoxical need for "progress by regression": More and more people are reducing their working hours, changing to lower positions with lower salaries or giving up employment altogether in order to gain time in return. Such *downshifting* aims at a more balanced life in which personal meaning and social relationships are valued more highly than economic success (Nelson, Rademacher, & Paek, 2007). While downshifting is only just gaining popularity in German-speaking countries, this is different in the UK: Already at the start of this millennium, 25 percent of a nationwide sample stated that in the past ten years, they had voluntarily made a long-term change in their lifestyle, other than planned retirement, which had resulted in earning less money (Hamilton, 2003). This did not even include those who gave up or reduced their employment because of a child or self-employment. Over 90 percent of the downshifters surveyed were happy with their decision. Fifty-two percent admitted that they missed the extra income but did not regret their decision (Hamilton, 2003).

For some of us, employment will continue to be the most important purpose in life. And this is probably a good thing given the challenging and enriching tasks that need to be accomplished. Other professions, however, are fairly monotonous and uncreative; they offer little opportunity for selfactualisation, selftranscendence or well-being and relatedness. This does not mean that such work is meaningless. *We should clearly differentiate between meaningful work and work that serves as a source of meaning.* Almost every type of work can be meaningful and should be designed accordingly. But not every type of work must be a source of meaning in life.

Let us look at two examples: a cleaner and a surgeon. A surgeon's work is highly complex and varied. It offers opportunities for personal development, achievement, power, knowledge, creativity – and it even saves lives. The cleaner does the same thing every day, has little opportunity for development and power and little scope for achievement and creativity. Nevertheless, the four criteria of meaningful work are relevant and implementable in both professions – and we can see a need for action for both in this respect. Let us first look at the situation of the surgeon. The *significance* of their work is obvious. In the case of surgeons, it is also highly probable that person and position fit well together, through selection processes and a long training programme. However, the organisational atmosphere in hospitals is often characterised by rigid authoritarian structures; here an open, appreciative and participative atmosphere could help to enhance a sense of meaning. In addition, many hospitals have a primary economic orientation. Doctors then see the core, or meaning, of their work threatened when the quality of their work is jeopardised by the need to economise.

Let us now look at the cleaner's work. It is of great importance to those who depend on clean rooms. The corporate atmosphere in the cleaning company can be more or less open, appreciative and participative. The company's orientation can be more or less selftranscendent, such as by putting environmental sustainability and health and safety issues, for example with regard to cleaning agents used, before maximum profit. The fit between person and position can also be taken into account, such as through flexibility in work schedules, job rotation, autonomy in the organisation of the workflow, team composition and so on. But although both activities are or can be similarly meaningful, they cannot be expected to equally generate meaning. It is unlikely that the cleaner will find the meaning of their life in their job. Personal sources of meaning can be realised within the framework of professional activity but also outside it – whether in family or social relationships, in social or artistic activities, in curious exploration or caring preservation or in sensual enjoyment or significant encounters.

As long as our professional life reflects the four characteristics of significance, orientation, belonging and coherence, as long as there are no conflicts of values and feelings of emptiness, isolation or alienation, any work that has a social benefit can be experienced as meaningful. The reference to social benefits is crucial, however. Some occupations do not show such utility, even upon deep reflection. David Graeber made this point succinctly in his book *Bullshit Jobs: A Theory* (2018). Under certain circumstances, a rigorous examination of your professional activity may make you aware of its meaninglessness. This is what happened to Fréderic Beigbeder, who vividly described his professional crisis of meaning in an advertising agency in the book *£6.99* (Beigbeder, 2014):

> My name is Octave and I'm dressed from head to foot in Tom Ford. I'm an advertising executive; yup, that's right, I pollute the universe. I'm the guy who sells you shit. Who makes you dream of things you'll never have. . . . No one in my profession actually wants you to be happy, because happy people don't spend. Your suffering boosts sales. In our own jargon we call this the "post-purchase downer." There's some product that you just have to have, but as soon as you've got it there's something else you have to have. Hedonism isn't humanism; it's cash flow. What does it say? "I spend, therefore I am." But in order to create a need I have to arouse jealousy, pain and dissatisfaction: they are my weapons. And my target . . . is you. . . . I spend my life lying to you, and I'm paid a shed-load for it.
>
> (Beigbeder, 2014, p. 5ff)

Wherever work primarily serves the benefit of individuals or companies, with potential negative consequences for society, change management strategies to enhance meaning in work are probably out of place.

13.6 Brief discourse: voluntary work – meaningful commitment

The work experienced as most meaningful is unpaid work: voluntary work. Volunteering is defined as a commitment to self-chosen tasks that meet personal interests and are seen as meaningful and useful for oneself and others (Bock, 2002). Such activities exhibit several characteristics that support its meaningfulness: They are oriented by selftranscendent goals (*orientation*), showing high *significance*. They are chosen according to personal interests, values, skills and time available, which allows for *coherent* and consistent integration into one's life. Last but not least, volunteering is mostly community based, and a feeling of *belonging* can develop from it (Schnell & Hoof, 2012).

It has indeed been shown that volunteers report higher meaningfulness than the general population does (Hoof & Schnell, 2009; Schnell & Hoof, 2012). A positive effect seems to occur when activities are carried out for at least two to three hours per week (Luoh & Herzog, 2002; Schnell & Hoof, 2012; Windsor, Anstey, & Rodgers, 2008). A connection between volunteering and meaning in life has even been demonstrated during unemployment, a period experienced as extremely stressful and associated with deteriorating health, well-being and vitality (Kroll & Lampert, 2012). Ina Dickel and Peter Schmuck conducted a survey of 145 unemployed men and women, 59 of whom were volunteers. As expected, meaningfulness was higher among these than among those who did not volunteer. The level even matched that of the general population. At the same time, crises of meaning were less frequent among those who engaged in voluntary work (Dickel, 2009).

Since these studies were cross-sectional, we do not know whether volunteering has a positive influence on meaningfulness or, vice versa, whether people with a sense of meaning are simply more willing to volunteer. Probably both are the case. However, there is anecdotal evidence that volunteering can create meaning. In the US, Steven Southwick and his colleagues treated war veterans who had PTSD. A central element of the therapy was voluntary work of ten to 20 hours per week. It turned out to be highly beneficial, as the authors described in three case studies. Patients experienced an increase in self-efficacy, sense of responsibility and, above all, sense of meaning (Southwick, Gilmartin, McDonough, & Morrissey, 2006). One patient described his experience as follows:

> We came to this hospital initially to be taken care of as "disabled veterans." We're realizing more and more with each project we dream up and complete, that what we do really matters out there. You can see it in the faces of the people we help, especially the kids.
>
> (Southwick et al., 2006, p. 171)

Southwick and colleagues were keen to ensure that their patients turned to projects related to their skills and personal experience. The activity's significance is thus further enhanced. Many people who are interested in volunteering are attracted to certain activities, associations or organisations at the outset. Others only know that they would like to do *something* but do not know what. For volunteering to be experienced as meaningful, it is important to find the best possible match between person and activity. Voluntary activities differ with regard to sources of meaning that can be realised through them. In a study of 168 volunteers, Matthias Hoof and I found that hospice volunteers differed from other volunteers in terms of their high spirituality and self-knowledge. Volunteers in secular organisations such as the Red Cross, food banks or the Volunteer Fire Brigade, on the other hand, were characterised by a stronger orientation towards power and fun (Schnell & Hoof, 2012).

13.7 Know thyself!

SELF-EXPLORATION: MEANING IN WORK

If you have a job, ask yourself the following questions:

- Why did I choose my profession in the first place?
- What were my original goals?
- Am I where I want to be?
- Am I overchallenged?
- Am I underchallenged?
- Do I enjoy my work? (If so, when is this the case, and when not?)
- What benefit does my work have for others or for society?
- Does my work correspond to my values?
- Do I experience myself as part of something larger than myself (e.g. a company, a team, a profession, etc.)?
- Can I discuss problems and conflicts openly with colleagues?
- Do I experience appreciation and support at work?
- Can I participate in shaping workflow or decision-making processes?
- Does my employer take responsibility for social and environmental issues?
- Are there conditions that oppose meaningful work?
- Where do I experience meaningfulness in work but am not aware of it?

If you encounter serious conflicts, this is a good opportunity to do the following:

- Say “no” when there is a conflict of values or interest.
- Take action against destructive working conditions (e.g. works council).

- Take time out for reflection.
- Talk to superiors about possibilities for changing your priorities (idiosyncratic deals).
- Come to a clear decision for or against the current position.
- If necessary, look for alternatives and find the courage to change.

13.8 Literature

Aßländer, M. S. (2005). *Bedeutungswandel der Arbeit: Versuch einer historischen Rekonstruktion.* München: Hanns-Seidel-Stiftung.

Al-Kattib, J. (2013, März 12). Unterforderung am Arbeitsplatz: 'Es ist wie eine Strafe.' *Der Standard.* Retrieved from http://derstandard.at/1362107773240/Unterforderung-am-Arbeitsplatz-Es-ist-wie-eine-Strafe

Allan, B. A., Batz-Barbarich, C., Sterling, H. M., & Tay, L. (2019). Outcomes of meaningful work: A meta-analysis. *Journal of Management Studies, 56*(3), 500–528.

Allan, B. A., Owens, R. L., & Douglass, R. P. (2019). Character strengths in counselors: Relations with meaningful work and burnout. *Journal of Career Assessment, 27*(1), 151–166.

Aristotle. (1999). *Nicomachean ethics* (W. D. Ross, trans.). Kitchener: Batoche Books.

Bailey, C., Madden, A., Alfes, K., Shantz, A., & Soane, E. (2017). The mismanaged soul: Existential labor and the erosion of meaningful work. *Human Resource Management Review, 27*(3), 416–430.

Bakker, A. B., Albrecht, S. L., & Leiter, M. P. (2011). Key questions regarding work engagement. *European Journal of Work and Organizational Psychology, 20*(1), 4–28.

Bauer, K. (2014, September 12). Unterforderung im Job ist häufiger als Überforderung. Bericht über Studie des Ifes-Instituts. *Der Standard.* Retrieved from http://derstandard.at/2000005453424/Unterforderung-ist-haeufiger-als-Ueberforderung

Beigbeder, F. (2014). *£6.99.* London: Picador.

Bock, T. (2002). Vom Laienhelfer zum freiwilligen Experten. Dynamik und Struktur des Volunteering. In D. Rosenkranz & A. Weber (Eds.), *Freiwilligenarbeit: Einführung in das Management von Ehrenamtlichen der Sozialen Arbeit* (pp. 11–20). Weinheim, München: Juventa.

Bruggemann, A. (1974). Zur Unterscheidung verschiedener Formen von Arbeitszufriedenheit. *Arbeit und Leistung, 28*(11), 281–284.

Brühlmann, T. (2015). Müdigkeit bei Burnout und Boreout. *Revue Médicale Suisse, 11*(471), 923–926.

Bunderson, J. S., & Thompson, J. A. (2009). The call of the wild: Zookeepers, callings, and the double-edged sword of deeply meaningful work. *Administrative Science Quarterly, 54*(1), 32–57.

Christian, M. S., Garza, A. S., & Slaughter, J. E. (2011). Work engagement: A quantitative review and test of its relations with task and contextual performance. *Personnel Psychology, 64*(1), 89–136.

Claes, R., & Ruiz-Quintanilla, S. (1994). Initial career and work meanings in seven European countries. *The Career Development Quarterly, 42*(4), 337–352.

Craig, N., & Snook, S. (2014). From purpose to impact. *Harvard Business Review, 92*(5), 104–111.

Deloitte. (2015). *Global human capital trends 2015: Leading in the new world of work*. Retrieved from https://www2.deloitte.com/content/dam/Deloitte/tr/Documents/human-capital/GlobalHumanCapitalTrends2015.pdf

Deloitte. (2019). *Global human capital trends 2019: Leading the social enterprise: Reinvent with a human focus*. Retrieved from https://www2.deloitte.com/content/dam/Deloitte/cz/Documents/human-capital/cz-hc-trends-reinvent-with-human-focus.pdf

Dempsey, S. E., & Sanders, M. L. (2010). Meaningful work? Nonprofit marketization and work/life imbalance in popular autobiographies of social entrepreneurship. *Organization, 17*(4), 437–459.

DGB-Index Gute Arbeit. (2013). *Der report 2013*. Retrieved from https://index-gute-arbeit.dgb.de/veroeffentlichungen/jahresreports/++co++20acc212-dec2-11e3-a855-52540023ef1a

DGB-Index Gute Arbeit. (2014). *Der report 2014*. Retrieved from https://index-gute-arbeit.dgb.de/veroeffentlichungen/jahresreports/++co++8192de46-7a3e-11e4-b422-52540023ef1a

DGB-Index Gute Arbeit. (2018, November 13). *Der report 2018*. Retrieved from https://index-gute-arbeit.dgb.de/veroeffentlichungen/jahresreports/++co++2710716a-e72f-11e8-891f-52540088cada

Dickel, I. (2009). *Erwerbslose Menschen mit freiwilligem Engagement und ohne freiwilliges Engagement: Ein Vergleich von Lebenssinn, Lebensbedeutungen und subjektivem Wohlbefinden* (Unpublished Master thesis), Technical University, Berlin.

DUW-Presseservice. (2011, September 15). *Kompetenz- und Talentmanagement in deutschen Unternehmen. Eine Studie der Deutschen Universität für Weiterbildung*. Retrieved from https://idw-online.de/en/attachmentdata10974.pdf

Ekstedt, M., & Fagerberg, I. (2005). Lived experiences of the time preceding burnout. *Journal of Advanced Nursing, 49*(1), 59–67.

Fairlie, P. (2011). Meaningful work, employee engagement, and other key employee outcomes: Implications for human resource development. *Advances in Developing Human Resources, 13*(4), 508–525.

Federal Ministry of Education and Research. (2018, March). *Berufsbildungsbericht 2018*. Retrieved from www.bmbf.de/upload_filestore/pub/Berufsbildungsbericht_2018.pdf

Förster, A., & Kreuz, P. (2009). *Spuren statt Staub: wie Wirtschaft Sinn macht*. Berlin: Econ.

Fouché, E., Rothmann, S. S., & Van der Vyver, C. (2017). Antecedents and outcomes of meaningful work among school teachers. *SA Journal of Industrial Psychology, 43*(1), 1–10.

Gaedt, M. (2014). *Mythos Fachkräftemangel: Was auf Deutschlands Arbeitsmarkt gewaltig schiefläuft*. Weinheim: Wiley–VCH.

Gallup. (2018). *Engagement index Deutschland*. Retrieved from www.gallup.de/183104/engagement-index-deutschland.aspx

Graeber, D. (2018). *Bullshit jobs: A theory*. New York: Simon & Schuster.

Grant, A. M. (2007). Relational job design and the motivation to make a prosocial difference. *Academy of Management Review, 32*(2), 393–417.

Grant, A. M. (2008). The significance of task significance: Job performance effects, relational mechanisms, and boundary conditions. *Journal of Applied Psychology, 93*(1), 108.

Hamilton, C. (2003, November). *Downshifting in Britain: A sea-change in the pursuit of happiness*. Discussion Paper Number 58, The Australia Institute. Retrieved from www.tai.org.au/sites/default/files/DP58_8.pdf

Höge, T., & Schnell, T. (2012). Kein Arbeitsengagement ohne Sinnerfüllung. Eine Studie zum Zusammenhang von Work Engagement, Sinnerfüllung und Tätigkeitsmerkmalen. *Wirtschaftspsychologie, 1*, 91–99.

Höge, T., & Weber, W. G. (2018). Das soziomoralische Organisationsklima und Sinnerfüllung in der Arbeit: Erkenntnisse über zwei Gesundheitsressourcen. In B. Badura, A. Ducki, H. Schörder, J. Klose, & M. Meyer (Eds.), *Fehlzeiten-Report 2018. Sinn erleben–Arbeit und Gesundheit* (pp. 225–233). Berlin: Springer.

Holbeche, L. (2004, June 26). How to make work more meaningful. *Personnel Today*. Retrieved from www.personneltoday.com/hr/how-to-make-work-more-meaningful/

Holbeche, L., & Springett, N. (2004). *In search of meaning in the workplace*. Horsham: Roffey Park.

Hoof, M., & Schnell, T. (2009). Sinn-volles engagement. Zur Sinnfindung im Kontext der Freiwilligenarbeit. *Wege zum Menschen, 61*, 405–422.

Hu, J., & Hirsh, J. B. (2017). Accepting lower salaries for meaningful work. *Frontiers in Psychology, 8*, 1649.

IMAS Report International. (2018, March–April). *Sinn im Beruf? Aktuelle demoskopische Studien zu Wirtschaft und Gesellschaft*. Archive-No. 018031. Retrieved from www.imas.at/images/imas-report/2018/14_Arbeitssinn.pdf

INQA. (2014). *Führungskultur im Wandel*. Retrieved from www.inqa.de/SharedDocs/PDFs/DE/Publikationen/fuehrungskultur-im-wandel-monitor.pdf?__blob=publicationFile

Kelly Services. (2009). *Kelly global workforce index 2009*. Source no longer available.

Kelly Services. (2012). *Kelly global workforce index 2012*. Source no longer available.

Kelly Services. (2014). *Kelly global workforce index 2014*. Source no longer available.

Kelly Services. (2016). *Work life design: The new balance*. Retrieved from www.kellyservices.com/global/siteassets/3-kelly-global-services/uploaded files/16-0004_kgwi_topic1_ebook.pdf

Kroll, L. E., & Lampert, T. (2012, January). Arbeitslosigkeit, prekäre Beschäftigung und Gesundheit. *GBE kompakt*, *3*(1). Robert Koch-Institut, Berlin. Retrieved from www.rki.de/DE/Content/Gesundheitsmonitoring/Gesund heitsberichterstattung/GBEDownloadsK/2012_1_Arbeitslosigkeit_Gesund heit.pdf?__blob=publicationFile

Lafargue, P. (1883/2012). *The right to be lazy*. Auckland: The Floating Press.

Lohmann-Haislah, A. (2013). *Stressreport Deutschland 2012. Psychische Anforderungen, Ressourcen und Befinden*. Berlin: Bundesanstalt für Arbeitsschutz und Arbeitsmedizin.

Luoh, M. C., & Herzog, A. R. (2002). Individual consequences of volunteer and paid work in old age: Health and mortality. *Journal of Health and Social Behavior*, *43*, 490–509.

ManPower Group Deutschland. (2019). *Bevölkerungsumfrage Jobzufriedenheit 2019*. Retrieved from www.manpowergroup.de/fileadmin/manpowergroup.de/Studien/MPG_190923_Jobzufriedenheit_2019.pdf

Maslach, C., Schaufeli, W. B., & Leiter, M. P. (2001). Job burnout. *Annual Review of Psychology*, *52*(1), 397–422.

Mercer. (2019). *Global talent trends 2019*. Retrieved from www.mercer.com/content/dam/mercer/attachments/private/gl-2019-global-talent-trends-study.pdf

Milliman, J., Czaplewski, A. J., & Ferguson, J. (2003). Workplace spirituality and employee work attitudes: An exploratory empirical assessment. *Journal of Organizational Change Management*, *16*(4), 426–447.

Musil, R. (2017). *The man without qualities*. London: Picador.

Nelson, M. R., Rademacher, M. A., & Paek, H. J. (2007). Downshifting consumer= upshifting citizen? An examination of a local freecycle community. *The Annals of the American Academy of Political and Social Science*, *611*(1), 141–156.

Nuremberg Institute for Market Decisions & St. Gallen Symposium. (2019). *Purpose beyond profit: Voices of the leaders of tomorrow 2019*. Retrieved from www.nim.org/sites/default/files/medien/359/dokumente/2019_report_lot_web_fin.pdf

Posch, R., & Köttritsch, M. (2015, February 6). Was sich von Non-Profit-Organisationen lernen lässt. *DiePresse.com*. Retrieved from http://karriere news.diepresse.com/home/karrieretrends/4656497/Was-sich-von-NonProfit Organisationen-lernen-laesst

Randstad. (2019). *Employer brand research 2019: Country report Germany*. Retrieved from https://workforceinsights.randstad.com/randstad-employer-brand-research-country-report-germany-2019

Rasmussen, V., Turnell, A., Butow, P., Juraskova, I., Kirsten, L., Wiener, L., . . . IPOS Research Committee. (2016). Burnout among psychosocial oncologists:

An application and extension of the effort – reward imbalance model. *Psycho-Oncology, 25*(2), 194–202.

Rosa, H. (2014). *Beschleunigung und Entfremdung*. Berlin: Suhrkamp.

Rosso, B. D., Dekas, K. H., & Wrzesniewski, A. (2010). On the meaning of work: A theoretical integration and review. *Research in Organizational Behavior, 30*, 91–127.

Rothlin, P., & Werder, P. R. (2014). *Unterfordert: Diagnose Boreout–Wenn Langeweile krank macht*. München: Redline.

Sabeti, H., & Fourth Sector Network Concept Working Group. (2009). *The emerging fourth sector. Executive summary*. Washington: The Aspen Institute. Retrieved from www.fourthsector.net/learn/concept-paper-request/

Schaufeli, W. B., Salanova, M., González-Romá, V., & Bakker, A. B. (2002). The measurement of engagement and burnout: A two sample confirmatory factor analytic approach. *Journal of Happiness Studies, 3*(1), 71–92.

Schnell, T. (2018). Von Lebenssinn und Sinn in der Arbeit. Warum es sich bei beruflicher Sinnerfüllung nicht um ein nettes extra handelt. In B. Badura, A. Ducki, H. Schröder, J. Klose, & M. Meyer (Eds.), *Fehlzeiten-Report 2018* (pp. 11–21). Berlin and Heidelberg: Springer Verlag.

Schnell, T., Höge, T., & Pollet, E. (2013). Predicting meaning in work: Theory, data, implications. *The Journal of Positive Psychology, 8*(6), 543–554.

Schnell, T., Höge, T., & Weber, W. G. (2019). 'Belonging' and its relationship to the experience of meaningful work. In R. Yeoman, K. Bailey, A. Madden, & M. Thompson (Eds.), *The Oxford handbook of meaningful work* (pp. 165–185). Oxford: Oxford University Press.

Schnell, T., & Hoffmann, C. (in press). Sinn im Beruf: Dimensionen, Konsequenzen und Gefahren. *Wirtschaftspsychologie aktuell*.

Schnell, T., & Hoof, M. (2012). Meaningful commitment: Finding meaning in volunteer work. *Journal of Beliefs & Values, 33*(1), 35–53.

Southwick, S. M., Gilmartin, R., McDonough, P., & Morrissey, P. (2006). Logotherapy as an adjunctive treatment for chronic combat-related PTSD: A meaning-based intervention. *American Journal of Psychotherapy, 60*(2), 161–174.

Stiftung Warentest. (2007, October 9). *Berufsberatung: Berater müssen nachsitzen*. Retrieved from www.test.de/Berufsberatung-Berater-muessen-nachsitzen-1573988-2573988/

Techniker Krankenkasse. (2016). *Entspann dich, Deutschland–TK Stressstudie 2016*. Retrieved from www.tk.de/resource/blob/2026630/9154e4c71766c410dc859916aa798217/tk-stressstudie-2016-data.pdf

Unterrainer, C., Jeppesen, H. J., & Jønsson, T. (2013). Different forms of job satisfaction: Does job satisfaction mean satisfied employees? *Psyke & Logos, 34*(2), 22.

Volpert, W., & Weber, W. G. (2018). Arbeitsgestaltung und Arbeitsorganisation. In F. Rauner & P. Grollmann (Eds.), *Handbuch Berufsbildungsforschung* (3rd ed., pp. 399–405). Bielefeld: wbv Media, UTB.

Waltersbacher, A., Zok, K., Böttger, S. J., & Klose, J. (2018). Sinnerleben bei der Arbeit und der Einfluss auf die Gesundheit. In B. Badura, A. Ducki, H. Schröder, J. Klose, & M. Meyer (Eds.), *Fehlzeiten-Report 2018* (pp. 23–46). Berlin: Springer.

Weber, W. G., & Unterrainer, C. (2015). Arbeit in demokratischen Unternehmen: Ihr Potenzial für eine demokratische Gesellschaft. *Zeitschrift für Sozialpsychologie und Gruppendynamik in Wirtschaft und Gesellschaft, 40*(1), 21–40.

Weber, W. G., Unterrainer, C., & Höge, T. (2008). Socio-moral atmosphere and prosocial and democratic value orientations in enterprises with different levels of anchored participation. *Zeitschrift für Personalforschung, 22*, 171–194.

Windsor, T., Anstey, K., & Rodgers, B. (2008). Volunteering and psychological well-being among young-old adults: How much is too much? *The Gerontologist, 48*, 59–70.

Xing. (2014). *Arbeit & Sinn*. Retrieved from https://spielraum.xing.com/2014/09/sinngetrieben-oder-karrieregeil-was-die-generation-y-von-ihrem-job-erwartet/

Xing. (2019). *Xing Gehaltsstudie 2019*. Retrieved from https://corporate.xing.com/fileadmin/user_upload/XING-Gehaltsstudie-2019-DE.pdf

Zinn, K. G. (2015). *Vom Kapitalismus ohne Wachstum zur Marktwirtschaft ohne Kapitalismus*. Hamburg: VSA-Verlag.

Chapter 14

Outlook

Existential psychologists Kirk Schneider, James Bugental and J. Fraser Pierson present an intriguing vision at the beginning of their handbook of humanistic psychology:

> What if psychology's next step were a holistic one, a rich mosaic consisting of each of the emerging trends but threaded throughout by the depth, breadth, and pathos of intimate human experience? What if artificial intelligence were complemented by poetic illumination, if neuroscience were supplemented by experiential inquiry, and if evolutionary psychology were matched by holistic reflection? What if positive psychology were linked with depth or philosophical investigation and if postmodernism were linked with personalism or transcendentalism?
>
> (Schneider, Bugental, & Pierson, 2001, p. xix)

This vision is not without justified hope. After decades of extensive research specialisation, we are now seeing initial approaches based on the principle of transdisciplinarity: Lifeworld problems are examined from various scientific and social perspectives, in accordance with their complexity. The overarching goal is to develop solutions oriented towards the common good (Hirsch Hadorn et al., 2008). Irrespective of the fact that this "selftranscendence" of disciplines in the pursuit of an overarching goal can be regarded as a highly meaningful undertaking that counteracts the isolation of individual subjects, transdisciplinarity has contributed greatly to making the complex, elusive subject of meaning in life empirically accessible. By linking the humanities, social sciences and economics and connecting them with medicine, neurology and immunology, practically relevant insights have been gained.

The question of meaning – as a lifeworld problem par excellence – affects individuals, organisations and societies. In *The Psychology of Meaning in Life*, the individual is in the foreground, as the subject that poses questions of meaning. Embedded in biopsychosocial structures, the thinking and judging person experiences more or less meaning. But if we broaden our view, we see that even organisations are not immune to the question of meaning. Our social system in toto seems to stand on unstable ground. What was long taken for granted is now called into question by reality: The primacy of growth and progress is crumbling in the face of a pandemic, economic crisis, climate change and widening income gaps. Our hope for a better life through highly technological, equipment-intensive medicine is being dashed by the simultaneous (or resulting?) inability to age and die with dignity. Higher educational goals are taken ad absurdum in overly regimented and instrumentalised educational institutions. Our self-image of an open and just society is shaken in the face of hundreds of thousands of asylum seekers.

"Wrong life cannot be lived rightly," said Adorno (2005, p. 39). It can, Frankl said. We are free in how we relate to the world; we can turn unchangeable suffering into accomplishment and preserve our personal meaning. But it is not just about our personal meaning. And at what point are painful situations really unchangeable?

People who care for meaning inevitably have an eye for the larger context. Anyone who searches for meaning asks why and will thus encounter dissonance and injustice that are inherent in social structures. Some such problems will be addressed in the following, with references to alternatives for action.

14.1 Caught in the system?

Compared to the majority of the world's population, most residents of Western industrialised countries are doing well in terms of security and material resources. Nevertheless, there is a high level of mental suffering. In Germany, one in three women and one in four to five men aged 18 to 79 years have had at least one mental disorder during the past 12 months (Jacobi et al., 2014). The use of antidepressants is rising continuously: Between 2000 and 2015, it doubled in EU countries (OECD, 2017).

The increasing relevance of the question of meaning must also be understood in the context of these societal developments.

> In a culture of performance and individual action, in which energy breakdowns can cost dearly, and in which we always have to be

> running at top speed and efficiency, inhibition is pure dysfunction, an inadequacy. The individual has an institutional need to act at any cost by being able to count on his inner strengths
>
> (Ehrenberg, 2016, p. 217)

If these inner strengths are not sufficient, then stimulants are available by prescription. What does it mean when, under such conditions, doubts arise about the meaning of everyday life? Must subsequent crises of meaning not even be understood as signs of mental health?

Clearly, this is not about trivialising existential suffering. Every person who experiences a crisis of meaning should be offered support and guidance in coping with it. But it is also important to reflect on the overarching goal thus pursued. In Petra-Alexandra Buhl's coaching blog, she has addressed the subject of resilience: "thriving despite adverse circumstances." Resilience means psychological robustness, the ability not to give up after a crisis and instead to carry on. From the perspective of the individual affected by a crisis, resilience is a highly positive characteristic. From a higher perspective, however, we should also consider that we don't have to endure everything. Thus, the chairperson of an insurance company's works council, Ralf-Giso Kutschker, reports on how, in the business world, resilience is used as a pretext to make people fit for even more stress:

> But the conditions are fundamentally flawed. Fewer and fewer employees have to do more and better work and achieve even higher quality and service levels. Human resource policy calculates with ever fewer people and these employees are then required to balance it with all their skills.
>
> (Buhl-Coaching.de, 2015; transl. TS)

At the same time, Kutschker sees alienation processes at work:

> I see a very strong individualisation up to isolation and loneliness, caused by constant competition. People have the feeling that they need to work so much and achieve so much more – yet their job is not safe, no matter how hard they try.
>
> (Buhl-Coaching.de, 2015; transl. TS)

This is one of many examples of how social structures obviously constrain personal meaning. In terms of sustainable counselling and therapy, it is important not only to (re)construct meaningfulness on an individual level but also to change the living conditions that cause the illness. There are plenty of alternatives. They may seem overly idealistic or utopian, but much is already being subjected to initial tests or being implemented on private initiative, on a small scale, by people who do not want to wait for the big system change but rather want to bring it about.

A universal basic income is discussed as a counter-draft to work intensification, exhaustion and alienation. In 2015, Finland decided to be the first country in the EU to test a universal basic income. Payment started at the beginning of 2017. The idea behind this is that every citizen receives a fixed amount of money on a regular basis without having to reciprocate in any way. This should enable the entire population to live in dignity and participate in public life. More specifically, it should lead to a destigmatisation of unemployment and part-time work. Professions would be chosen according to criteria of fit, not according to whether they secured one's existence. The absence of fear of losing one's job would mean less pressure to perform, excessive demands and exhaustion. Monotonous and unpopular work in the low-wage sector would be upgraded and paid more highly. There would be more scope for activities with children/family, for education, voluntary work and social commitment (Hohenleitner & Straubhaar, 2008). The Finnish experiment was terminated after one year. The people who received a monthly amount of €560 (much less than suggested by most initiatives) reported a higher level of well-being, but initial analyses showed no effects on their employability. The final report is due to be published at the beginning of 2020; no decision has yet been made on whether the experiment will be continued (Laufer, 2019). The concept meets with both strong rejection and euphoric approval. According to a study by the German Institute for Economic Research, almost half of Germans are now supporters of the idea, with greater approval among young people, the better educated, those with a more left-wing political orientation and those on lower incomes (DIW, 2019).

Several analyses support its economic feasibility and convincing social benefits. The economists Ingrid Hohenleitner and Thomas Straubhaar come to the conclusion that because the universal basic income relies on voluntariness in the choice of occupation, it would promote an optimal division of labour. This in turn would increase productivity, gross domestic product (GDP) and overall economic welfare (Hohenleitner & Straubhaar, 2008).

In October 2019, the German organisation My Basic Income had already financed 435 basic incomes through crowdfunding. Basic incomes are raffled off as soon as sufficient money is available. The individual sum is €1,000 per month for the duration of one year. Michael Bohmeyer, the founder of the organisation, visited and interviewed 24 randomly selected winners. Their conversations yielded an essential insight: It was not the money that was important but the unconditional nature of the payout. As Bohmeyer and his coauthor, Cornelsen, point out, more than half of all Germans already live on public or private transfer payments. The payment of money is therefore not what is special in this experiment but rather the way in which this is done: unconditionally. Recipients experienced this as a gift of trust. As a result, many of them succeeded in breaking free from inner compulsion and existential fear and became actively involved:

> Our winners report that without pressure, they have learned to love their job anew and have become more productive. If you are no longer forced, then intrinsic motivation can unfold. . . . They do not calculate their lives economically like a company, but they discover a meaning and do everything they can to serve this meaning.
>
> (Bohmeyer & Cornelsen, 2019a, p. 280f; transl. TS)

Last but not least, the trust that the winners experienced, manifested in the monthly payment, resulted in commitment to others and a greater willingness to take on responsibility and to rethink the consequences of their own actions, also in the long term (see also Bohmeyer & Cornelsen, 2019b, 23 January).

To counteract climate change and dwindling resources, a wide range of initiatives has developed, including conscious consumption, the primary use of regional or local resources and food and energy sovereignty. Vegetarians avoid food that comes from killed animals. They thus withdraw their purchasing power from ethically and ecologically controversial factory farming. Vegans avoid any animal food or food containing animal ingredients, often also clothing, cosmetics or medicines containing animal products. In so-called food co-ops, individuals or households join in and organise the purchase of (mostly) organic products from local farms, market gardens, beekeepers and so on. Local farming is thus supported and short transport distances are achieved, and by excluding intermediaries, members of a food co-op can usually buy at lower prices than they can at retail outlets. Similar objectives, only organised externally, are pursued by organic or farmers' box initiatives, which deliver a range of foods from selected farmers to households. Urban gardening and community gardens serve the purpose of partial or complete self-sufficiency while initiating communication and integration processes (e.g. see https://gartenpolylog.org [as of 01.02.2020])

In repair, share and exchange initiatives, the accumulation of property is questioned. Furthermore, they take into account that the production (and disposal) of electrical appliances has environmentally harmful consequences and that in many cases, appliances enter the market with planned obsolescence: a reduced lifespan built in by the manufacturer, independent of use. So-called repair cafés offer temporary self-help workshops in which everyday objects can be repaired together (e.g. see https://repaircafe.org/en/start/ [as of 01.02.2020]). Local exchange trading systems (LETS), or time banks, exchange skills or knowledge that are useful and valuable to others via an (interest-free) account. Calculations are based on time units; all activities have the same value. Vehicles and equipment whose purchase would not be worthwhile for individuals are also shared and exchanged. At clothing exchange markets (not only) parents can find well-preserved clothes and toys, which – after naturally short use by a growing child – bring multiple benefits and joy. Online thrift stores satisfy an interest in producing less waste and saving resources while offering affordable fashion. Public handicraft workshops, sewing studios and virtual and analogue networks for handicrafts make a frugal lifestyle possible – that is, a status-independent, fashion-conscious life, which considers the origins and ecological balance of garments as important criteria. Neighbourhood help is also being revived with online support: taking care of pets, trimming hedges, looking after children, watering flowers and so on. Anonymous residents of a district or block of flats can thus find each other via the Internet.

Regional currencies are another way of decoupling trade from global markets and instead pooling and promoting regional resources. In 1932, in the wake of the world economic crisis, such an initiative was launched in our neighbouring town of Wörgl, Tyrol. It was so successful that it has been called the Miracle of Wörgl. As an engine driver in the First World War, the Tyrolean Michael Unterguggenberger came across a subversive magazine, *Der Physiokrat*, in which coeditor Silvio Gesell published an article on his concept of free money. Gesell had observed that hoarded money paralysed the economy. Such hoarding was even rewarded by high interest rates. His suggestion was for money to lose its value over time, so that it would be advantageous to put it into circulation immediately. When Unterguggenberger became mayor of Wörgl in 1931, life there was marked by unemployment and hunger. Unterguggenberger, who had extensively studied industrialisation and capitalism, now recalled Gesell's theory and put it into practice. Municipal employees were paid by a complementary currency, the Wörgler schilling. With this, they were able to pay for local businesses. If they kept it, the shilling lost value each month; by buying a stamp at one percent of the nominal value of the note, it was possible to maintain the original value. And Gesell's idea worked out: The money cycle was revived, unemployment fell and income and tax revenues in the community grew (Uchatius, 2010). But only just under a year and a half after the start of the experiment, which had been so successful, the Austrian Administrative Court ruled that the Wörgler schilling was in breach of the law: Only the National Bank may issue banknotes. Although to this day the legal situation has not been fully clarified, there are several hundred regional currencies. A continuously updated list of complementary currencies can be found on Wikipedia ("local currency").

Meanwhile, it has become apparent that our economic system and the lifestyle associated with it cause personal, social and ecological dangers. Accordingly, this raises questions of meaning for individuals. The foregoing selection is intended to indicate that there are alternatives and that even now "other worlds are possible." They open up forms of life that have an *orientation* towards justice and the common good, can be lived *coherently* with personal values, make it possible to experience the *significance* of one's own actions in a new way and strengthen one's sense of *belonging*. Many publications bring the vision of a better world to life while linking it to fundamental scientific findings (e.g. Felber, 2019; Hellbrück & Kals, 2012; Paech, 2012; Plöger, 2011; Rohde & Koglin, 2016; Rosa, 2019; Schmuck, 2015; Schmuck & Schultz, 2012; Schumacher, 2019; Welzer, 2019).

14.2 Meaning is subjective – eudaimonia calls for justice

In the course of this book, I have repeatedly pointed out that meaning is not inherent to anything. It is always attributed by a person in a particular situation. This subjectivity of meaning implies that people may find different things meaningful. We must imagine Hitler, Stalin or the members of the Islamic State as full of meaning – at least over a certain period of time. We might be reluctant to accept this; but as soon as we define the concept of meaning normatively, we severely limit its explanatory power.

This value neutrality with regard to the definition of meaning does not mean, however, that science must, or even can, be value-neutral in principle (Feyerabend, 2010; Putnam, 2002). On the one hand, unconscious valuation processes play a role everywhere, from the choice of the research subject to the development of theories. These must be made conscious as far as possible to avoid distorting influences. In addition, the question arises whether science should also take a normative position. In terms of the principle of transdisciplinarity as formulated earlier (Hirsch Hadorn et al., 2008), I see this, though depending on the field of research, as possible and desirable: Science (also) has the objective of developing solutions to problems, oriented towards the common good. To this end, I finally return to the theorist who has repeatedly contributed to this book: Aristotle. His concept of eudaimonia is not value-neutral. He resolutely puts one value in the foreground: justice. In this, he (exceptionally) agrees with his teacher Plato. Justice for Aristotle is

> complete virtue, but not absolutely, but in relation to our neighbour. And therefore justice is often thought to be the greatest of virtues, and "neither evening nor morning star" is so wonderful; and proverbially "in justice is every virtue comprehended."
>
> (Aristotle, 1999, p. 73)

As "unjust," Aristotle describes not only lawbreakers but also greedy people who think that they are entitled to more than others, who thus exhibit an "attitude of inequality." To understand a meaningful life as the consequence of a eudaimonic lifestyle (Section 10.1.2) is to say: Meaningfulness is based on a self-determined and responsible practice of personal talents, which does not ignore the needs of others and does not place itself above others.

14.3 Literature

Adorno, T. W. (2005). *Minima Moralia: Reflections on a damaged life*. London: Verso.

Aristotle. (1999). *Nicomachean ethics* (W. D. Ross, trans.). Kitchener: Batoche Books.

Bohmeyer, M., & Cornelsen, C. (2019a). *Was würdest Du tun? Wie uns das Bedingungslose Grundeinkommen verändert–Antworten aus der Praxis*. Berlin: Econ.

Bohmeyer, M., & Cornelsen, C. (2019b, January 23). 1.000 Euro mehr im Monat – auch für Managersöhne und Sozialamtbetrüger. *ZEIT Online*. Retrieved from www.zeit.de/arbeit/2019-01/bedingungsloses-grundeinkommen-michael-bohmeyer-buchauszug

Buhl-Coaching.de. (2015, May 1). *Interviewprojekt "Hindernisse machen uns groß: Resilienz und Digitalisierung"*. Retrieved from www.buhl-coaching.de/blog/2015/05/rp15-interviewprojekt-hindernisse-machen-uns-gross-resilienz-und-digitalisierung/

DIW. (2019, April 10). *Wer kann der Idee eines bedingungslosen Grundeinkommens am meisten etwas abgewinnen? Studie zeichnet Profil der Befürworterinnen und Befürworter*. Retrieved from www.diw.de/de/diw_01.c.618785.de/themen_nachrichten/wer_kann_der_idee_eines_bedingungslosen_grunde inkommens_am_meisten_etwas_abgewinnen_studie_zeichnet_profil_der_befuerworterinnen_und_befuerworter.html

Ehrenberg, A. (2016). *The weariness of the self: Diagnosing the history of depression in the contemporary age*. Montreal: McGill-Queen's University Press.

Felber, C. (2019). *Trading for good*. London: Zed Books.

Feyerabend, P. K. (2010). *Against method*. London: Verso.

Hellbrück, J., & Kals, E. (2012). *Umweltpsychologie*. Heidelberg and New York: Springer Verlag.

Hirsch Hadorn, G., Biber-Klemm, S., Grossenbacher-Mansuy, W., Hoffmann-Riem, H., Joye, D., Pohl, C., & Zemp, E. (2008). The emergence of transdisciplinarity as a form of research. In G. Hirsch Hadorn et al. (Eds.), *Handbook of transdisciplinary research* (pp. 19–39). Heidelberg: Springer.

Hohenleitner, I., & Straubhaar, T. (2008). Bedingungsloses Grundeinkommen und Solidarisches Bürgergeld – mehr als sozialutopische Konzepte. In T. Straubhaar (Ed.), *Bedingungsloses Grundeinkommen und Solidarisches Bürgergeld – mehr als sozialutopische Konzepte* (pp. 9–127). Hamburg: Hamburg University Press.

Jacobi, F., Höfler, M., Strehle, J., Mack, S., Gerschler, A., Scholl, L., & Wittchen, H. U. (2014). Psychische Störungen in der Allgemeinbevölkerung. *Der Nervenarzt*, *85*(1), 77–87.

Laufer, N. (2019, August 26). Was ein garantiertes Grundeinkommen in Finnland brachte. *Der Standard*. Retrieved from www.derstandard.at/story/2000107782132/was-ein-garantiertes-grundeinkommen-in-finnland-brachte

OECD. (2017). *OECD health statistics 2017*. http://dx.doi.org/10.1787/888933605540

Paech, N. (2012). *Befreiung vom Überfluss: Auf dem Weg in die Postwachstumsökonomie*. München: Oekom.

Plöger, P. (2011). *Einfach ein gutes Leben: Aufbruch in eine neue Gesellschaft*. München: Hanser.

Putnam, H. (2002). *The collapse of the fact/value dichotomy and other essays*. Cambridge, MA: Harvard University Press.

Rohde, M., & Koglin, I. (2016). *Und jetzt retten wir die Welt: Wie du die Veränderung wirst, die du dir wünschst*. Stuttgart: Franckh-Kosmos.

Rosa, H. (2019). *Resonance. A sociology of our relationship to the world.* Cambridge: Polity Press.

Schmuck, P. (2015). *Die Kraft der Vision. Plädoyer für eine neue Denk- und Lebenskultur*. München: Oekom.

Schmuck, P., & Schultz, W. P. (Eds.). (2012). *Psychology of sustainable development*. Heidelberg and New York: Springer.

Schneider, K., Bugental, J., & Pierson, J. (Eds.). (2001). *The handbook of humanistic psychology: Leading edges of theory, practice, and research*. Thousand Oaks, CA: Sage.

Schumacher, E. F. (2019). *Small is beautiful: Die Rückkehr zum menschlichen Maß*. München: Oekom.

Uchatius, W. (2010, December 22). Das Wunder von Wörgl. *Die Zeit Online vom*. Retrieved from www.zeit.de/2010/52/Woergl

Welzer, H. (2019). *Alles könnte anders sein: Eine Gesellschaftsutopie für freie Menschen*. Frankfurt am Main: S. Fischer.

Index

actions 32
Adorno, T.W. 238
affective commitment for an organisation 98
alcohol and drugs use 164
alienation 99, 110, 127, 222, 240
allostatic load 158, 159
Alzheimer's disease 148, 154, 160
angst 106, 109
antiviral response 159
Antonovsky, A. 13, 33, 96, 149, 150, 151, 158
anxiety 161
Aristotle 98, 139, 140, 141, 214, 244
atheism 45, 81
authenticity 3, 109, 121
authenticity profile 22, 83
authoritarian regimes 34
autobiographical retrieval 185
autonomy 54, 140

belonging 8, 9, 88, 211, 212, 213, 222, 225, 243
binge learning 55
biomarkers 157
boreout 219
bright-siding 171
Bullshit Jobs 228
burnout 219, 222

calling 224
cancer 155, 160, 164, 165, 179, 184, 187, 190, 193, 195
cardiovascular disease 149, 157, 160
children 41, 93
chronic pain 189
chronic stress 157, 160
climate change 238
cognitive deconstruction 95
cognitive functioning 147, 194
cognitive reminiscence therapy (CRT) 185
cohabiting 94
coherence 8, 9, 180, 194, 211, 212, 213, 222, 228; horizontal coherence 32, 36; vertical coherence 32, 36
common good 237, 244
communicative validation 19
competence 121, 127
comprehensibility 150
corporate citizenship 210
corporate social responsibility 217
cortisol 157, 162
counselling 188
crisis of meaning 6, 8, 13, 36, 50, 64, 106, 111, 163, 239
CTRA (conserved transcriptional response to adversity) 159
cynicism 217, 221, 225

death 108, 167, 171
dementia 186
depression 109, 166, 167, 187
despair at the end of life 165
diabetes 157, 160
dignity therapy 181
downshifting 226
downward comparison 136, 137
dying 171, 181, 194

Easterlin paradox 136
economic crisis 238
education 47, 119
employability 47
Erikson, E.H. 40, 62, 95
eudaimonic well-being 134, 139, 141, 160
exhaustion 222
existential communication 178
existential indifference 117
existential isolation 7
experience-sampling 52
exploitation 224

family 8, 88
feelings 35
food co-ops 241
forgiveness 192
fourth sector 217
Frankl, V. 3, 4, 6, 64, 65, 109, 117, 142, 195, 197, 198, 238
Fridays for Future 119
friends 7, 88
frugal lifestyle 242
functional differentiation 9

Gallup Engagement Index 207
gender differences 119
Generation Y 123, 216
generativity 182
genetic disposition 52, 138
gestalt 28
giftedness 48, 141
gnothi seauton 3
goals 29
gratitude 138, 143
grounded theory 14

happiness 2, 49, 51, 134
HDL cholesterol 157, 162
health behaviour 150, 152
healthcare 178
hedonic treadmill 135, 137
hedonic well-being 134, 141, 160
Heidegger, M. 4, 106, 117, 121, 198
hierarchic model of meaning 29, 30, 31, 32, 33, 54, 110, 120, 151, 159, 212
hikikomori 125, 128
Hillesum, E. 142
Hölderlin, F. 51
horizontal coherence 32
hormonal contraception 47

identity 179
ikigai 148, 149
illusions 2
income 136
inflammation 158, 159, 161, 162
intelligence 49
interindividual differences 38
interview 14, 15
intrinsic motivation 139

Jaspers, K. 110
justice 139, 244

Kierkegaard, S. 110, 198
knee surgery 154

laddering technique 14, 15, 92
legacy 182, 192
life review 179, 192, 194, 199
life-review therapy 185
life story 180
local currency 242
local exchange trading systems 242
logotherapy 197
loneliness 96
long-term blood sugar 157, 162

manageability 150, 158
managing cancer and living meaningfully (CALM) 193
marital status 92, 119
marriage 92
meaning: as attribution 28; balance 64, 84, 188; breadth 62, 84; depth 64, 84; as dynamic and relational 6; etymology 5; gender differences 43; in life 1; of life 1; measurement 6; as moderator 153, 156, 157; as motivator 150, 153; as multidimensional 6; not an emotion 34; relativity of 34; as result of evaluation processes 35; stability of 42, 52; as a story 31; as subjective 5, 243; surplus 28, 29, 30, 31; very old age 108

meaning-centred interventions 178
meaning-centred psychotherapy 195
meaningfulness 6, 7, 19, 33, 35, 51, 150
meaningful work: correlates 221; definition 211; predictors 213; risks 222
meaning in work 207
meaning-making intervention (MMi) 190
mental disorder 168, 238
mental health 147
meta-perspective 52, 179
mindfulness 138
mobile spiritual and existential care teaching team 179
mood 52, 54
mortality risk 148, 157
multi-optional society 2, 33
myths of happiness 144

NEET 126
negativity bias 137
neighbourhood help 242
neuronal reserve 154
nursing homes 187

objective meaning 198
order 34
organisational identification 98
orientation 7, 8, 212, 225, 243
outlook 191
over challenge 218

pain 148
palliative care 166, 179, 181, 184, 188, 189, 191
paradox of parenthood 93
perception 28
perfectionism 50
personality traits 38
physical health 147
pilgrimage 111, 112
pleasure 140
positive feelings 160
positive illusions 50, 113, 114, 155
posttraumatic growth 156, 169
posttraumatic stress disorder 111, 147, 155, 160, 229
precarious working conditions 208
profit maximisation 208
pro-inflammatory cytokines 157
prosperity 122
psychological ownership 99
Purabheda-Sutta 130
purpose 6
purpose-driven management 224

religion 77
religiosity 43, 155, 170
remembering yesterday, caring today (RYCT) 186
repair cafés 242
resigned work satisfaction 208
resilience 239
responsibility 128, 129, 140, 220, 224
Rilke, R.M. 110
ritual 111
rumination 155, 170

salutogenesis 149
school experiences 49
search for meaning 155
secular 77, 78, 81, 83, 230
selfactualisation 39, 40, 83, 113, 246
self-control 38, 51, 95, 138
self-exploitation 223
self-optimisation 65
selftranscendence 40, 64, 66, 112
sense of coherence 150
Shakespeare 4, 98
short-term life review 184
significance 7, 8, 128, 150, 161, 212, 214, 225, 233
single 93
sleep 157, 162
social and historical processes 33
social belonging 96
social comparisons 136
social connectedness 97
social entrepreneurship 217
social genomics 159
social inclusion 97
social relationships 88, 165, 169
social support 96
socioeconomic status 157, 160
socio-moral atmosphere 99, 213, 216
sources of meaning 8, 14, 19, 25, 31, 38, 60, 190; achievement 71;

attentiveness 76, 170; care 16, 76; challenge 69; comfort 15, 75; communion 74, 170; creativity 16, 72; development 16, 70; freedom 71; fun 75; generativity 16, 17, 39, 60, 69, 97; harmony 75; health 68, 151, 170; individualism 69; knowledge 72; love 75; morality 17, 74; nature relatedness 67; power 70; practicality 73; reason 74; religiosity 66, 77; self-knowledge 68; social commitment 16, 17, 67, 170; spirituality 66, 79; tradition 78
Sources of Meaning and Meaning in Life Questionnaire (SoMe) 6, 19, 45, 60, 92
Sources of Meaning Card Method (SoMe-CaM) 25, 187
spirituality 43, 170
stress buffer 156
stress theory 162
study experiences 55
subjective well-being 108, 141
suffering 108, 143, 170
suicidality 50, 105, 168
super-diversity 9
sustainability 217

task significance 213
testosterone hypothesis 45
Tillich, P. 84, 110
transdisciplinarity 237, 244
trauma 154, 169
true self 120, 130

underchallenge 218
unemployment 208, 229
universal basic income 240
upward comparison 137
urban gardening 241

veganism 241
vegetarianism 241
virtues 139
vocation 224
volunteering 81, 111, 141, 228
vulnerability 170

waist–hip ratio 157, 162
well-being and relatedness 40, 43, 45
work as a source of meaning 226
work engagement 221
work-role fit 213
work satisfaction 208
worldview 91, 169

Yalom, I. 7, 88, 100, 109, 117, 198
youth 119, 124, 125, 128, 152, 164, 168, 220, 240